Judaism, Human Rights, and Human Values

Judaism, Human Rights, and Human Values

Lenn E. Goodman

New York   Oxford
OXFORD UNIVERSITY PRESS
1998

Oxford University Press

Oxford   New York

Athens   Auckland   Bangkok   Bogotá   Buenos Aires   Calcutta
Cape Town   Chennai   Dar es Salaam   Delhi   Florence   Hong Kong   Istanbul
Karachi   Kuala Lumpur   Madrid   Melbourne   Mexico City   Mumbai
Nairobi   Paris   São Paulo   Singapore   Taipei   Tokyo   Toronto   Warsaw

and associated companies in
Berlin   Ibadan

Published by Oxford University Press, Inc.
198 Madison Avenue, New York, New York 10016

Oxford is a registered trademark of Oxford University Press

Library of Congress Cataloging-in-Publication Data

Goodman, Lenn Evan, 1944–
Judaism, human rights, and human values / Lenn E. Goodman.
p.   cm.
Includes bibliographical references and index.
ISBN 0-19-511834-0
1. Human rights—Religious aspects—Judaism.   2. Human rights—
Philosophy.   3. Mill, John Stuart, 1806–1873.   On liberty.
4. Liberty.   5. Ethics, Jewish.   I. Title.
BM645.H85G66   1998
296.3'82—dc21   97-36235

1 3 5 7 9 8 6 4 2

Printed in the United States of America
on acid-free paper

Wisdom has built her house; she has hewn her seven pillars.
   She has carved her meat, poured her wine, set her table.
She has sent forth her lasses.
   Now she calls over the roofs in the heights of the town:
"Let all who are simple come hither!"
   And to those who lack understanding, she says:
"Come, eat my food, drink the wine I have poured,
   Leave behind your simplicity, and live.
Set your feet on the road to discernment. . . .
   The first step of wisdom is awe of the Lord,
And to know what is holy is insight.
   For I give your days their abundance
And add length to the years of your life."

Proverbs 9:1–11

In Memoriam
Madeleine Joyce Goodman
1945–1996

Preface

Rights have always been a vexed issue, a ground of public contention, and, more privately, a marketplace of compromise and exchange. Today that ground has grown soft. The market slopes toward an international bidding war whose commodities, if they are publicly discussed at all, are rarely displayed among the rhetorical wares that are the boast of politicians and the pride of statesmen. Child labor, forced prostitution, ethnic cleansing, pollution by policy, famines planned and tolerated — even advocated — environmental degradation, sabotage and poisoning, medically supervised torture, ritual mutilation, cult slavery, mind control, and group suicide exacerbate the ancient abuses of genocide, to close the twentieth century with horrors as ghastly as any of the past, but perpetrated on a far broader scale and with industrial efficiency.

The commodification of violence, in land mines, chemical defoliants, and agents of mass murder like Sarin gas, or in cheap consumer goods from the gulags of the Second and Third Worlds or the sweatshops of the First, has spawned a ready apologetic for all these terrors and more: Free trade, global competition, and constructive engagement (if not the lifeboat ethos) create a climate in which rights talk grows problematic. And the new slogans are abetted by one very old one, which urges, in liberal language, that we not impose *our* values on *their* ways — that liberalism may be fine for the West but not necessarily for China, Burma, or Africa; that our troops, our boys and girls, and treasure, as politicians say when they want money to sound like something sacred, should not be inserted into age-old and endemic conflicts in Bosnia or Kurdistan (or Iraq, it was argued not too long ago), where the quarrel is not ours and the issues may be too complex for our understanding (meaning: too remote for our concern). As often happens with slogans, the subtext is far more eloquent in its silence than the spoken words. Here the subtext is the moral dichotomy of "us" and "them."

Meanwhile, at home, rights claims proliferate, as Bentham predicted they would, in a way that cheapens the rhetoric of rights to the point of worthlessness. Small wonder that Bentham sells short the entire concept. What anyone could claim with equal vehemence and could demand of a naturally uninterested public would of course appear to be of no value to begin with. But devaluation does not stop inflation. Rights at home are fiercely defended and aggressively dilated even as they are quietly compromised abroad, or in the moral margins of liberal societies, the fiduciary favellas where advocacy does not find ready sustenance — at the margins of human life, for example. Today there are rights for cars and buildings. There are those who say that food additives should be presumed harmless until proven otherwise. And I have met serious philosophers who refuse to call their dogs their pets but refer instead to "the dog who shares my home." There are jurists who claim not only differential rights to employment and to university and professional school admissions but even a right to weighted and multiple votes in elections for public office.

The advocates who use such inflated discourse seem to share the pragmatism of those who treat the very idea of rights as a notion of limited temporal or geographic application. They too would be just, *sed non modo* — not just yet. For now, there is ground to be gained. What can a philosopher do or say about any of this? Is all rights talk special pleading? Is there any way of appealing over the heads or behind the backs of what others say are their basic intuitions, or cultural presuppositions, or received traditions about justice? One can try.

One problem with the familiar discourse about rights, the discourse that we in the West have been using and enlarging over the last three centuries, is that fear of intolerance has stripped the idea of rights of overt metaphysical grounding. Relativism has not assured tolerance among its tenants, but the yearning for tolerance has nurtured a robust and invasive relativism. Skepticism (including moral skepticism!), secularism, positivism, romanticism, and historicism have long been urged, severally or in curious or muddled alloys, along with relativism, as marking out the one sure path to tolerance. Today, in the same spirit, many who call themselves Postmoderns condemn all forms of foundationalism, charging that such views are constitutively intolerant. It is as though the very belief that one's value claims might be grounded in reasons rather than in shared prejudices amounted to a license for political and ideological murder and mayhem. Even as classical a Lockean liberal as John Rawls defines political liberalism as a doctrine that prescinds from any comprehensive metaphysical scheme[1] — as if such basic metaphysical questions as the ontic standing of the individual or the ontic relation of that individual to a community had no bearing on questions of right and wrong or political legitimacy!

In Rawls's ideal, political discourse will be conducted solely by appeal to an underlying body of political assumptions that is sustained (ardently if necessary) without any visible support from a metaphysical or religious doctrine — a body of prejudices, in other words, although its elements preserve too attenuated a hold on the common life for them to pass muster and function even as respectable bits of prejudice. For, by Rawls's reasoning (and many share this view), to bring into the public square the values, insights, or perceptions of what Rawls calls a "comprehensive" scheme — be its primary and familiar idiom the symbolisms of religious myth and ritual or the conceptual dialectics of philosophy — is *eo ipso* to violate the only social compact upon which the natural pluralism of a healthy and stable human society can rest. The assumption seems to be that at home or perhaps in our places of worship we may all believe (within reason) what we like, but that when we come together in public, beliefs, like zipguns, should be checked at the door: We have nothing to teach one another about basic values or the nature of things, at least not when it comes to our common public life.

Fortunately, that is not the way any human society works, and it is not the way civilizations have grown. The most dynamic epochs of human cultural evolution, historically — whether in technology or in the realms of morals, spirit, science, and exploration — have always been the periods of greatest openness and exchange. Sometimes that interaction has been eager, sometimes hostile, sometimes ambivalent, or all of the above. Critical thinking, and the spread of critical thinking, have been by-products. Philosophy itself repeatedly has been a by-product and beneficiary of the clash and complementarity of cultures. Politically, it is not liberal but repressive to bar metaphysics and religion from the political realm. The intention may be to declaw religious and metaphysical discourse, but the effect is to emasculate political discourse.

The assumption that religion is about intolerance, or that the comprehensiveness of metaphysics is achieved by oppression rather than argument, is an unwholesome assumption, reflective of the misuse of religion and the abuse of metaphysics. Adoption of that assumption as a norm of liberal politics will not dislodge political thought and action from its metaphysical moorings or purge the religious motivations from political thought and action. Indeed, the assumption that comprehensive schemes are illiberal by nature fosters obscurantism and misdirection, for it assumes that metaphysical schemes and religious ideas are logic-tight, incommensurable, and pragmatically sterile. The implicit demand is that core human motives be camouflaged or disguised. Those whose work it is to create and elucidate religious and metaphysical schemes may sincerely adopt the intellectual asceticism proposed by those who find no net social gain in the teachings of religions or the reasonings of metaphysicians. But the required self-restraint leads only to the degeneration of their work. For a religion that is not public is esoteric or occult, and a metaphysics allowed no public expression becomes not private but hermetic. It does not lose but sublimates its pragmatic nisus. What it loses is its claim to self-critical rigor. When a "comprehensive scheme" loses the challenge to convince the unconvinced, premises slide into conclusions and psychic desiderata fuse with facts. Both the hearers and the makers of such schemes come, then, in the end, to equate metaphysics with arbitrariness, religion with superstition, and philosophy with pursuit of the unexamined life.

The aim of this book is to lay metaphysical foundations for an idea of rights and to apply the idea that these foundations anchor to several of the vexed issues of our day. The metaphysical theory I deploy is the general theory of deserts that I have been developing in several recent books, principally *On Justice* (1991) and *God of Abraham* (1996). What this theory says is that deserts are to be found in all beings, proportioned to and indeed identical with the extent of their claims, as equilibrated against the corresponding claims of other beings. Among the strengths of this theory are several that will emerge in the pages that follow:

1. It is not perspectival. The worth of a being or the merit of its claims does not depend on its notional similarity to ego or its pragmatic propinquity to ego's interests.
2. It does not presume that competition over a single type of resource in a zero sum game is the core theme of human interactions, since all beings exist in communities, and the realization of one being's project will often complement or enhance the interests of another.
3. The theory is naturalistic but not reductionistic. It obviates the search for a natural or non-natural quality of goodness by understanding the good as the aggregate interest of all beings. That interest in turn is contained in the natures of those beings. In fact, it *is* their natures, when the essence or identity of each being is construed dynamically, as its conatus.
4. By locating value in all beings, we achieve a *general* theory of justice, one that is not confined to contracting parties or even to human beings.
5. At the same time, we avoid the naturalistic fallacy: Value is not facticity; it is not a state of affairs at all. The reality of beings is what is of value; and it is that value, understood dynamically, as a project, that makes its appeal for recognition to all conscious choosers.
6. Further, the dynamism of being intends transcendence, so we can see the worth and beauty of all beings as expressions of their divine creation. We can reason from being to God, and we need not derive the preciousness of beings by appeal to their createdness. The goodness of being is evidence of God's love. We need not derive it from suppositious appeals to divine authority.
7. Since desert is proportioned to the claims a being makes, the special status of persons is preserved: The deserts of all beings are relative to the standing of those beings as claimants. Persons have a special standing, as subjects, as choosers, as potential fashioners of their own destiny.

Rights are a special class of deserts. They belong only to persons or to groups of persons, that is, communities such as families, nations, neighborhoods, and tribes. Rights, strictly construed, do not supersede or subordinate other rights. But many of our rights claims are in fact the built-up expectations that are made feasible by our social and specifically civil cooperation. Just as the prima facie deserts of all must be reconciled and coordinated in those cases where we need to establish legitimate deserts (the child or the virus), so rights claims need to be equilibrated (by laws and courts, but also by accommodation, economic cooperation, and social coordination) to establish what shall count as rights in a given context, that is, as deserts not to be overridden.

In reflecting on the anatomy and dynamic of rights in this book, as in *On Justice* and *God of Abraham*, I have drawn heavily on the Jewish sources. I think these sources have a great deal to contribute today, as they have in the past, to human understanding of the issues we are addressing—issues that have grown vexed conceptually, in part because they are contested politically. I am under no illusions about the power of philosophy to persuade. Many readers are innocent of the basic skills required to follow a philosophical argument; and professional philosophers have many skills for armoring themselves against conviction, not least of which is the ingrained bias of some against whatever looks too foreign, or insufficiently secular. Yet I think it helps philosophy to hear from quarters not typically heard from; and I know that some philosophers, and some non-philosophers too, are attuned to ideas that are not mere repetitions of a familiar cant.

Much of modernity as we know it is a form of secularism. It originates in a kind of adolescent rebellion against the authority of an ancestral tradition that infused law with morality and morality with religion. The old tradition built norms that were global in rationale but fragmented and local in application. Seeking to correct the oppressiveness and disorder of medieval authority structures, the makers of modernity created its mirror image, norms intended to be global in application but minimal in overt cosmology. The old abuses were widely displaced by a new and more efficient order, with its own characteristic excesses, manifested, in the extreme, in bouts of statist absolutism, secular hubris, and (if we trace the continuum from street gangs to the SS) organized anomie. The new traditionalism of the former Soviet lands and the communalism emergent in the West are both responses to the excesses of secularist modernity. They bear with them a host of historically familiar dangers — not least, the recrudescence of atavistic superstitions, religious oppression, destructive ethnic passions, and groupthink. At several points this book reflects on some of the weaknesses of the still prevalent liberal orthodoxy (to coin an oxymoron), an orthodoxy that can trace its roots back to the Epicurean individualism of the Hellenistic age. But my criticisms are made not in a hostile but in a constructive spirit, since I too am a child of the liberal dispensation, and a philosopher committed by conviction to the humanistic aims of liberalism, if not to the impatient secularism that is its frequent historical concomitant. Perhaps the more ancient tradition that antedates both modern liberalism and the excesses against which it reacts will serve (despite its own ancient problems) as something of an outrigger, offering some moment of balance, against which both the medieval (or neomedieval) and the modern varieties of excess can be checked.

Let me say a word about what I do not intend to do. This book is primarily a normative book. It is not a descriptive survey of the Jewish sources and does not profess to contribute to the positivist project of *Jüdische Wissenschaft* by tracing a single theme or group of themes through the sources with a view to extracting "the" pertinent Jewish belief or practice — or even with a view to tracing the history, dialectic, or dynamic of rival Jewish views or competing Jewish practices. In a fair-minded review of *On Justice*, Warren Zev Harvey writes: "On the question of justice, one finds different and conflicting views in the Jewish sources. Goodman's book is no less 'authentically Jewish,' even if some books defending rival theories are also authentically Jewish."[2] Here Harvey takes the reference to authenticity that he draws from *On Justice* (p. x) in a strictly historicist sense. But if authenticity is to evoke commitment, then argument and the coherence of the sources with one another and with the whole of human knowledge and experience must have their say. Philosophically, our concern is not with what is Jewish among the documents in the common human legacy but with what is credible and livable, including what is credible and of enduring worth in the Jewish canon. Such questions are not answered from a purely positive historical standpoint.

The philosophical method is powerless without its historical basis, a fact that many philosophers seek to ignore; but outcomes reached by the historical method must also be informed, their standpoint enlarged and their biases counteracted, by the thematic and dialectical tests of philosophy. Even the most sheerly descriptive work, I find, when it tries to avoid engagement with the philosophical issues, typically adopts categories, distinctions, and above all dichotomies that lead not to the sidestepping but to the begging of the critical philosophical questions — so that, for example, an opposition is presumed, say, between reason and revelation, and then any philosopher who seeks to overcome the projected opposition is branded incoherent or confused.

Since it is not my intention to write a natural history of all the notions that can claim Jewish ancestry, this book will not work too well as a catalog of ideas already well formed in the Jewish tradition. Many themes will be omitted, and some may be included that are not found fully elaborated in the canon. One does not find what is appropriable in a tradition by sheer repetition. Indeed, no living tradition perpetuates itself by rote. Encyclopedic surveys are typically a way of closing the books on a tradition. They are headstones, not incubators.

My surveys of the Jewish sources are highly selective. But what they find is representative of important themes in the tradition — themes important for their intellectual depth, and often for their positive penetrance and historical impact on the ethos of Israel and beyond. It would be easy enough, and perhaps entertaining, to cull other themes and patterns from the sources. One might write a history of misogyny, or of textual ciphers, for example. Or one could work instructively at a higher level of abstraction, tracing the rhetorical tropes, syntactical connectives, or associative linkages in the canonical and non-canonical literature. But what I have looked for, and found abundantly, are the appropriable norms and the insights that provoke philosophical reflection. Thus, the spine of this book, as of *On Justice* and *God of Abraham*, is its philosophical argumentation. The proof texts it contains are used, as they have been used by all the great Jewish philosophers, to exhibit a continuity between the present argument and the tradition that nourishes it. The book may prove useful to readers of cosmopolitan interests who are less familiar than they might like to be with what is to be gleaned from those sources. But the argument is not simply derived from those sources. Still less is it an apologetic for their positivity.

What Jewish philosophy must do, as sharply distinguished from the history or even the philosophy of Judaism, is to work out a viable line of argument about the large issues, in dialogue with the Jewish sources and the general discourse of philosophy. Doing this means securing the truth philosophically to the best of one's ability, allowing the sources to inform one's understanding — and allowing one's understanding, even as one reads, to inform one's reading. The method is not novel. It has been used throughout the many epochs in which Jewish thinkers have had to reconstitute and recapture the ancient insights of their tradition, from the writing of Deuteronomy, to the recasting of the Mosaic message by the Prophets, to the reappropriation of its norms by the Judges, the rabbinic Sages, the medieval philosophers, the Moderns, and, of course, the Postmoderns, like Levinas and Leibowitz.

Although what I am writing is intended as a normative book, it is not a book of prescriptions but a book of philosophical theory. It seeks the basis of a decision about what our idea of rights should be, and it seeks that basis in reasoning. Thus, it is not my aim, here or anywhere else, to argue from authority. That means in part that I do not intend to urge a normative conclusion on the grounds of its Jewishness. Such argumentation is inherently self-defeating. It appeals only to those who are committed to the normativity of Jewish imperatives, and, among that group, only to the tiny subset who subscribe precisely to one's views about Judaism and the content and application of its norms. As the discussions grow more specific, that subset rapidly approaches one — unless, of course, an author bears some traditional or charismatic authority. But then argument becomes a mere ornament of discourse. My beard has never been long enough to help or hinder me in that way, and my hope and plan are to keep that beard well trimmed.

A sympathetic Catholic philosopher, after reading *On Justice*, remarks that the book "never deviates from a naturalistic interpretation of the Hebrew scriptures," which it presents "as an important, although literary source of insight into human nature and its fulfillment."[3] That, I think, is as it should be. How else, I wonder, can we read our sources in a multicultural context, where those who read with us can hardly be expected simply to adopt our traditional perspectives? Our own community is not united in its vision of the status or authority of Scripture. And even if there were a text that held unquestioned authority, one still would face the task of interpreting it. In this circumstance, let us read Scripture, and the larger canon, with an open mind and see what we can find there that we are able to deem worthy of divine inspiration. That approach holds itself open to revelation but does not presuppose it. The presumption that scripture (any scripture) is revealed yields only suppositiousness and, when that fails, dogma, skepticism, and loss of interest.

Similarly with appeals to God himself as the ultimate authority, an option that has been urged upon me by friends both wise and simple. Surely, one might argue, a Jewish theory of justice must be theistic. This expectation, I think, is right in one sense but dead wrong in another. If what is meant is that the theory should acknowledge holiness and assign a higher than merely material or exchange value to beings in general and persons in particular, I think the claim is true. Every religion assigns special value to the objects of our encounter, and Judaism does so by regarding all beings, and human beings especially, as works of divine creation and recipients of divine grace, love, and concern — repositories of the value that is rightly celebrated and respected in our treatment of those beings and our responses to their preciousness. It is that celebration and respect that the Law seeks to interpret and enhance.

But if the idea is that a Jewish philosophy of justice must ground its normative claims in the authority of God, then the idea is wrongheaded, not because God issues no such commands in behalf of His creation, but because arguments from authority prove nothing to anyone. Those who do not know or acknowledge the reality, let alone the rule of God, far from being impressed by such appeals, are only put off by them. And even among committed monotheists there are material disagreements about God's expectations.

Natural theology, I believe, should link the idea of the good with that of God, for the core insight of monotheism is the recognition that God's commands speak only in behalf of the good. We can be sure of this nexus, since the idea of goodness is, for monotheists, constitutive in our idea of the divine. It is this linkage, I have argued, that is intended when Genesis calls the mountain where Abraham did not sacrifice Isaac "the mountain where the Lord revealed Himself" (Gen. 22:14). For Abraham was blessed even though he did not carry through his initial intent to sacrifice his beloved son. Indeed, he was blessed in that very choice, the choice forced upon him when he had to decide between God's explicit and unambiguous command that he sacrifice Isaac and the angel's urgent plea that he refrain from such a horror and do no harm to his son. His blessing, shared with all nations, lay in the recognition that divine holiness is found not in the tremendum of violence but in acts of kindness, generosity, and justice.[4]

Tracing this paradigm, we can allow the growth in our idea of goodness to inform our idea of God, even as our recognition of God's perfection and abso-luteness makes clear to us key facets of the metaphysic of morals — for example, that moral requirements are as unexceptionable as the laws of nature, and for the same reason: Both are temporal expressions of God's immutable grace, wisdom, and love. But again I emphasize that we compromise our ability to rise episte-mically from the recognition of moral truths or material gifts to acknowledgment of their source in divine law or grace if we have derived the worth of those gifts or the sanctity of those obligations from the authority of the divine in the first place. How, then, can we anchor moral claims?

A Jewish philosophy of justice, as I will argue, should be ontological. It should ground the deserts of beings in the nature of their being, according respect, rec-ognition, or dignity to all things in accordance with what they are. I would not claim that a sound philosophy of justice must be Jewish, or ontological. There are many ways of pointing toward the widely shared ideals that cluster under the idea of justice. Indeed the effort to give grounding to such ideals might seem otiose — an ironic attempt to justify justice itself — were it not for the broad areas of controversy about the footings and the coverage of the idea. Such controversy can make even the ideal of justice seem problematic and can, at times, undercut important ele-ments of it. Appeal to the worth, beauty, and dignity of the beings we encounter can help steady the picture and stabilize the commitment that practical justice calls for.

Thus the first chapter of this book argues for the ontological theory of deserts as an objective and inclusionary anchor to normative claims. The second chapter traces the metaphysical foundations of the idea of human rights in the classic Jewish sources. The third considers the vexed issue of abortion. In the phased approach of the Judaic canon it finds an application of the idea that entitative claims are the basis of deserts. This leads in turn to the delineation of a middle ground between the strident extremes that claim on the one hand that abortion is murder and on the other that it is no more a concern of the law than is a woman's decision to pare her nails or cut her hair. The fourth chapter is a critique of Mill's idea of liberty and of some of its current overextensions. The intent is to show how our ontic theory of deserts affords broader coverage and surer protection to positive and negative human rights than are available from Mill's Utilitarian argumentation. Addressing several topical concerns, including issues of pornography and commercial persuasion, the chapter seeks to expose some of the inconsistencies and moral problematics that arise among the more high-voltage applications of Mill's defense of free expression, the area where Mill tended to focus his interest in liberty. The final chapter deals with nations and nationhood. It argues that national states are legitimated by the good they can do for their members and for the world at large. Like any sound legitimation, this argument bears within it the parameters of its own limitation, in the corollary, that these states may not rightly violate the principles that legitimate their very sustenance.

Thanks are due here to all the philosophers, colleagues, and friends who discussed the contents of this book with me. Chapter 1 grows out of lectures presented at Harvard and at the Universities of Arizona, Colorado, and Hawaii. Those lectures became the basis of two papers presented, respectively, at the Academy for Jewish Philosophy meeting in Evanston and at the American Academy of Religion meeting in Chicago. Kenneth Seeskin of Northwestern University and Hava Tirosh-Samuelson of Indiana University organized those sessions; Elliot Wolfson of New York University and Daniel Frank of the University of Kentucky edited the proceedings; one of these papers appeared under the title "Prescriptivity" in the *Journal of Jewish Thought and Philosophy*, and the other, in the SUNY Press volume *Commandment and Community*, under the title "Toward a Jewish Philosophy of Justice." The two papers are combined and much revised here. Further thanks are due to Robert Audi of the University of Nebraska, Jean Bethke Elshtain of the University of Chicago, Mark Murphy of Georgetown University, and Gregg Horowitz of Vanderbilt for their insightful comments on the matter of chapter 1.

Chapter 2 began its life as a paper written for a session of the Society for Medieval and Renaissance Philosophy at the American Philosophical Association meeting in Atlanta. My thanks to all the discussants there, especially A. S. McGrade, and to Mark Murphy for his comments on an intermediate draft. Pamela Huby of Tunbridge Wells and Susan Wiltshire of Vanderbilt made valuable contributions that are noted in the text.

Chapter 3 was written in response to an invitation to the Constantinus Colloquy organized by G. R. Dunstan at the University of Exeter. This early version was published in the proceedings volume, revised and expanded in the Samson Levey Festschrift edited by David Ellenson and Stanley Chyet, and more fully revised and updated here. I fondly recall the memory of David Balme, the brilliant Aristotle scholar. I learned much from his comments at the Exeter colloquy and in subsequent exchanges. Thanks to David Novak of the University of Toronto and Menachem Kellner of Haifa University for their careful reading and helpful comments as the chapter evolved, and to Stephen Ricks for information about abortion in the Ancient Near East.

Chapter 4 was first presented at the Vanderbilt meeting of the Academy for Jewish Philosophy, which I chaired. I thank my Vanderbilt colleagues Robert Ehman, Elijah Millgram, Henry Teloh, and John Lachs for their comments on the early drafts.

Chapter 5 was first written for the East West Philosophers Conference in Honolulu, where it was presented as a plenary address. I took the argument further after presenting the paper in the Vanderbilt Philosophy Colloquium. Thanks to Mark Murphy and to my Vanderbilt colleagues David Steiner, Don Sherburne, and Ben Walter for their thoughtful and provocative comments on the early drafts.

For comments, advice, and suggestions that were relevant and helpful as the preparation of this book itself proceeded, I thank all of the above, as well as Rabbi Zalman Posner of Nashville, for his stimulating conversation and personal warmth. I acknowledge here my student helpers Jonathan Born of Emory University for help with the general index and Ben Wolf of Yeshiva University for help with the index locorum. Shelly Zilberfarb of Bar Ilan University and Ben Wolf were of great help in double-checking the biblical and rabbinic citations. Thanks too are due to Amani al-Bedah for her substantive comments as well as her technical help.

Among the stimulants to the writing of this book were the many comments I received about *On Justice* and *God of Abraham*. Notable among these were the reviews of *On Justice* by Alfred Ivry, Oliver Leaman, and David Novak and the commentaries on *God of Abraham* organized by Michael Zank at the first American Philosophical Association session of the Academy for Jewish Philosophy and in further sessions on the Internet. The A.P.A. symposiasts, besides Michael Zank, included David Novak, Heidi Ravven of Hamilton College, and Norbert Samuelson of Temple University. Hilary Putnam of Harvard held the chair. The Internet respondents included David Burrell of Notre Dame, Allan Arkush of Binghamton University, Menachem Kellner, and David Weininger of Boston University. I also received formal or written responses to *On Justice* from Allan Arkush, Robert McLaren, and David Novak, and from my Vanderbilt colleagues in a colloquium dedicated to discussion of this book and its theory of deserts. The speakers were Robert Ehman, Peter Haas, Gregg Horowitz, and John Lachs. These critiques and appreciations, along with the reviews, played no small role in my thinking as the new book took shape.

All but one of the learned friends with whom I discussed the ideas of this book are still numbered among my friends and collaborators. But the friend who was the closest to me is no longer here to share my pleasures and delights. Madeleine Goodman died October 2, 1996, just two years after becoming the first woman Dean of Arts and Science at Vanderbilt University, and a scant 31 years after our marriage in August 1965. The cancer that took her just four months after its appearance did not rob her of her spirit, integrity, creativity, or hope. Even in the hospital her laughter remained. I have never known a better or more beautiful person. The elegance of her musical and artistic soul clothed itself in gentle power, intellectual rigor, human warmth and fairness, generosity and openness of spirit.

This book was completed in the intervals of her illness, as I struggled to care for her. It was finalized during a semester's research leave granted me by Vanderbilt shortly before her death. I place it as a pebble on her grave.

Nashville   L. E. G.
February 1998

Contents

Abbreviations

ARN	*Avot de-Rabbi Natan*
B.	Babylonian Talmud
ED	Saadiah Gaon, *Kitāb al-Mukhtār fī 'l-Āmānāt wa-'-'I'tiqādāt (Sefer ha-Nivhar ba-Emunot ve-De'ot* — The Book of Critically Selected Beliefs and Convictions)
EI²	*Encyclopedia of Islam*, second edition.
Guide	Maimonides, *Guide to the Perplexed*
K.D.	Epicurus, *Kyriai Doxai* (Principal Doctrines)
JPS	Jewish Publication Society
MT	Maimonides, *Mishneh Torah*
SUNY	State University of New York
TF	Al-Ghazālī, *Tahāfut al-Falāsifa*
TP	Spinoza, *Tractatus Politicus*
TT	Ibn Rushd, *Tahāfut al-Tahāfut*
TTP	Spinoza, *Tractatus Theologico-Politicus*
Y.	Jerusalem Talmud

Judaism, Human Rights, and Human Values

The Idea of Deserts

Philosophers may seem to pay inordinate attention to questions about the source of legal or political authority. Is it man or God or nature, fact or convention, the consent or acquiescence of the governed or the dictum, tacit or explicit, of that by which they are governed—whether law or ruler, institution or individual, the collective wisdom of a society or its counterpart of unwisdom? The metaphor of a source from which authority flows may mask a damaging confusion between the fruitful and morally imperative quest for justification and the historical question of beginnings. For, whatever else authority may be, it is not the same as authorship. Thinkers who would never dream of judging another by an accident of birth blithely or anxiously seek the normativity of the law in the circumstances of its origin—as though legitimacy here meant what it once did in genealogy and was rather a test of rectitude than a mark of good fortune in the birth of a polity, or a person.

The debate over the sources of authority is made the more acrimonious by an unseemly squabble for control over human inclinations and aspirations that has persisted as long as there has been talk about norms. The arms and armor of those who continue that struggle today inevitably bear the battle scars of the long fight for the emancipation of the individual human spirit and the concomitant segregation of the sacred from the secular. Inwardly, too, the participants are scarred, by the wary presumption of an inevitable adversarship between individual and community, freedom and tradition, creativity and conformity. It would be valuable to outflank or at least mitigate such struggles by showing the complementarity rather than egging on the hostility of the rival sources of prescriptive claims—sacred and secular, public and personal, innovative and traditional.

Some seek objectivity for law by anchoring its demands in the absoluteness of God, or in a surrogate for divine rule, the authority of nature. But no one who loves freedom will accept mere or sheer authority—not even divine authority—without the imprimatur of consent. For authority that is not accepted is not authority at all. And the name of God, and of nature too, seems everywhere at risk of misappropriation. Any standard can be misappropriated. So no badge or name or seal of authority gives proof of normativity. There is no tyrant too low to claim divine approval, and no tyranny too base to find apologists who will describe its crimes as responses to the imperatives of nature — as, in subtle and intellectually impressive ways, A. J. P. Taylor did for Hitler, E. H. Carr for Stalin, and Arnold Toynbee for virtually every despotism known to the historical record. The graver and more heinous the villainy, the higher the authority claimed for it. Thus the rightful fear of sensible persons, and of cautious friends of Thomas Hobbes, toward those who claim to talk with God and act directly at His word. Thus too, ironically, the quest for sources of authority not above us but within us. I say ironically, because Hobbes feared appeals to private conscience for the same reasons as he did appeals to divine voices. The two were typically interchangeable in the recalcitrant individuals and refractory movements that most drew his fears.

Then there is the social process of consent. Beyond questions of imposture, one reason why appeals to God and nature accomplish little when offered as anchors of normativity is that justice, to be done, clearly must be instituted. Neither God nor nature *institutes* the laws, defines the rights and wrongs, the crimes and punishments that a polity ordains. Even if God is the legislator, and His laws of life, incipient in the laws of nature, undergird the laws of the courts, or even if God is taken literally to thunder His laws from on high, along with every detail of their penalties and rewards, conditions and exceptions, procedures and formalities, still it is we humans who must implement or ignore, interpret and apply those laws. It is with this thought in mind that I do not think it wise to begin the quest for the basis of authority by appealing to the presumptive authority of God or that of nature. For even those who accept the often controversial notions that God or nature *have* authority seem to hold widely divergent views about what that authority commands or expects of us. Abe Lincoln wisely answered questions about whether God was on the Union side in the American Civil War by saying that his hope was that the Union was on God's side. The powerful reminder of Deuteronomy (30:12), "It is not in heaven," was cited in the same spirit by the Rabbis (B. Bava Metzia 59b). The working edge of the law is ours to discover and devise, in full awareness of our responsibility — all the more so if it is God's will that we are called upon to execute and institute.

Since we alone can implement the norms we will call our own, consent is of the practical essence in establishing normativity — and consent in no mere formal, mythic, idle, or wishful sense, but the living interactions that make a written law a way of life or a dead letter. Not surprisingly, we read that when some of the Rabbis wanted to extend to olive oil restrictions like those they had applied to wine, the proposed norms died by desuetude: They were not accepted by the people (B. Avodah Zarah 36a).

Since a law is law only where there is some measure of consent, the illusion arises that there would be no norms at all, no right or wrong, apart from human assent. Indeed, many humanists believe that man can do what God and nature cannot: create a law where there was none. But note the necessary distinction: Only man can institute. But it does not follow that man is the sole and sufficient fount of authority in the law. Even for man to be the measure, there must be something to be measured and so some standard of accuracy or consistency in the measurement.

Laws, I believe, are devised to implement respect for certain values. With this idea in mind, I would like to shift attention away from the legislator, whether located within us or beyond us, and to focus on beings, the beings that norms in general and laws specifically seek to protect and respect. This seems so natural and appropriate an approach that I am surprised it is not more widely adopted. I can certainly understand the sense of urgency that leads some to make a backstop of divine authority or that prompts others to turn to sanctions of social disapproval, ostracism or punishment, condign or subtle, as if sanctions, somehow were justifications. The voice of God may seem more monitory than the mere imperatives of what is right. Or, if God's voice is muted and dulled into the rough noise of nature, perhaps that noise may seem to gain a sharper articulacy when broadcast as the voice of convention and consent among the multitude. Still, we must ask, why would God command — or why should society sanction — anything other than the right?

When consent becomes paramount in justifying norms, the quest for moral objectivity shifts its gaze to the undeniability of the subjective and comes to rest in intersubjectivity, first as the mark, then as the test, finally as the substance of objective justice. The shift gives force and credence to the ancient fiction that justice is a compact or convention among contracting parties. Higher claims are dismissed as mere pretexts or pretensions. Yet popular consent is as readily wooed or bribed, deceived or seduced, as are the pens of historians, cosmologists, or theologians. And the rationales for its omnisufficiency smack of the law courts or their atria: "If Smith agreed to this, he has no one to blame but himself." "Jones was an adult, unhoodwinked and uncoerced. So what jury now would say that he was wronged in what he once thought would be right for him?" Is consent the same as justice?

1. Prescriptivity by Agreement?

No one who lives free and loves justice will pay lip service to tyrannous laws. So defenders of justice are no friends to the idea that laws can draw their rightness or moral force from a mere fiat. God, who is the traditional repository of such fiats, becomes, as a result, the paramount and most hated of tyrants to be overthrown. The theory of popular consent takes its birth and first infant steps as the biblical twin and counterpart of the idea that God's legislation must be just (see Exod. 19:8, 24:3, 7; Josh. 1:16; cf. Num. 32:31). But it reaches adolescence in the Renaissance and Enlightenment by throwing off such claims to kinship. Like Jacob and Esau, the two ideas come to maturity distanced from one another.

The view that justice is a compact or agreement is proposed by Plato's brothers Glaucon and Adeimantus when they speak as devil's advocates in the *Republic* (II 357–60). Glaucon, "always an intrepid, enterprising spirit, in everything," argues for "the view of the multitude" that justice is a bother. It has its rewards, to be sure, but no intrinsic worth — and worse, it interferes with our natural desires. It is tolerated, even sought after, only because men have gotten together and agreed that they would rather give up the chance of harming one another than risk each others' constant depredations and attacks. Any one of us, Glaucon argues, would surely rather take advantage of the rest than submit to rules. But recognizing the exposure we all would face if force and fraud were universal, ego, never setting aside its egotism, submits to a law. The essence and basis of that law is the understanding that I will not take advantage of you, if you, on pain of punishment, agree not to take advantage of me.

Justice here is a mean between extremes — between ego's presumptive preference of aggression with impunity, and a countervailing fear of becoming the butt and victim of everyone else. No definition of advantage is offered beyond the presumptions as to the desiderata of interacting parties. So the most basic questions about right and wrong, good and evil, are begged or finessed in favor of an unreflective subjectivism. Desire and aversion become determinative of objective value. The fact that desires may vary or conflict, from person to person or even from moment to moment, is both exploited and ignored — exploited in the image of justice as a kind of deal or compromise; ignored in the nonce suspension of any thought of the tensions that might undermine such deals or of the standards that might call them into question, including, crucially, any standards that individuals might use to moderate or guide their own demands and expectations. Rather, Glaucon confirms the claim that aggression without risk is indeed ego's absolute preference, by telling the tale of Gyges and the criminal acts by which the Lydian dynasty was founded.

Epicurus, who held the conventionalist view mooted by Plato's brother, sums it up perfectly: "Natural justice is a compact of mutual advantage to restrict the parties from harming or being harmed by one another" (*K.D.* 31; cf. Lucretius, *De Rerum Natura* V 1010–27). "For all living things which have not been able to make contracts not to harm or be harmed by one another, there is no justice or injustice. The same holds true of those peoples who have been unable or unwilling to make compacts not to harm or be harmed" (*K.D.* 32). That last dictum is a ready rationale for enslaving tribal peoples. But it is simply a corollary of the general axiom Epicurus has laid down: "Justice is not anything in itself, it is just a compact among men in their various relations in a particular time and place, mutually undertaking not to harm or be harmed" (*K.D.* 33). By the same token: "Injustice is not an evil in itself but only in the fear arising from the apprehension that one will not escape those appointed to mete out retribution" (*K.D.* 34).

On this account there is nothing intrinsically wrong in injuring another, but there is a prudential reason for avoiding harm to others: to avoid trouble, especially trouble of mind; for friends or family of those injured, or agents appointed for the purpose, will seek out the author of an injury. He can never be sure that some Javert will not hunt him down for the most venial of offenses: "It is not possible for one who surreptitiously violates the compact not to injure or be injured ever to be confident that he will escape retribution, even if he has done so ten thousand times. Down to his death he will remain uncertain of his escape" (*K.D.* 35). So criminals will never enjoy the Epicurean goal, *ataraxia*, peace of mind.

The aim and upshot of this theory, with all its prudential suasions in behalf of moderation and its sometimes wishful warnings against giving free rein to our impulses and desires, is relativism. All genuinely prescriptive norms remain personal, tied to an objective standard only by the limitations of human physiology and sociality. We can see the limits of such a position clearly in the immediate consequences of the Epicurean argument. For the reasoning proves too much. It not only counsels against wrongdoing but also urges us to do nothing, even to defend family dignity or personal property, loved ones' lives, or our own liberty, against a criminal or tyrant. Indeed, the account makes no distinction between the unease of the criminal and that of the victim. By the stated standard, no one should ever testify in court, especially not against a criminal, given the ungovernable threat of reprisals. Right and wrong have now become contingent on the efficacy of "those appointed to mete out retribution"—a task of the sort that Epicurean philosophers, of course, are advised to shun.

"In general terms," Epicurus tells us, keeping one eye on the naturalism that anchors his hedonism, "justice is the same for all, a kind of mutual advantage in their relations. But in terms of a particular country or circumstances the same thing is not just in every case" (K.D. 36). "Among the things regarded as just, that which has proved mutually advantageous in human relations is what is just, regardless whether or not it is the same for all. If one makes a law and it does not remain mutually advantageous, then it no longer has the character of justice. But if the advantage in terms of justice should shift and agree with the general notion only for a short time, still for that time that law was just in the eyes of those who regard the facts and do not confuse themselves with empty sounds" (K.D. 37.) "Unless circumstances have changed, actions which have been considered just but do not accord with the general notion in their actual effects are not just. Where circumstances have changed and actions which were held to be just no longer lead to advantage, then they were just when they promoted the common welfare of citizens in their mutual relations; but when no longer advantageous they were no longer just" (K.D. 38). Here we see vigorous roots of progressivism, utilitarianism, Deweyan experimentalism, Hobbesian nominalism, Benthamite reformism and hatred of legal fictions—even a precedent for Rawls's appeals to ordinary (civil) notions—much that is wholesome, wise, and refreshing, but also much that is misleading.

I want to raise two problems about the view that justice is a convention. The first is what I call the Skyhook Problem. The second is a problem about the exclusion of those—like the animals and savages tellingly paired by Epicurus—who are not parties to the political or social contract.

First the Skyhook Problem. If justice is by agreement, and agreements are conventions, how can any law be binding? I do not mean permanently binding, but binding at all, even for the moment of its immediate utility? The fact that some practice is useful does not in itself entail that any person or institution has the authority to impose it, especially not if the utilities are transferred and, like tax revenues (or pollution credits), arise in one quarter and alight in another.[1] But even if the prospective benefit is confined to the actor (hardly a typical *social* benefit or a prima facie demand of law), where does anyone get the right to tell another what goods to pursue or how to pursue them?

If it is argued that individuals have agreed to accept some common authority or rule (and the fiction is maintained that present actors are somehow, by ancestry or patrimony, parties to that agreement), we still must ask where societies acquire the authority to bind individuals to adhere to their undertakings. Hobbes would have it that it is irrational to break an agreement into which one has rationally entered. But that argument violates the basic Epicurean claim that any norm applies only as long as its benefits continue. How can self-interest bind us to an undertaking no longer seen or believed to be in our interest? Hobbes here simply throws up his hands and speaks of reprisal, since the organism that consent has created now has the power to enforce adherence.

If one objects about the rightness of such enforcement, or asks how the state or the society acquires the authority coercively to sustain a relationship that for some at least, *ex hypothesi*, no longer seems worthwhile (if it ever did), we are reminded of the Machiavellian axiom that right is nothing more than power. That sounds like Galileo being shown the rack, and we wonder, has the aim of justifying authority somehow been forgotten? If raw hegemony is the only issue, there was no need for elaborate appeals to the self-interest of the contracting parties. But why should even self-interest be heeded—unless there is some intrinsic worth in the individual?

Conventionalists and relativists, of course, want no truck with the idea of intrinsic worth. Hobbes equates worth in general with price, and worthiness with usefulness, as gauged by that most social of all measures, monetary exchange: "The value or worth of a man is, as of all other things, his price; that is to say, so much as would be given for the use of his power: and therefore is not absolute; but a thing dependent on the need and judgment of another. . . . Worthiness . . . consists in a particular power or ability . . . fitness or aptitude."[2]

Spinoza criticizes Hobbes on the first of these points, the legerdemain that wants to keep agreements in force beyond their perceived usefulness. Hobbes's exertions here yield the entertaining spectacle of an avowed nominalist trying to work word magic with the fact that promises have been made. Marx attacks the second point, the economic reduction of human value, when he shows that the labor market may drive the replacement cost of human beings below the level of subsistence. But Marx's materialism gives him no words in which to voice the moral abhorrence of such outcomes. The root of the trouble is the false assumption that human worth can be rightly and exhaustively measured in economic terms.

A. E. Taylor comes to Hobbes's defense, charging Spinoza with bad faith for allowing some pledges to be broken.[3] But the criticism misses the mark. Spinoza exempts us from our undertakings only insofar as they preserve no inherent value.[4] In such a case, he reasons, the contract has been nullified by the misfeasance of one of the parties, and there is no ground for insisting that the other remain bound by it. The Elizabethan sting of the Hobbesian charge that rebels are "forsworn" is blunted by Spinoza's recognition that only worthless or noxious enterprises are rightfully abandoned. When an agreement or convention is sustained by nothing more than the fact that it once was viable, why need there be any compunction in walking away from it? And if only words sustain what has become an unwholesome arrangement, why not simply leave it to its fate?

As Mendelssohn makes clear, communities and societies, generically, do have an inherent value, in virtue of the interests they serve.[5] Crucially, to put the matter in Aristotelian terms, civility and civilization can humanize human life. Yet tyrannies can dehumanize it. History shows us many more instances of both possibilities than the ancients knew. Avoiding what I call the generic fallacy (treating genera as though they were species, whose members share the same nature and effects), we can see that it would be wrong to abandon all social engagement. But that fact does not legitimate all modes of government; nor does it legitimate all established states, or any of their rivals. Hobbes may be right, as apologists of authority before him were often right, in arguing (with concrete cases in mind) that a bad government is better than none at all. But he was wrong in supposing that the only alternative to a bad government is none at all.

Governments as such have no authority whatever. The authority of a state, its legitimacy, rests on what it does, in its particularity, for the interests it was founded to serve, or rather for the interests in behalf of which its survival is sustained, and those that need its aid. Past or even present acts of consent confer no such authority. To pin authority to consent, as though consent sufficed to legitimate laws, states, or other institutions, is to suspend justice from a skyhook. It legitimates too much, sweeping up into its embrace bad arrangements along with good ones. And it appeals to the putative rationality of choices made under duress (the threat of anarchy) and then seeks to enforce adherence to those choices on the notional grounds that a choice has been made. When the arbitrariness of that appeal is exposed, the positive (as opposed to rational) sanction of authority is unlimbered: the threat of punishment, and behind it once again the threat of anarchy, wishfully invoked, like the fanciful avengers of Epicurus's moral fable, or the *ayenbite of inwit* that moralizers hold up as a bogey to threaten ever less sensitive "pale criminals." Our concern, however, is not with the sanctions of authority but with its warrant, not with the likelihood of retribution but with its legitimacy.

Here the conventionalism of Hobbes and Epicurus contributes little. It remains as vulnerable as ever to Mendelssohn's dialectic: "If men are not bound by nature to any duty, they do not even have a duty to keep their contracts."[6] For the conventionalist account does not adequately answer the question, 'On what basis do individuals band together?' And it gives no answer at all to the deeper question about the grounds on which they might rightfully expect one another's loyalty or support. Hobbes's intent was to derive obligations by assuming none and thus to traverse the no-man's-land that Hume would later demarcate between the *is* and the *ought*. His strategy was to argue that no one can deny man in a state of nature the right, identical with his power, to defend his life and any interests he might deem conducive to self-protection. Fear and vanity, in such conditions of lawlessness, will no doubt motivate many actions. But no civil society yet exists to call any act wrong, and what has not been named wrong is, by Hobbes's standards, done with perfect right. The proof (apart from appeal to an abstract state of nature in which no one, *per hypothesi*, has forbidden anything as yet) lies in the futility of seeking to forbid the intended acts of self-protection that are done "by a certain impulsion of nature no less than that whereby a stone moves downward."[7] Thus even in a state of nature, Hobbesian men have rights, or they act by right, although they have as yet no obligations.[8] They acquire obligations by their natural desire to protect their rights, or lives, or powers. Reason sees the bootlessness and fruitlessness of continued life in a state of nature, and men enter into civil society like fish into a trap: Reason advises them to give up their powers of aggression and self-defense in the interest of creating a sovereign, who will use their several powers collectively to exact obedience from each and enforce the protection of all.

To say that no one has yet forbidden (or effectively forbidden!) an act is not to make it justified; and I may well have obligations to others prior to making any undertakings about them. But I fail to see how I can have even an obligation to myself unless I have some worth. The plea that no one should be surprised if I take what measures I deem necessary to protect myself is not a justification but only a warning. The notions that warning employs—of self, of measures, of interests, and even of warrant—are suspiciously moral in tone,[9] parasitic on conceptions made possible through the work, if not of civil society, then at least of some form of community that fosters a sense of personal identity and enlightened self-interest.

Myths often presuppose what they overtly explain,[10] and the idea of the social contract is no exception. Thus, those who enter civil society, whether on Hobbes's or Rawls's terms, are somehow expected to know pretty much what the new society will be like. More troubling than that bit of projective thinking, and the related notion that men who acknowledge no responsibility to one another will have a clear conception of their social wants, is the notion that such wants can somehow be cranked up into a normative program. That can be done, I argue, only by imputing deserts. Even Hobbes imports suppositions of desert into the dialectic of his argument, or it would collapse entirely. For justice and its demands are not creations of social convention but in some form or another prerequisites of the legitimacy of such conventions as promise keeping and good faith. It follows that the claims of justice may go much further than any explicit societal arrangement may acknowledge, and that no such arrangement, no state, nor even any informal communal body like a family, tribe, or nation—groupings that antedate the state and prepare the conditions for its creation—is above moral criticism, dismantling, or reform.

The conventionalist account declines into circularity when it presupposes communal or indeed civil values that it is intended to derive. If we look for the hook on which the loop of that circle is to be hung, we find it suspended in midair, sustained by nothing but wind and bluster—appeals to the power of words and the force of threats. Then, with the characteristic dialectic of good-cop/bad-cop, the language subtly shifts to more inviting talk about consent, not as the mark of past commitment but as the hallmark of acceptance. All the while, nothing has been said about what we should consent to.

Describing "a pure contract-theory" as "one that holds all other duties and obligations to stem from a contract to assume them," Urmson wrote:

Anyone holding this view would have to maintain that the duty to respect liberty and all other duties and obligations were such only because of a contract. I may, perhaps, have a duty to deliver you a sack of potatoes only if I have contracted to do so. For the pure contract-theorist all our conventional moral duties would be on a par with delivering a sack of potatoes; if we were to allow that there were independent moral reasons for observing these duties . . . the contract would have become at best a reinforcement and very likely superfluous.

Addressing Hobbes directly and the whole tradition that extends from Hobbes to Locke and down to Rawls, Urmson adds: "There seem to me to be as good reasons for respecting the life and interests of others as for respecting any contract, so that the fact, if it be a fact, that the rational self-interested man would contract to accept these duties in certain circumstances is interesting but irrelevant. Can one seriously believe that the sole moral objection to personal violence is that it is a form of breach of contract?"[11]

The second difficulty I want to raise about contractual schemes of legitimation is the exclusion problem: If societies are simply collections of individuals bound by some common covenant, what is to stop them from arbitrarily excluding certain "others" whose interests thereby simply do not count? If justice is the way we agree to treat one another, then we face not only the very real possibility that we may agree to treat one another badly, but also the problem that we do not seem to have any obligations, on this account, toward those who are not party to our agreements. Not only does this possibility apply to persons who live beyond our boundaries — although in an age of active international trade and global environmental exigencies, they are certainly a morally important class — it also involves those whom the devisers of an agreement may exclude intentionally, inadvertently, or of necessity: the weak, the ignorant, those who cannot "pull their own weight" or who have no effective advocate or lobbyist, and those who have been dehumanized, demonized, or damned to ethnic cleansing.

Historically all sorts of individuals have been deemed non-persons: slaves, aliens, persons of marked race, caste, or lineage. But there are also the unborn, the members of future generations, and the large class of persons who for social or intellectual, moral or political reasons, through disability or disadvantage, penal servitude, geographical distance, or social isolation, are in no position to take part in the lively debate and deliberative activity of a free society, let alone the ceremonial consent and declaration of homage, fealty, or allegiance characteristic of history's less participatory societies. Even in a republic there are those whose will is overridden by the majority or outbid by the influential. And democracies are well-known in the annals of imperialist adventurism. If the state is a contract, are the non-participants not parties to it, and are those who are not parties fair game?

Plainly, non-persons can be harmed by human agency — species, eco-niches, monuments of nature, triumphs of art and architecture, institutions, texts, wildernesses, and individual plants and animals. It is contested, in a legalistic sort of way, whether such beings can have interests in a sense relevant to the concerns of justice. Clearly they are not the beings that our American system of law, or the theory to which it was built, was designed to protect. Yet surely at least some of them have worth apart from the social or commercial value that convention may assign them. Many, indeed, are protected in existing laws—the spotted owl, for instance, or the snail darter, which may have little social value and perhaps no market price at all. Political contractualists seem to have no basis for considering such beings, except insofar as they become the clients of some economic or political interest. At that point the graves of the ancestors or the habitat of the timber wolf suddenly vault from nullity to legal prominence, and we are given the assurance (by contract theory) that right has been done by them when the political process has worked to its conclusion in their regard, quite without reference to their inherent worth or relational impact.

But confining ourselves to persons for the moment, are all non-citizens or non-signatories of a formal civil constitution thereby non-persons? Are those who are not equal partners in our joint undertakings thereby excluded from the resultant harms, benefits, and responsibilities? This question could be called the Mafia problem, since the Mafia observes very different standards toward insiders and outsiders. It could also be called the "lifeboat earth" problem, in view of the modest proposals of Garrett Hardin and others to exclude from the human covenant those who seem in their view only to add to the load and risk swamping the boat we all share.[12] Does the metaphor of a social contract mask the fact, which it ought to convey, that the human situation, history, and destiny link us together in ways that we may never fully know and that some of us are loath to acknowledge?

Defenders of slavery before the American Civil War professed a version of Lockean liberalism but did not acknowledge their chattel slaves as rights bearers. Their Whiggish creed excluded Tory or feudal notions of a static hierarchy of caste or class. The sharp division of the inalienable rights of persons from the sheer passivity of property, it has been argued, exacerbated the polarity and heightened the violence of the war: Blacks were either persons or property, and if they were property they could not be persons.[13] Biological models were widely invoked, before and long after the Civil War, aiming to show that Blacks were less than fully human.[14] Indeed the Smithsonian movement, which led to the founding of physical anthropology as a discipline, was an offshoot of that invidious campaign. Still worse was reserved for Jews. As Uriel Tal and others have shown, the Nazi theorists of race dehumanized their targeted victims semeiotically as a prelude to the Final Solution. Dehumanization placed the victims in the crosshairs; and the depiction of persons as vermin placed their caricatured images into a foreground whose setting was the blueprint of gas chambers and crematoria. Likewise the fetus was made notionally a non-person before its interests were legally undermined or negated.

Yet having interests that deserve regard does not require being party to an agreement. The agreement of gang members to rape or kill or rob some passerby is not legitimate just because the victim is no party to it. Nor does the gang's agreement have the same moral standing as the determinations of, say, the state, the neighborhood, or the police. Consent to a social, political, or economic arrangement is clearly a critical index of its legitimacy. In normal circumstances there is no better judge of a relationship than those whose interests are affected;

nor is anyone more likely to be affected than the participants. But not all circumstances are normal, and the effects of a relationship are not confined to its parties. Covenantors may be shortsighted about their own interests and acutely myopic about those of others, so the consent of covenantors is not a sufficient condition of justice. Consider Japan's imposition of enforced prostitution on women from Korea during World War II. Korea was a subject state and had no effective government. Japan was a modern nation state, whose duly appointed officers decided the fate of the Korean women with a view to the morale of Japanese troops and the vital state interests that those troops were pledged to serve. What then of the Korean women? Can the notion that justice is an agreement among contracting parties even find the words to describe the enormity that one Japanese government committed and another concealed for decades after the fact?

The exclusion problem works telling damage on that variety of contractual theory that rests on the notion of passive consent. The notion of passive consent arises from the recognition that even the participatory citizenry of a modern commonwealth are not parties to its full panoply of laws and institutions. They were not present at the creation, and they cannot agree to or even know all the laws and regulations enacted, implemented, and enforced in their name. Even in a representative democracy, there will be rules or provisions to which individuals might take exception. And even where consent was freely given item by item, as in a referendum, it might be argued after the fact that some of those consenting did not fully comprehend the impact of their agreement until damage was done to their interests or until it was too late to dismantle the now suspect institutions or to slow their momentum and halt or reverse their effects.

There is tacit recognition of such facts as these when champions of the idea that states and their actions are legitimated by consent argue that those who find themselves sufficiently dissatisfied always have the right, at least in a free society, of departing. Their continued presence, it is argued, is sufficient warrant of their consent, showing that they themselves deem their engagement with this society to bring more benefit than harm to the interests they cherish. I call this appeal to acquiescence an argument from passive consent, because it substitutes the absence of an effectuated decision to emigrate for the explicit, but always ambiguous, affirmation of allegiance that traditionally signified consent. The appeal to passive consent, which is a common feature of popular discussions and debates about political legitimacy ("If you don't like it, you can always leave"), weakens the claim that agreement is a sufficient ground for the legitimacy of a polity by exposing tellingly its exclusionary character. If departure is necessary to prove any governmental action illegitimate, and remaining in place is sufficient to legitimate a government and its actions, then any policy that does not provoke abandonment of a nation by a significant number of its people would appear to be legitimate.

Clearly, by our standard, if consent is an important index of legitimacy, the departure from East Germany of large numbers of its people prior to reunification, and the desperate flight of much smaller numbers prior to the opening of the borders, provide overwhelming evidence of the illegitimacy of the government of the German Democratic Republic. But desperate people can jump out of the frying pan into the fire. The escapees' choice of a nation other than their homeland does not clearly show the legitimacy of every state in any land to which they might flee. And if we take remaining in place as sufficient proof of governmental legitimacy, then we can clearly envision a programmatic policy in which a government might rid itself of a minority of "undesirables" or non-conformists simply by imposing some form of discrimination upon them, such as differential taxation or restrictions on education or reproductive opportunities. Then the argument might be made — if it were assumed that a government is as just as its people think it is — that a discriminatory government is only marginally unjust, or not unjust at all, as long as it allows departure to victims or dissenters.

Sticklers for human rights (among whom I would hope to be numbered) might wonder how any arbitrarily invidious policy can be just. But if second-class citizens, excluded minorities, dissenters, and the dissatisfied are given free rights of egress and do not leave — because they fear they might lose more by leaving than by staying, or because of normal human inertia or social ties, or through human hope — the advocates of the idea that passive consent is a sufficient condition of our labeling a social arrangement just would be in the embarrassing position of defending the view that a state (or any group) might justly impose any disability upon some community or individual, or upon the populace as a whole, up to the limit of the tolerance of those invidiously treated or oppressed, without injustice, since the continued presence of these victims is clear proof that they find their conditions acceptable and the alternatives freely open to them unacceptable or less acceptable than acquiescence or silent suffering.

The forms of discrimination and oppression that might be tolerated by some or all the members of a group are limited only by human imagination and the stoical or spiritual capabilities of human endurance. Yet it would seem strange to make the justice of some proposed policy contingent on the risk averseness of the members of the target class or the asperity of the alternatives available to them elsewhere — allowing legislators or tyrants to make unjust or unhappy conditions elsewhere their accomplices and allies, not only to ensure the continued presence of those they plan, say, to exploit, but also to reassure their own conscience as to the rightness of a vicious policy, on the grounds that its victims seem to find submission to it less undesirable than the available alternatives.

Clearly, then, legitimation by passive consent — although it has its uses in rhetoric and in scaling to reality the extent of the sufferings or disabilities about which persons may feel moved to complain or rebel, and although it harbors more verisimilitude than the notion of a mythic moment of consent or the notion that some ritual affirmation can bind allegiance rather than merely signal it — is fatally holed below the waterline. It is no sufficient foundation of political legitimacy, for it will legitimate an almost unlimited array of (tolerated) tortures and depredations. Indeed, one can readily envision circumstances in which the excluded are deceived, kept under the illusion that they or their children might one day join the ranks of those who profit from their expropriation or oppression. In such a case, the vision of glittering rewards held up by exploiters (and extracted by exploitation) would heighten the tolerance of the exploited and, by the standards of passive consent, heighten the levels of oppression that could be imposed legitimately, if passive consent is tantamount to legitimation.

I do not think this last case should be sought too breathlessly in America. This is not simply what we have done — certainly not all that we have done, although it is a part of the record. But my present point is criterial rather than judgmental: The possibility of ignoring or shrugging off unfairness on the grounds that the disadvantaged are free to leave displays a deep flaw in the contractual model of authority. The practical moral is that states and their patriots should not take too much pride or comfort in the continued presence within their borders of the people whom they govern. For there are many reasons that might induce long-term residence. Not least among them, the hope that the oppressed may nurture of overthrowing a hated oppressor.

Attempts to legitimate the rule of law, or any sort of authority, by appeal to agreement, then, rest on a fiction, dissolving into stories about the past or into thought experiments about what certain imaginary persons might do. Passive consent theories are not theories at all but rhetorical challenges and dares. They seem better designed to put a defiant front on disabilities than to legitimate civil authority. They even invite those who wield power or can sway it to push the envelope by mounting up piles of constraint or corruption, inefficiency, or annoyance that fall short of the threshold of political irritability, anger, social sabotage, mass self-exile, or revolution — fostering the opinion that the people is a great beast to be milked and goaded, baited and bred, but never trusted.

All appeals to convention, covenant, or consent as the foundation of political legitimacy suspend from nowhere the power of an individual or a group to make an agreement with the expectation that it will be fulfilled. For an objector who questions the authority of laws, whether theoretically or in practice, might ask the same questions and raise the same objections about contracts and promises. Consent theories do not explain how consent can bind the self, let alone another. And they systematically, if sometimes unwittingly, exclude from the scope and sentence of the law all who are not somehow party to an agreement which they may never have heard of or might gladly see destroyed.

2. Autonomy

Despairing of social mandates and alienated from the groups and institutions in whose names such mandates are most often pronounced, some thinkers have imagined that autonomy is the source of prescriptivity. Here the noose of subjectivity is drawn more tightly than in appeals to consent. It is no longer the group but only the self that legislates. No one, it is assumed, has any right to issue commands to another — at least not with any moral expectation of being obeyed. The paradoxes of this view do not stop at the anarchism that it biblically calls to mind (Judg. 21:25). Just as conventionalists seem to mistake the need for an institution with its adequacy, so personalists make self-legislation somehow its own arbiter, incorrigible, either because of some mysterious property of individual choice and conscience, or simply because moral decisions are assumed to be non-transitive and so can have no external source. But surely the truism that no other person can make my choices for me does not imply the outlandish claim that no one can tell me rightly what I must or must not do. And even that would not imply the adequacy of all my judgments.

The basic and profoundly sensible argument underlying the claims of autonomy rests on the ideal of authenticity: Surely an act that is no act of my own is of no moral relevance on my account, although it may be on someone else's. Strengthened into the generalization that an act is morally relevant in my regard only insofar as I am its chooser, this becomes the principle that my choices are the necessary condition of estimability (or its opposite) in my actions or omissions. If I act not by my own choice, the reasoning goes, but out of mere conformity to some external prompting or standard, I have not yet entered the moral sphere.

This argument starts out soundly enough, although grave questions must be raised about the choices I may have made (or avoided making) to land in a posture, say, of mere conformity. Moral abdication itself may be a choice fraught with moral significance. But the notion that all appeals from the external world, of duty or pleasure or even the will of God, must somehow be morally alien, ill-formed, or out of order in my internal deliberative councils is simply misguided. For how can I make judgments at all without motives or standards of choice, or make them well without reference to the insights of others?

The idea of authenticity is distorted beyond workability when autonomy is elevated from a necessary to a sufficient condition of moral adequacy. We slide from recognizing the necessity of appropriation (I choose this act, this course, this standard or pattern of action or of life) to presuming the self-sufficiency of my choices. The slide is greased by the notion that no one else's opinions or desires are relevant, since (it is falsely argued) my choices are not mine to the extent that they are based on the demands, concerns, or even counsels of anyone or anything other than myself.

Such reasoning misses the core idea of appropriation: that of making some value or standard of choice one's own, not in being blindly ruled by it as though it were a mere external cause impinging on one's being, but in the active sense of accepting it as an expression of one's own and thereby making it a part of the self. Thus we find Rabbi Yohanan arguing: "Whoever performs one *mitzvah* for its own truth is as if he ordained it himself and bestowed it at Sinai." The homilist finds a verbal hint of his theme in Deuteronomy. Glossing a seeming redundancy in the discourse of Moses as an allusion to the moral power of appropriation, he reads: "*Ve-shamarta ve-ʿasita otam,*" "You shall keep and do them" (Deut. 26:16). Rabbi Yohanan asks, "What is the point of adding 'do them'?" And punning on the duality of meanings in the Hebrew verb *la-ʿasot* (to make *or* to do), he answers his own question: "It is only to teach you that whoever fulfills the Torah and does so for its own truth is as if he himself ordained it and gave it at Sinai." Pressing the same theme, R. Yohanan argues: "Everyone who fulfills the Law for its own truth is esteemed scripturally as though he had created himself, as it is said, 'The Lord commanded me at that time to teach you statutes and laws for your doing of them' [Deut. 4:14]. It does not say, 'That you might do them,' but '*For your doing of them*' [that is, for your being made by them], whence we learn that one who fulfills the law is regarded as though he had made or created himself" (Midrash Tanhuma, *Ki Tavo*, 1, ed. Buber, 3.46).[15] Fulfilling the revealed law on the basis of an understanding and appreciation of the values for whose sake it was legislated ("for its truth") is tantamount to legislating for oneself, and indeed, to creating oneself. Such actions form our character. The law here is not opaque to the understanding, and the understanding is not opaque to the wisdom that underlies the law.

Examining the phenomenology of choice, which the midrash vividly portrays, we can see that the choosing self is not some Cartesian or Lockean spectator watching from the back of the theater, perhaps operating or tampering with the projection equipment. Rather, the self that chooses is the self that is chosen, and the values by which it chooses are those that it makes its own. I am at once the subject and the object of choice, for it is of the essence of subjecthood that the subject constitutes itself in the very act of choosing. Each self is its own project. The authenticity of its actions lies not in its ex nihilo creation of its standards but in its taking ownership of them.

The creativity requisite in any action, then, is the creativity of self, not the absolute creation of norms. Creativity of self is a high and sacred office and responsibility. Like skill in art or music, it is not to be had for the asking, or by the mere fact of willing or wishing. Indeed, no one can fashion norms who has not learned to love and live by them, just as no one can compose music who has not learned to play or sing, and no one can make poetry who has not learned to love words and their power.

Restiveness with old norms may foster the illusion of a creative antinomianism. But moral or legislative creativity is not love of novelty or change for its own sake; still less is it love of anarchy. Rather, it is the love of a higher or better law that makes a lawgiver, just as it is not love of obscurity but of truth that makes for creativity in science. Love of novelty is never the same as love of truth, and autonomy should never be confused with idiosyncrasy, any more than creativity should be confused with eccentricity. If one can learn, by precept or example, then it is absurd to imagine that one cannot act authentically in doing what one is commanded to do, even on the grounds that it is commanded. One needs a basis for accepting any standard or counsel, and clearly one's sheer personhood does not, without further art or insight, amount to such a basis. If it did, we would never be in doubt about the course to take, let alone ever morally mistaken.

The idea of the good is so resistant to capture and confinement by its various claimants that even personal choice is often resisted as its test, not just with the obvious recognition that a wrong choice is not really good but also with the claim, made by philosophers from Plato to G. E. Moore, that the good itself inevitably eludes analysis or verbal formulation. Correspondingly, we are met with denial: A false choice, we are told, is not really ours but is a product of false consciousness, self-deception, introjection, the highjacking of the higher self by pleasure or passion, by the demand of others, or by its own unreality, when notions of selfhood are dismissed as illusions and freedom itself is collapsed into just another reflex of socio-linguistic convention.[16] Wrong choices, on this account, are no choices at all, or at least they are not ours. They represent nothing more than the immature attachment of a real but undeveloped self to what it thought were solid values. Or they are the expressions not of our selves at all but of our victimhood.[17] But all this is rationalization. When I choose bad reasons as the ones on which to act, it is not someone else who has chosen for me. I am as authentically the chooser of my actions, and of the self who acts, as when I choose good reasons. By the same token, when I choose rightly, it is not because it is I who did the choosing but because I have found and chosen the right grounds on which to make my choice.

The illusion of the moral sufficiency of authenticity arises out of extreme versions of the deontological way of schematizing ethics, where moral obligations are conceptualized not only as commands but as commands that must be heeded regardless of any consideration beyond the command itself. The illusion is furthered by the idealization of individual conscience, by the secularization of the mystic's notion that one's conscience is the voice of God, and by mystification of the rationalist's idea that reason as such cannot err. But one must inquire how the dicta of secular conscience retain their absoluteness once they are divorced from the divine authority formerly thought to guide or inspire them. And how does reason retain its infallibility when it is not reason per se but your reason or mine to which appeal is made?

The purism of extremist deontology sparks a disdain for any norm that would prostitute ethics to the mere demands of consequence, or that would compromise its imperatives in the face of any merely external authority. Such purism is at its peak in the moral theories of the Cynics on the one hand and of Nietzsche and the Existentialists on the other. Where Stoic purists treat all mere "externals" as morally indifferent, since praise or blame rightfully attaches only to the sphere of my control (and this, the Stoics held, extends no further than the inclination of my will), the Cynics judged more categorically, making moral originality and independence (so alienated were they from the declining polis) the sole and sufficient moral criteria. Where Kant makes the irrelevance of pleasure and pain, authority or inclination, the hallmark of moral authenticity, Nietzsche will treat Kantian duty itself as a mere "ghost of God," an external, which is therefore morally inconsequent, to be overcome, on the very grounds of its claims to objectivity, universality, or fixity. The outcome in both cases is a moral theory that makes sincerity the only virtue and inauthenticity the only vice.

But consider the resultant paradox. For what does it mean to command oneself? If the self that commands is different from the self that is commanded, then alienation has gone beyond the isolation of ego from other, walling off the I from itself. In that case, the same alienness that is thought to prevent others from issuing commands with moral impact upon me is now found within me, or between my no longer integrated parts. The inner voice of the Stoic *hegemonikon* or Kantian conscience has now become external. It may beg or plead, cajole or threaten. But ego, as the recipient of its commands, will have no more reason to heed it (even if it speaks in ego's voice) than it had to obey the voice of another. Indeed, ego may well come to suspect this seemingly inner voice as an introjection of some social standard that it cannot or must not (on this account) make its own—much as saintly ascetics, driven half-mad by the rigors of meditation and self-mortification, once called certain promptings demonic when they seemed alien or unacceptable, or as schizophrenics battling for their sanity must somehow seal their inner ear against the voices they so clearly hear ordering them to commit obscene or outrageous acts. But the promptings are rejected now no longer on the grounds that they are morally suspect or irrational, but because they are somehow not one's own, not of one's own devising, perhaps not strange enough to the common thread and bread of human decency to be identified distinctively or uniquely as one's own. In this direction lies the bizarre counter-logic that breeds the willfulness of Plato's tyrant, who can recognize and seek acknowledgment for the working of his own will only in perversity.

If, on the other hand, the self that commands is recognized as none other than one's own, so that I indeed command myself, and it is the selfsame I who commands and is commanded, then the very idea of command dissolves and I am left with nothing more than my own will, or wish, or desire, self-alienated or well-integrated to some degree or another. But whether self-possessed by self-acceptance or tormented by self-rejection and self-doubt, I am back outside on the grass, a deontologist no longer, but just an ordinary human being who feels the cold wind at his back, who has hungers and fears, longings and inclinations, some of which have gone to college and can dress up in pretty names and costumes, but none of which bears its own warrant in its hand. I am as much in need of moral counsel as I ever was. Now being told to do what I am or choose as I must[18] — or even (with a faint whiff of Kantian universalism) to choose as I would wish to choose again (as though there were any moral reason for an existentialist to bind his future to his past) or to choose for the world, in full knowledge that in reality I can choose only for myself — gives me no more guidance than does the instruction blindly to obey all laws, respect all authorities, perform all commands without a thought. Which is to say, it gives me no guidance at all. For why, morally speaking, should I heed my own will any more than any other? And how can I be justified in assigning its dictates even relative precedence to any others I might encounter — let alone countenancing those dictates to the exclusion of all other claims? Isn't one who obeys only his own conscience just another kind of egoist, and, indeed, the severest kind? And what difference is there between the thoughtless spontaneity of a Nietzschean blond beast or *Übermensch* and the equally thoughtless spontaneity of the customs house bureaucrat or the storm trooper?

What then should count as authenticity and when should an action be regarded as authentic or inauthentic, autonomous or heteronomous? It is pertinent to address these questions, for it is no part of my intention to demean or diminish the importance of autonomy or authenticity but rather to distinguish their legitimate from their illegitimate roles. Clearly we should stand close to the arguments and criteria that brought us to these concepts: An act that we have appropriated as our own, through our own choice (including the choice of omissions or acquiescences) can in no way be cleared from our own moral account. Our choices are our own, even if they are complexly mediated by other agencies — natural or artificial, psychodynamic or appetitive, communal or institutional. Our actions are our own to the extent that by our choices we might have altered their outcome, or even modified our participation in that outcome, by so much as signifying or failing to signify an attitude with respect to it. But actions in which we do not take part or acquiesce, which happen in spite of us or in an ignorance on our part which we could not have alleviated, are not our own. We deserve no credit and share no blame on their account.

Heteronomy would be the adoption of a maxim that one does not or will not acknowledge as one's own. Heteronomy does not mean acceptance of a sense of duty before the law or of creatureliness before God, but rather refusal to appropriate, inability to internalize or declare the maxim on which one acts. It is a matter of false consciousness or bad faith. The Hebrew word is *ma'al* (Job 21:34). False consciousness does not negate or neutralize the moral significance of one's actions or make them other than one's own, any more than alcohol does. The moral character of the choice to close one's eyes or stop up one's ears or refuse to think is transitive to its utmost impact, just as the moral character of one's first decision to experiment with cocaine, or leave one's child's fate to chance, or nurse one's wrath to keep it warm, or any other act or abdication is transitive to the utmost reach of its consequences.

Thus the kind of moral surrender to God that is idealized in the name of creatureliness, or even romanticized under the title of heteronomy, does not make our actions less our own. The pious or devotional surrender of choice or will is our choice, as muscular in its insistence on its purpose as ever was the Stoic act of willful resignation. When we surrender our choice-making to God or to God's law, we remain responsible for the tenor and the consequences of our actions. It is only the supreme confidence of the pious in the goodness of God or the perfectness of His law that can render such surrender a morally responsible act. Even then, the surrender may be tinged with the colorations of abdication if it masks some form of false consciousness or mutes the voice of conscience. That would be heteronomy in the morally objectionable sense. It affords a perfect target for the dictum of Naḥmanides that one can be a wretch within the province of the Law.[19]

Authenticity, on our account, would be a virtue, just as bad faith or self-deception is a vice. One might be better or more poorly integrated volitionally, more or less keenly self-aware, more or less capable of grasping the intentions that underlie one's choices or of subjecting the grounds of those choices to scrutiny — whether in one's own eyes or by the sometimes more objectifying gaze of others, as manifested in the rules and maxims they approve, or in the pleased or shocked or confused glance or gaze of one's peers or parents or one's children. Joseph, as the Talmud imagines, might have been seduced by Potiphar's wife, but for the appearance at the crucial moment of his dead parents' image at the window. Why, then, does Joseph's chastity remain his own? Because it was he who chose to heed the message that he and he alone could see encoded in his mother's eyes and hear articulated from his father's lips. According to the midrash (B. Sotah 36b), Jacob appealed to Joseph's sense of history and destiny; immediately, "his bow abode in strength" (Gen. 49:24) — that is, his lust abated. But even in this ancient homily Joseph was cautioned, not unmanned. What the apparition offered him was a choice — inscription of his name on the ephod of the High Priests or its erasure from the stone reserved for it, his virtue blotted out by his dissoluteness, his memory preserved only as a whoremaster (Prov. 29:3). The cautionary vision clarified Joseph's choice against a backdrop larger than history—but it did not make his choice for him.

Integration is a virtue, and self-acceptance is a sign of it, but no more a guarantee of internal wholeness than is acceptance by others—who may also, and sometimes more easily, be deceived. And integration, of course, is not the only virtue but is part of a family, in isolation from which integration alone is worthless and self-esteem is worse than worthless, since it then amounts to nothing more than complacency, which is a vice and source of other vices. Autonomy is the gift of personal integration but is no guarantee of moral soundness or good judgment. Heteronomy is the mark of moral confusion but is no exit visa from the realm of moral responsibility.

3. A Foundation for Justice

Bearing in mind the bankruptcy of conventionalism and recognizing the powerlessness of self-legislation to provide its own warrant or to offer any more than an emblem of sincerity, I have proposed that we seek value in the only place it can be sought: in beings. For nothing exists but beings. These are the loci of value. Indeed, the being of things is their value. One strength of this ontological approach to values is that it obviates the quest for a "property" of goodness, which we then must deem natural or "non-natural." The being of things is their nature. That is no static and neutral fact, however. Each being constitutes itself in a telic groping of its own toward perfection. For that reason, being varies in kind and in degree.

The perfection that beings seek is unitary at its source, but not in its expressions. It is not a preordained goal, but an end that the actions of beings define and redefine creatively, open-endedly—as with any creative work, whether that of the artist or poet, or that of biological or cosmic evolution. If we ask, in Plato's terms, why Eternity needs a "moving image," or in scholastic terms, why time exists at all, the answer, clearly, is that the work of creativity is not over but just begun when creatures reach the shores of existence. Just as a novel does not have an end until it is written, and the face in a portrait does not have an expression until it is painted, so no being is finished with its work until it has played its part. This is what we mean by saying that creatures play a role in their own creation.

Many thinkers, playing upon the varied senses of the term 'value,' focus on the verbal sense, in which 'value' means 'valuing' or 'valuation.' They argue that there is no value without a valuer. But even if that is true, or trivially true, of the sort of values that are of interest in an atlas of subjectivities or a marketing survey, such an insight, or purported insight, is of no help in our quest for the basis of all norms. What concerns us is the discrimination of legitimate from wrongful impulses, claims, or inclinations. It does us no good at all in such a quest to learn that there is no judgment without a judge; and it is pernicious nonsense to pretend that because there is no judgment without a judge, no judgment can be more right or wrong than any other or can have more legitimacy or make any greater claim upon us than its alternatives.

On the contrary, I argue that there is no claim without a claimant. Claims (which might be made by or in behalf of all sorts of things) belong ultimately to the beings that make them and have a legitimacy reflective of the reality of those beings. The appraisal of claims remains a task for intelligent beings. That such appraisals demand intelligence and indeed negotiation does not imply that possession of a modicum of intelligence or a stable forum for social negotiating renders any individual or social agency infallible or unbiased in the task. But it does mean, in principle, that we can see our way across the notorious passage from subjective to objective interests. What we see is that all beings make claims equivalent to their being (identified, Spinozistically, with their project or conatus), that all have prima facie deserts equivalent to their claims, and objective deserts that are the resultant of those claims, equilibrated by the countervailing and complementary claims of all other beings. It is in the deserts of beings, where the intrinsic value of all things and of persons par excellence makes its claims, that we find the anchor point of prescriptivity. We locate the moral force of norms in the worth and beauty of beings, and above all, of persons, since finitude finds its most powerful means and most compelling meanings in the lives of persons.

Our fallibility and liability to bias in evaluating deserts may seem to argue their subjectivity or conventionality, but such limitations on our part, I think, prove just the opposite. For the notions of bias and error, long pled as evidence for subjectivism or relativism of some other sort, presuppose a legitimacy that can be strayed from. Where there is corrigibility, there is a truth to be known. Where unfairness can be detected — as it is when bias is uncovered — there are Socratic grounds to hope that fairness can be found as well. Found, not merely imposed — for some standard of fairness was implicit in the knowledge by which bias was exposed. The fact of subjectivity, then, is not the ally but the enemy of subjectivism. Subjectivity has no meaning if there is no truth or objectivity against which it can be disclosed.

My present concern, however, is not with moral knowledge, nor with the adjudication of rival claims or the reconciliation and integration of potentially complementary ones. Human judgment will be no less fallible in recognizing and adjudicating claims than it is elsewhere. What concerns me here is how deserts anchor norms and provide a touchstone for the legitimacy of laws. Justice is the imparting of what beings deserve. All beings have deserts, insofar as they are beings; and deserts reach a plane of sanctity and mutuality in the case of persons. The legitimate claims of all beings are scaled to the stature of their projects; and the claims of persons (and so of human beings) are grounded in their subjecthood — not their club or class membership, their affinities to one another, or their similarities to us, but in the splendid prospects opened up by the possibility of choice and consciousness.

All beings are dynamic in some measure. All affirm, as it were, a certain character, which is their own and which they define in the very act of affirmation that is their history. A being, viewed telically, from the standpoint of the nisus manifest in its activity, just is the agency that stakes out for itself a project, an identity grounded in a system of interests constituted in part through its own activity. Any claim or interest is worthy of concern and attention. The interests of a being, prima facie, lie in the furtherance of its project, an open-ended goal. Any dynamic claim is implicitly or potentially infinite in some respect. Yet wisdom demands recognition of the limitations inherent in all claims made by finite beings.

My view that beings are constituted by and through their claims is akin to the Existentialist identification of a being with its project, and to Spinoza's equation of the essence of each being with its conatus, its striving to preserve and promote its reality. A being is not the mere sum of its history or amalgam of the facts about its static self-identity. Still less can it be identified with its apprehension by other subjects or its impact on other objects. For both impact and apprehension are aspectual. Perception or conception can apprehend only some abstract or sampling of a thing; to engulf it would not be to know it but to eat it, absorb it, destroy it. By the same token, a thing cannot be its impact on another, or even the sum total of its impacts on all other things. For what, then, would remain as the cause of all those impacts?[20]

The moral realism of our theory of deserts rests on an ontic realism: It is because beings are not just aspects of our experience or functions of their effects that they have deserts of their own. The world contains a great variety of beings, each actively affirming its identity, setting out its own project and interests. If there were nothing to contradict such interests, their affirmation might well warrant their legitimacy. But in a world of multiple particulars, interests will collide. They may also harmonize or complement one another. Because interests can conflict, however, we cannot simply equate deserts with claims. Interests are prima facie deserts. To find the legitimate deserts of all beings, we must attend to their specific and particular projects, consult the conflicts and the potentials for complementarity. Ecology and the economy of the garden are valuable models here—but models, not oracles. They yield no trivial or automatic resolutions to all conflicts.

To map the hierarchy of deserts in detail is not a necessary part of the philosophical theory of justice, and efforts to do so might seem only to appeal, suppositiously, to familiar notions of the relative worth of beings and their projects. The normative task of regulating our practical and notional responses to claims of all sorts is a task of culture and morality in general and of law and religion in particular. Indeed, it is chief among their tasks; philosophy cannot successfully usurp it. But philosophy can observe and thematize the criteria in use and criticize intellectually and morally the outcomes of various systematizations and axiological schemes.

We can say that the interests of a being, its project or conatus, are the very essence of that being as it expresses itself in the world. That means they are the being; they are what it is. Sensation, sensibility, considerateness, and consideration are strengths, not weaknesses in conatus. They enable a being to seek, discover, or even devise its own good, and to confront its own limitations without first being brought up short by them. Sentient beings are adept at finding complementarities that will optimize the realization of deserts. Conscious beings, that is, persons, can uncover or create intellectual realms in which even infinite claims are not invidious or self-undermining. And as self-conscious beings, persons can expand their individual identities to accept as their own the interests of other beings. But for all beings, legitimate deserts are grounded in claims. Indeed, deserts and claims are identical if the claims are evaluated contextually and not taken as if in isolation (where they are never found). Justice will be the recognition of each being's deserts, equilibrated against those of all others. For there is no reason why one being's deserts should count more than the equivalent claims of another.

But not all claims are equivalent. Beings vary in ontic worth; their deserts must be scaled to their reality. Claims vary in merit, and their equilibration is not easy. Yet even without a recipe for assaying the relative worth of all rival claims, I can say with confidence that justice cannot be achieved, or understood, if we do not assign deserts to beings; and it will never be complete or universal if we confine deserts to ourselves.

The primary rule of the general theory of deserts is that all beings should be treated in accordance with what they are. This demand for a proper response to the claims all beings make can be compared to the recognition called for by facts: Just as facts demand acknowledgment cognitively, deserts claim moral recognition. In both cases we have an obligation to respond to things' being as they are. In neither case do we have a tautology. For the according of recognition goes beyond the demand for it, although the demand is implicit in the self-affirmation of a being (or a fact). Otherwise the demand would not be needed.

To implement so broad and potentially nebulous a rule as the demand that the reality of things be recognized, two cardinal principles are needed:

1. Deserts are scaled to the reality each being claims. We do not rightly sacrifice a child to a virus, as though their claims were equal — even though the quasi-life of the virus is all it has.

2. The interests of persons take special precedence and make a special claim. Persons need not be human. They do not win their special consideration on the grounds of looking like us or behaving as we do but rather on the grounds of their subjecthood, a precious achievement in nature. Persons invoke special recognition, not simply because they are capable of returning it — for a dog can respond to recognition and a person often cannot, whether because of infancy, incapacity, ignorance, or simply absence — but because only subjects are capable of giving or receiving moral regard or intellectual recognition, to other persons or to anything at all. It is the status imparted to persons by their moral cum intellectual standing in the hierarchy of being, not their affective claim on our sympathies or their effective impact on our interests, that grounds their deserts — their rights and dignity as subjects, as moral persons, choosers of their life patterns and their destiny.

Persons, then, stand on a moral plateau. Personhood, in whatever form it discovers itself, is never to be sacrificed to interests of some lesser order; and even the highest subjects may not rightly subordinate or negate the subjecthood of the rest. All subjects deserve a level of consideration that can be called absolute, in the sense that nothing can be traded for it; it has no price or counterpart, and it is not measured on a scale commensurate with other interests. Underlying the special regard deserved by subjects is our primary rule: that all beings must be treated in accordance with what they are. Subjects, in self-consciously constructing their own life projects, call upon one another, in a language that is not to be ignored, not only for cooperation but for recognition of the intensionality of their aims.

The moral consideration that is the due of non-persons can be treated as an extension of the model used in assigning deserts to persons. That is a political, rhetorical way of stating the case, however, and can foster the error of claiming the status of subjects for non-persons. In ontic terms, subjects are the special case, and the general rule is to respect beings for what they are, not for their approximation to our self-image. Living organisms, species, ecosystems like the riverbank or the canyon, the mountain range or the shore, implicitly claim recognition, as virtual subjects. Persons claim recognition explicitly. The difference is one not of degree but of kind. It is not simply a matter of language or commerce, any more than it can be reduced to a matter of appearance and sympathy. Persons genuinely are subjects, whereas non-persons are analogous to subjects in having projects and thus interests. In both cases recognition is deserved by the reality that is each being, but those realities differ crucially because of the role that consciousness plays. The interests of non-persons deserve consideration, other things being equal. But those of persons are in some sense inviolable, so long as the persons can be treated as such and not, like the sniper in the tower, as a public menace or a pest.[21]

The ontological theory I have proposed assigns a special status to persons, but it does not confine interests to persons. The relative deserts of animals, plants, species, monuments of nature and of art, institutions and practices, make claims upon our consideration. But the legitimacy of such claims never extends as far as the categorical claims of personhood. To underscore this point, I would say, for example, that I believe it is an error of moral judgment to compromise the nutritional needs of a child to meet the demands of vegetarianism. But norms of stewardship can be derived from an ontic account of justice. They cannot be derived from a strictly Kantian view,[22] still less from a consistently contractarian account. The effort to derive them from Utilitarian precepts is fraught with paradox and inconsistency. For appeals to sentience like those of Bentham or Tom Regan try to warrant rights by identifying a lowest common denominator of sensibility among the various forms of animal life. By proposing susceptibility to pain as that denominator, they transform an emotive appeal for the "rights" of sentient beings into an undermining of the special place of subjecthood, upon which the idea of rights depends, and still fail to regard the claims made by trees and other non-sentient life forms—let alone species and ecosystems, institutions, practices, cultures, and ethnicities.

An ontic theory can and should acknowledge a hierarchy of deserts, in which personhood makes singular claims. Some romantic programs deny such hierarchies—engratiatingly, for the element of ritual necessary in implementing any value system can grow so familiar as to become at once transparent to view and irksome. But to exclude hierarchies of value is to negate deserts, for recognition, like nourishment, must be shaped to the contours of beings' claims. Once the special claims of personhood are made commensurate with those of lesser beings, the principle of ontic recognition is violated, and no sound basis for the allocation of recognition remains. The same is true even if deserts that are lesser only in degree are placed on a par with others that exceed them, as, for example, when a whole ecosystem, such as a forest, is placed at risk by the protection in it of some feral species or invading weed.

Efforts to "extend" the rights of persons to other sorts of beings, then, are not just inappropriate (since animals cannot vote and plants cannot enjoy an art museum) but misguided. The effect is not an extension of rights (as though plants were now given the vote), but rather the spread of the relativity of deserts into the realm where deserts are properly conceived as rights and are not relative at all. The outcome is not the announced expansion of the moral franchise but debasement of its meaning. Animals and plants, species and eco-niches, deserve protection, for what they are as well as for what they may mean to us. But persons have dignity as well as the more graded sort of value that every being attains in its own way. Persons are holy. Genesis expresses this idea by saying that humans are created in God's image. Rabbi Akiva draws the moral message of the verse: "Cherished is man, being created in the divine image; but all the more cherished is he, in that this was made known to him, as it is said: 'For in the image of God did He make the man' " (Avot 3.18 in Hertz; 3.15 in Mishnah, ed. Danby).

Does the dignity of persons entail the inevitability of tragedy? Popular thinking is encouraged to suspect that it does. Sophists and dramatists are fond of projecting conflicts among absolutes—dramatists, for the emotive energies sparking from the clash of values; sophists, in an impatience with absolute claims. Reconciliation may have its dramatic appeal, but vendettas make more sensate theater. Mediation, by the same token, might well seem to open a stonier and steeper path to a livelihood than do nostrums about the impotence of reason to conciliate in politics, let alone to broker in the marketplace, or to prosecute specific interests in the matter of gored oxen and violated or affronted dignities. Most conflicts of principle can be reconciled by reference to a higher principle; but we do need non-linear thinking to inquire after higher principles, and some professionals see an advantage to be gained in denying our access to such principles. Yet we are not helpless. Whenever we make value judgments, we compare incommensurables, making reference to an Absolute above all lesser absolutes.

Several gifts restrain the absoluteness of dignity from inevitably provoking irreconcilable conflicts. The first is language. We can communicate; life need not be so prickly as a minefield. The second is cooperation. As Spinoza noted, we are useful to each other; nothing is more useful to us than each other's aid.[23] The third is modesty. We are capable of consideration and reserve. We can accord as well as demand privacy, consult each other's interests even as we pursue our own. The Talmud voices the exigencies of the last case negatively when it says that Jerusalem was destroyed because its people pressed for their rights under the Torah (B. Bava Metzia 30b). The stability of any social system depends on accommodation.

The special recognition deserved by persons is singled out in the Kantian imperative to treat humanity in ourselves and others never merely as a means but always also as an intrinsic end. A person, as such, is a chooser of ends. To respect a person as a person is to respect not necessarily those ends but the freedom and dignity of the self-conscious and self-choosing subject. The content of this imperative is, of course, not Kant's invention. Kant, like Aristotle and Maimonides, would have thought an ethics without prior history or tradition, and a resonating echo in common moral sensibility, an anomaly, not an achievement. Humanity has not survived and learned as long as it has without any inkling of the fundamental principles of morals. But Kant's achievement in moral philosophy was to retrieve the Socratic rigor in which logical analysis was first used, for the sake of ethics, and to place it once again in the service of ethics. Specifically, Kant laid bare the inner incoherence that Socrates had discovered at the heart of wrongdoing. Kant found a contradiction in any maxim that professes to pursue the good by vicious means. Just as Socrates found incoherence in the idea that courage can be stupid or pigheaded, or piety harebrained or unfilial, Kant found a contradiction in the notion of enhancing one's wealth by undermining the security of property, fidelity, or trust; or of finding comfort through suicide. Such implicit contradictions become explicit when attempts are made to treat the underlying maxims as matters of principle, that is, as universal laws.

But the ethics Kant renders scientific by reviving Socratic logic is not the relative ethics of Plato, whereby a lofty enough end inevitably justifies the means. Nor is it the virtue ethics of Aristotelian eudaimonism. It is the positive ethics of Scripture, the ethics of love for our fellow human beings and of concrete obligations and prohibitions that give effect to that love. The austere formalism of the Kantian moral law can yield such obligations only by invoking an idea of the good. It was the appeal to the good typically implicit in human motives that bred the contradictions crucial to the Socratic elenchus. And, although Kant's deontology sharply distinguishes the right from the good and excludes the value of ends from moral relevance, thereby making rightness a purely formal matter, Kant does not exclude the good from our maxims but acknowledges it as their core material content. A vicious maxim bears a contradiction because of its implicit appeal to some good, taken as an object of desire.

Many goods might be consistent with the formal demands of the idea of right. Only one, however, will express it, and that is love, regard for being. Here we must supply the missing nexus between Kant's formal and material formulations of the categorical imperative, generalizing the theme Kant voices when he focuses the moral law on its application to humanity and instantiates the universal moral law in the command to treat humanity in ourselves and others never solely as a means but always at the same time as an end, that is, to regard each person as a subject, and so worthy of respect, a bearer of dignity.

In reaching this formulation, Kant's moral formalism, in search of a viable material foundation, has traded places with the usual concreteness of the biblical idiom. The categorical imperative, when fleshed out in the end-in-itself formulation, demands in concrete and material terms what the Torah prescribes formally in God's commandment to love one another as we love ourselves. What the Golden Rule intends is not that we perform on one another just the behaviors we wish to have performed on ourselves, but that we treat one another with love, esteem for human subjecthood, a deference measured and given content, at least in the first instance, by our self-knowledge and the understanding it imparts of the universal human claim to dignity and to the fulfillment of wholesome desires. What is called for is practical recognition of the moral personhood vested in human beings as choosers of their own ends.

The resultant ethics requires clear imperatives and cannot be confined to guidelines, although there must be those as well, since ethics will make demands beyond the minimal expectations of its laws. The biblical ethics, whose groundworks Kant retraced, is not solely and simply an ethics of tendencies, then, as some forms of virtue ethics can be. It is not an uninterpreted "love one another." The Torah, in fact, tells us concretely *how* to love one another, spelling out the minimal demands of human dignity and painting vivid ethical and ritual pictures of the behaviors it deploys to improve human character and reflectiveness — paradigmatically in the command (Exod. 23:4–5) to assist even an enemy with his lost ox or his ass that lies sprawling by the wayside. Thus the immediate context of the command to love one another as we love ourselves is a tiny, tightly balanced system of obligations regarding reproof.[24] These cover a range of engagements, from what we might call whistle blowing to the subtle dynamics of human tact in sensitive situations of admonition. The Golden Rule is invoked as the general governing principle here. Its scope is hardly confined to the contexts of this specific application, or it could not be invoked a priori, as it is. But the concreteness of its relevance is typified by these applications.

4. A Different Kind of Naturalism

Our ontological approach to ethics does not rest the prescriptivity of norms on the fact that they are prescribed. No mere command has moral force merely by virtue of being a command. There are those who issue commands with every rightful expectation of being obeyed. Parents do so, for example, although not in every instance. So do God and nature and the laws of a legitimate state — one reason, I suppose, why God and nature and the laws of such a state have been compared to parents, as when we acknowledge God as our father, or nature as our mother, or when Socrates has the laws address him as his parents. But despite the rhetorical force of the metaphor, it does not locate or anchor the prescriptivity of the commands it endorses.

What makes parental commands prescriptive is not that they issue from a parent's mouth, as though whatever a father or a mother ordered must be obeyed, regardless of content or consequences, intentions or implications. On the contrary, the commands of parents to their children are prescriptive in virtue of the presumption that they are issued with a clear and committed view to the children's good. When that presumption is shaken or defeated, so is the moral force of those commands. Others who might share parental concerns or insights do not normally have the same authority. The presumption that no concern for a child's welfare will normally be greater and no insight into that child's interest keener than that of the parents powerfully shields the privacy and privileges the authority of parents. But, in the marginal cases where the familiar presumption is refuted roundly enough, societal interventions pierce the protective membrane; parental authority lapses, and society rightfully intervenes and reassigns both the responsibility and some measure of the authority. The same must be said of the laws. They draw their prescriptivity from the interests they serve and are undermined and hollow to the extent that they serve no interests or misevaluate the interests they affect. Thus a law that is exploitative is unjust, and a law that serves no interests is a dead letter.

Our ontological account fosters an objectivist idea of justice, and it allows, indeed requires, a general rather than a restrictive assignment of deserts. Far from confining attention to the interests of some consensual body, it extends consideration to all beings, subjects and non-subjects, animate and inanimate, natural and artificial. It finds deserts in animals and plants as well as in humans; in mountains, rivers, species and ecosystems as well as in sentient beings; in works of art, institutions, memories, traditions, sciences, and ideas as well as in planets and galaxies. Not all value depends on the value of persons or on the values assigned by persons. Claims may deserve recognition even if they are not our own, even if they are not of the type we make. Indeed our ability to recognize claims other than our own is part of what gives precedence to human claims.

What a general theory of deserts entails is that utility, to ego or to us, is not the sole basis of worth. Recognition of deserts extends to those persons who are not in league with us. Nor need we cloak our impulse, say, to save the rain forest, solely in appeals to the usefulness of its biomass as a source of oxygen. Mere instrumental values, after all, might be secured by alternative means, perhaps technologically; the interests they once protected might then be overridden by the commercial value of the lumber in the Mato Grosso or the gold in its streams. Discovery of intrinsic worth in persons, and in all beings, obviates embarrassing appeals to Epicurean anxiety fables: Even if the rain forest harbors no cure for cancer or AIDS and will never be enjoyed or appreciated as wilderness by the great majority of humanity, its intrinsic value is none the less for that. The worth of things does not depend exclusively on their use or appreciation. On the contrary, these rest on intrinsic worth.

The theory I have proposed is a form of naturalism. It is not, as some may fear,[25] a form of materialism. The natures in which it finds value are dynamic seekers of goals, which they themselves help to constitute but which are never reducible (as matter traditionally is) to the mere facticity of the given. Part of what is precious in beings, signaled by the open-endedness of their quest, is their linkage to eternity. We see evidence of that linkage clearly in human becoming. But even beings that are not sentient at all show their linkage to the divine, in the transcendent reach of their projects.

Because the ontology underlying this general theory of deserts avoids the reductionism familiar in most forms of naturalism, it avoids the naturalistic fallacy. The theory equates being with value in the classic way that regards being as a perfection—and in the case of finite, contingent beings, as a gift. The theory is naturalistic in equating interests with claims and claims with prima facie deserts. 'Interest' here is understood objectively rather than subjectively, as in Ralph Barton Perry's famous equation of value with the object of any interest. Interests need not be consciously articulated. Value need not be instrumental, because interest need not be external. It need not belong to someone else. A being can have interests, and so deserts, even if no one cares about it. Its worth is not proportioned to the extent and intensity of the concerns of others for it, let alone their desires to consume, possess, or appreciate it.

Relativists, in their rationalizing mode (the tack of the defense attorney, or of Kinsey explaining that all sexual behaviors are normal because they are natural), equate every state of affairs with what ought to be. This posture is radically at variance with their critical mode, which sharply distinguishes what *is* from what ought to be. Hume, for example, sunders the discourse of *is* and *ought*. But he also seeks to rationalize human moral sentiments, epistemic and political practices, habits of the mind, and even prejudices on the grounds of their facticity. Moore, similarly, not only pinions the naturalistic fallacy but also commits it. He does so subtly in his attempted refutation of idealism, where he assumes the legitimacy of our penchant to presume the reality of the bodies we perceive. And he does so far more blatantly in offering a utilitarian account of 'right' as a counterpart to his Platonizing, even mysticizing account of 'good.'[26]

But the naturalism I have proposed avoids the naturalistic fallacy, because it does not equate any mere fact about a thing with what constitutes its value. Still less does it entail that whatever exists should exist. Rather the thesis is that the claims of beings deserve recognition, prima facie, simply because they are the claims of beings: Beings deserve recognition *insofar as* they are beings. It follows that recognition of claims should be scaled to the magnitude of the claims. But of course claims are made (and can only be made good) in a world where there are other claims. They could never be made in isolation; and they can never be recognized unless they are equilibrated, balanced or reconciled, with one another. Justice, classically understood as giving each his due, here would mean the adequate or optimal recognition of the deserts subtended in the claims of beings.

What, then, is the relation of our naturalism to the idea of natural law? Nature, in its way, does issue commands, but in quite a different way from that of human lawmakers. Natural laws are prescriptive only insofar as their imperatives are hypotheticals, which, if voiced in words, would inform those subject to them of the conditions of their survival or flourishing. They are hypothetical imperatives given in the context of a grace that does not just define but proffers the conditions of success.

Ultimately, all beings perforce obey the laws of nature. But nature's sentence may be delayed, as when the Soviet Union, for example, had not yet fallen under the growing weight of its long battle with history. Such denouements, darker than the tragedies of the house of Atreus, are not inevitable. We humans, unlike other creatures, can study nature's imperatives, which the biblical idiom calls the laws of life. We can adapt consciously, not just genetically, grasping and even rethematizing nature's commands, accepting or rejecting what we find. We may celebrate and enhance or despise and degrade the values we encounter in nature, seeking to ignore them or struggling to enshrine and enlarge them in individual memory and communal practice. It is because nature lays out the parameters of every creature's project, defining what it is for each being to be and to become, that the laws of nature are prescriptive. Their prescriptivity rests on the worth of each ontic status that nature provides and on the conatus of each being to which nature opens a path, or a fork in the road.

The same is true, of course, of the laws of nature's God. Each being has its own worth; each person, his own dignity. This worth or dignity is the substance of God's existential gift and is nothing different from the project imparted by the act of creation. In the riot of nature, such projects may and will encroach on one another. The exuberance of the lightning or the tornado, the easing of the earth in its traces, relaxing the tension along fault lines—the Lisbon earthquake and Job's stormwind—acknowledge no face. But persons, as persons, have the power and responsibility to give names to one another, to recognize faces and acknowledge individual worth and dignity. We persons and we alone can grant one another recognition, not just as objects of use or annexes of ego but as subjects. That is part of the special worth and dignity of persons—where the worth inherent in all things reaches the pitch of awareness and so is capable of returning or acknowledging, but primally of according and receiving, consideration and regard.

The special deserts of personhood, like the general deserts of all beings, issue a demand for recognition. Like any demand, it is rightfully curbed only to the extent that it is undermined by incoherence or overreaching. Exploitative demands, like those of a pimp, a thief, a tyrant, or a traitor, are undermined by the incoherence of the notion that one person grows in stature by threatening the being or negating the dignity or trust of another. Pestilent demands, like those of a virus, a spot of mold, or a serial killer, are overruled by the victim's higher standing or more innocent claims, and by the demands and presumptions of civil society, on which the realization of all human claims depends. The serial killer, of course, is not a virus or a spot of mold, but a person. Yet, in negating the deserts of others, he becomes, pragmatically, little more than the threat he represents, and the responsibility devolves upon society of removing that threat while preserving what it can of the killer's residual deserts.

The moral scheme, like being itself, is hierarchical, since deserts arise in the measure of the beings they constitute. But the laws of nature are not the same as the laws of God. For natural beings have latitude to aggress; and persons have the freedom, whether out of ignorance or out of willfulness, to withhold recognition they ought to accord, or to allow intrusions, encroachments, neglect, and violation of legitimate deserts. The withholding of recognition is the natural counterpart of the capacity to recognize deserts, cherish worth, and sanctify dignity. Freedom and naming are counterparts. Both are gifts of God, for God loves freedom as much as He loves the play of nature; and God's explicit law makes room for and presupposes freedom in the same way that His implicit law, the law of nature, leaves room for and gives energy to the play of nature while allowing freedom to those who claim it. Negligence is the natural concomitant of freedom. Without freedom, humans would never rise above the blind justice of nature or attain a dignity beyond the animal claims of the organism, in which subjecthood is given body and thereby is comprised as an actor and compromised as an object in the world. Nature allows the wildfire to overwhelm the forest, although man must not; and nature allows man to drain the wetlands, but God (as we now think) commands us to restore them.

All things, even inanimate objects, have a worth and beauty, not merely *for* or *to* anyone else, but in themselves, in virtue of what they are. Thus the Torah commands us not to make an enemy of the tree in the field (Deut. 20:19–20) and warns us that even the land will be requited for the sabbaths of fallow years that it may be scanted (Lev. 26:34). The world is the better for the existence of Mauna Kea or Diamond Head, the Mona Lisa or Venus de Milo. We would not suffer the destruction of these in equanimity. Yet the first two were not made for us, and none of these is human.

Clearly persons have and deserve a lexical priority to things in our moral calculus, and the fetus is no person. But it is a work of art, or rather a marvel of nature that far outshines Diamond Head. It is the only marvel of nature that will ever become a person. So I find it hard to see the moral grounds for according it less worth than the rain forest or the wetlands. The moral problematic of abortion will be explored in chapter 3. I will say here only that it is a daunting display of the social power of conformity and opinion over conscience that a woman who would not dream of marring a Michelangelo would not hesitate to destroy the fetus within her or would stridently defend the right of others to do so, for any reason at all, or for none. My point here is a broader one: the anchoring of norms in the being of things. This is what laws must respect. It is by reference to the value of beings that laws can be made, enlarged, applied, revised, and even— insofar as they fail to respect the worth of things and the dignity of persons— rescinded.

I do not possess some algorithm for adjudicating all conflicts among claims. Nor do I have some divining rod for discovering all the complementarities that might arise among the claims that beings make. The "art of measurement" capable of assaying ontic claims, adjudicating among them, and discovering their comple-mentarities will be no mere Benthamite calculus but a broad appreciation of the open potentialities of nature in general, and human nature in particular. We can readily understand why Plato would urge that only by access—direct or indirect, clouded or clear—to the pure idea of the Good can we adequately assay the relative worths among which our finitude calls on us to assign priorities. But even without reference to such thoughts, the aspirations visible in the projects of all beings make me confident that the naturalism I am broaching is non-reductive. If being is so variously realizable and is always dynamic and creative, as I have suggested, there is no danger of its being confused with mere facticity.

I find value in all beings and argue that if value does not reside in beings, there is nowhere else to find it. The legitimate criticism of the naturalistic fallacy by Hume, Moore, and others shows that facticity does not entail or amount to legitimacy. But being is more than facticity. To assume that reality is a bare or neutral fact, devoid of value, is to beg that question, and in a direction belied by every natural quest and attainment. To deny the identity of being and value is to deny that being is an achievement and thus to deny the most manifest fact of our experience, the dynamism of being.

Part of what I am arguing is that existence is better than non-existence. Cer-tainly there are many things that the world might be better without. But I do not think that any reality is purely evil, for as evil in a thing increases, so does its incapacity to sustain itself. Evil tends to self-destruct, partly because it saps the strengths (for which read 'virtues') of those in whom it takes hold, and partly because it tends to destroy the milieu on which any being must depend. Thus evil disappears long before it can reach totality. Beings are sustained only by the perfections they win. The things we picture as evil are such by their destructiveness to other things; but what preserves even the most destructive is their small measure of good. So a universe could not survive, let alone come to be, if it contained only evil. (That is not a truth of logic but a fact of metaphysics; its necessity arises from the nature of being as it is constituted; its universality is the hallmark of God's handiwork.) A universe of beings whose perfection is only partial and relative, however, can exist and does sustain itself. That, I believe, is the sort of universe we live in.

The weakness of my position is that it is metaphysical. That problem is unavoidable. One cannot answer the relativism of the claim that values subsist only notionally without saying something about what values really are, and so about what is real. Talk about what is real is metaphysics. I can argue dialectically that one who thinks that values are purely notional is as committed to metaphysics as I am. Such a person too has very general notions about what there is and how reality and goodness are related. Yet siting the metaphysic of morals in metaphysics and not in morals does not cause argument to dry up, as if, when one turns to such very basic questions, one opinion were suddenly no better than another and there were as good grounds for holding all values to be conventional as for denying it. The natural *tu quoque* response to such denials becomes especially enticing when, say, the relativist urges tolerance and an irenic posture in behalf of relativism. Are these too mere matters of convention?

Dialectical arguments can be powerful, and they are not neutral on the metaphysical question about whether values can be found within the world. I find relevant and compelling what Kenneth Seeskin argued years ago in defense of Leibniz's assumption that we are qualified to judge one possible world superior to another: "If a metaphysician cannot express preferences *qua* metaphysician, then he cannot disapprove of universes suffering from the most severe forms of impoverishment when he is acting in an official capacity. He would have to be able to reflect on any of the infinite number of possible worlds with complete equanimity. A universe containing nothing but a whiff of smoke or a taste of cheese, for example, could not be rejected in favor of a universe as luxurious as the one we inhabit."[27]

I think what has fostered conventionalism about values from the beginning is neither argument nor skepticism but a powerful alliance of marketing and minimalism. Marketing, because attorneys and those who train them (originally Sophists) have a service to sell under the slogan, "Who's right and who's wrong depends on whose ox is gored." Minimalism, because deference to diversity in moral outlooks is not a new invention but an ancient form of tact. Conventionalism proffers a common ground for a modus vivendi that does not demand ultimate agreement about values, the gods, lifestyles, or any matters other than certain procedural protocols, rules of the game, canons of etiquette, or terms of trade. Thus at least part—the political part—of the discomfort with metaphysics.

The market appeal of conventionalism I grant; but the minimalist pretension I deny. Conventionalism can be smothering, all-encompassing, and highly demanding of conformity in all sorts of ways—intellectual, moral, spiritual, and above all stylistic. Its liberal and pluralistic posture proves a sham, if conventions are to have any force at all *as conventions*, and then the outlook becomes oppressive and dogmatic.

For the most part relativists incline, at least overtly, to dismiss metaphysical disagreements as differences of style. But I do not find even such differences inconsequential. In nature in general and in the human case in particular, style often marks or makes the difference between conflict and accommodation. Consider Spinoza's distinction between *ambitio* and *humanitas*.[28] Where intention is the only inner difference, style becomes the only outer one between what classical philosophers would readily, and rightly, distinguish as a virtue and a vice.

What I have claimed is that to make all values subjective and to find none in reality is to deny that anything has any real worth. That position, I believe, cannot be sustained. It is refuted, I argue, by every act we make, including every speech act. One who speaks affirms implicitly the value of his speaking. Even in taking a breath one implicitly affirms the value of life—denying it perhaps in words, but affirming it again as one inhales. Yet, lecturing around the country about the ontological theory of justice that I have been advocating here, I have often heard professional philosophers deny that there is any value in being at all. Some defenders of the idea that values are only notions are apparently so committed to that view that they would rather deny that there are any values at all than admit that there is value in things. This leads me to ask again: What else is there, besides beings in general and persons in particular, that could warrant our acts of valuing? Or is valuing always irrational?

One who actually thought being itself devoid of value would be committed to the view that the universe at large might just as well not exist. I find it very hard to understand such nihilism about being, but moral conventionalists and subjectivists, in earnest conversation, seem not to shrink from it. Against such a rejection of realism about values, I respond that even to affirm a subjective value seems to entail an affirmation: that what I choose is good or right, objectively, even if only for me. To act at all seems to entail that something in the world is worthwhile—if only my will and the assertion of its desires. Obliquely, it seems to affirm the worth of the willer. But all such arguments are only dialectical.

I cannot refute the nihilism I reject without appealing to some value. So there might seem to be an impasse between my affirmation and the nay-saying of those who voice disagreement—unless I beg the question in favor of being. For it is the value of anything at all that is in dispute. But the position is not quite so symmetrical as might seem. If I assume what my interlocutor denies, at least I do not assume the contrary of what I hold, as one who denies all value to reality must do to affirm anything at all.

Dialectically, I can say that one who rejects all value in being would have no grounds for staying the hand of some nuclear or ecological terrorist bent on destroying the universe. If there were a doomsday machine (a possibility far more readily envisioned than a real person who found no value in anything), and if some maniac had his finger on the button, the nihilist would have no reason even to try to prevent the madman from pushing the button. I do not rest my affirmation of the value of beings on such negative and dialectical considerations, however, but on an open appreciation of being as we know it. In such an appreciation, scientific understanding, aesthetic awe, and religious celebration all respond to the same underlying givens.

The Jewish sources are of help here. They attest to the value of being and invite our appreciation of it. When God surveys the newly created world and sees that it is good, He might appear to be making a redundant judgment. Was He not the almighty author of it all, who made exactly what He wanted? Who was present or qualified to judge His work? Yet, like a craftsman who has made a table or a cabinet, God assays His creation and judges that it meets His expectation and intent. And more, that it is a good thing, good in itself, a thing that should exist, that deserves to exist, for the beauties it now bears, through no prior claim, but for its value now — not to God, who stands in need of nothing, but in itself, as a work of art might be valuable, not because it can be sold or put to some use, but intrinsically.

Although the world holds many utilities, they serve no function beyond it but are perfections relative to *its* purpose, which is the sustenance and flourishing of all sorts of beings — all the myriad things, as the Chinese philosophers might say. All these things, in their diverse ways and to their diverse degrees, exist for their own sakes and plot their own projects. Maimonides writes:

> According to our doctrine of the creation of the entire world out of nothing, the search for a final cause of all existence might well seem necessary. Thus it might be supposed that the end of all existence is simply that the human species should exist to worship God and that all things are done solely for man's sake, even the heavens turning solely for his benefit and in order to bring his needs into being. . . . If this view is examined critically, however, as intelligent men ought to examine views, the fallacy in it is exposed. For the advocate of this belief has only to be asked, "This end, the existence of man — is God able to bring this about without all these preliminaries, or is it the case that man cannot be brought into being until all these things have been done?" If he replies that it is possible for God to give being to man without, say, creating the heavens, then it must be asked, "What is the utility to man of all these things which were not themselves the object but which exist 'for the sake of' something that could have existed without any of them?" Even if the universe does exist for man, and man's end, as has been said, is to serve God, the question remains: What is the object of man's serving God? For His perfection would not be augmented by the worship of all things that He created, not even if they all apprehended Him as He truly is. Nor would He lack anything if nothing but Him existed at all. . . .
>
> For this reason, the correct view, in my judgment, in keeping with religious belief and in consonance with the theories of reason, is that all beings should not be believed to exist for the sake of man's existence. Rather all other beings too were intended to exist for their own sakes, not for the sake of something else. . . . We say that all parts of the world were brought into being by God's will,

intended either for their own sake or for the sake of something else intended for its own sake. . . . This view too is stated in the prophetic books: "The Lord made each thing *le-ma'anehu*" (Prov. 16:4). The reference might be to the object [each thing for its own sake]; but if the antecedent is the subject [God], the sense is 'for Himself,' i.e., His will, which is His Identity . . . also called His glory. . . . Thus His words, "All that are called by My name and created for My glory, I created, yes and made" (Isa. 43:7). . . .

If you study the book which guides all who seek guidance toward what is true and is therefore called the Torah, this idea will be evident to you from the outset to the end of the account of creation. For it never states in any way that any of the things mentioned was for the sake of something else. Rather, of every single part of the world, it is said that He created it, and its being agreed with His purpose. This is the meaning of its saying, "God saw that it was good" (Gen. 1:4). For you have learned what we have explained on how "Torah speaks according to human language" (B. Bava Metzia 31b, cited at *Guide* I, 26; cf. I, 46, citing Gen. Rabbah, 27.1). 'Good,' for us, refers to what agrees with our purpose (*Guide* III, 13, citing *Guide* I, 2).

In saying that God created all things by His own will and intent, Scripture is saying that God created them for their own sake and only secondarily for the uses they may afford one another. If we judge anthropocentrically, we shall inevitably find many things whose "purposes," in terms of utility to us, baffle us; many will seem to have no purpose at all or to be "detrimental." Yet all serve God's purpose, which is their existence. That is what is meant by their existing for His glory, distinguishing God's purpose from any merely instrumental end. God's glory is found in the creation of all things for their own sakes. Maimonides is aided to this view by the Neoplatonic response to Stoic anthropocentrism.[29] But the thesis, which he aims at the occasionalists and anthropomorphizers of providence in his own day,[30] is clearly biblical. His reading of "God saw that it was good" is borne out in Isaiah's vision (6:3) of the complementarity of God's transcendence ("Holy, Holy, Holy") with His immanence: "The fill of all the earth is His glory."

Where Genesis envisions God examining His creation and seeing that it is good, we see neither the bending of God's judgment to the world's standards nor the capricious imposition of God's demand—as if we were ordered to call the world good because it is the work of a powerful artisan. Rather, nature, the world, is God's, not only in the sense that He is its Creator and the Author of the values nature displays but also in the sense that God has scrutinized His work and found it a fair expression of the values intended. Even here God's judgment cannot substitute for our own, but it can instruct ours, aid us in seeing God's more universal goodness exemplified in the multiplicity of things. The varieties of goodness in nature make it a text in which we can recognize God through the references to His goodness and wisdom implicit in His handiwork. The finite goodness in things intends the Infinite. It points beyond itself, toward the Ultimate that is its Ground. Frost says it well in a sonnet[31] that records the lesson of a country walk:

It took that pause to make him realize
The mountain he was climbing had the slant

As of a book held up before his eyes
(And was a text, albeit done in plant).
Dwarf cornel, goldthread, and *Maianthemum*,
He followingly fingered as he read,
The flowers fading on the seed to come;
But the thing was the slope it gave his head:
The same for reading as it was for thought,
So different from the hard and level stare
Of enemies defied and battles fought.
It was the obstinately gentle air
That may be clamored at by cause and sect
But it will have its moment to reflect.

Naturalism, the doctrine that the laws of nature can ground moral and social laws, biblically finds warrant in the idea that nature bears a goodness that is of God — that its patterns, read with prepared eyes, contain instruction for the morally adept, even though they are not themselves moral patterns. But note the need for prepared eyes. To a cow, letters are mere marks. Only moral subjects will find the matter of moral injunctions in natural laws, just as only sapient beings will find instruction there at all, whether to the spirit or to the understanding.

For sapient subjects, there is always multiplicity in meaning, and for the morally adept, there is always polyvalency in intension. The Talmud tells us, "If the Torah had not been given, we might have learned modesty from the cat, not to steal from the ant, chastity from the dove, and solicitude for our wives from the cock" (B. Eruvin 100b). But note how selective the illustrations are, and how pointedly moral are their applications: We do not learn chastity or humility from the cock, friendliness or loyalty from the cat, thoughtfulness or love of liberty from the ant, wit or insight from the dove. Again, the discovery of an imperative to perfection in the nisus of evolution, rather than of a license to rapine and exploitation, is a morally mediated choice, not one that natural models alone can make for us. Thus the worth of revelation, and the complementary possibility of our receiving it — for without moral sensitivity on our part, even God's direct word would be of no more value to us than the dumbshow of nature.

The naturalism that flows from the idea of creation, unlike the unqualified or isolated kind that treats nature as an absolute or its patterns as warrants for an empty pragmatism, finds both its meaning and its limit in the idea of nature as God's work: There is a goodness beyond the goodness inchoate in nature, a wisdom beyond the wisdom that is objectified but for that very reason only implicit in the works of nature. When we see God's goodness and wisdom as the source of goodness and wisdom in nature, we acknowledge a lack of ultimacy in all merely natural values, and we recognize God's goodness as the ultimate measure of nature's adequacy and truth. Naturalism here seconds theism rather than second-guessing it. Humanism becomes, as it should be, not the rival but the ally of theism. For man is part of creation, the consummate realization of God's creative act on this planet, since man, like God, can judge the goodness of all things and can look beyond the immediacy of self-presence. God's regard for man, his breathing into Adam of His own breath, is not a mark of arbitrary favor, then, but a concrete manifestation of universal grace and justice. For God assigns to all beings a desert commensurate with, indeed equivalent to the reality they can attain. In man this desert is dignity. Man's regard for God, correspondingly, is not just a matter of prayer or other explicit modes of worship. It is a matter of self-transcendence raised to the pitch of self-awareness. It is thus the power to devise the parables and choose exemplars everywhere in nature, but nowhere more adequately than in the figure and idea of humanity itself.

Man, like all beings, must be treated as what he is, but what he is is a self-conscious and self-choosing being. His personhood morally requires recognition *as* personhood. It is for this reason, before any biological exigency is fixed, that God can judge (not as a fiat or imposition but as a statement of fact), "It is not good for the man to be alone" (Gen. 2:18): Humanity needs society. No being, not even God, but only another person can accord the friendship and mutuality that personhood requires. Thus when we examine the often contested ground of human sodality and sociality, we find complementarity where Sophists typically see conflict. Spinoza argues for the complementarity of human interests from the similarity of human projects—a similarity that points to congruity. A more linear thinker might argue on the same grounds that conflict is inevitable and unceasing. But that is to mistake the character of the likeness, which for Spinoza devolves into a quest for goods that are real only insofar as they are shared—the goods of civility and civilization; above all, the goods afforded by knowledge and indeed constituted in understanding itself.[32]

Pressing the argument further, we can say that if the deserts of beings are proportioned to their interests and their projects, it is as master builders, devisers of our own projects that we reach the plateau of personhood which makes our interests estimable above those of lesser beings and unassailable even by greater ones. If we consider the nature of those projects, it will be clear that most if not all of them (and not least those that regard the most basic biological needs of sustenance, growth of its various kinds, and reproduction) rely on social means to extend human acts and identities beyond the confines of the atomic ego and its minimal reach. Every act that enhances human capability or identity, to the extent of its worth or even feasibility, depends on the capacity to make common cause with our fellow humans and with other beings in our environment. Correspondingly, for humans to be valued and recognized as persons is, in large measure, for them to be valued and recognized as social beings. Human fulfillment is attained, then, not at the expense of other humans but largely through the perfection of our cooperation with them. This dictum is not just a prudential prescription about the means to our fulfillment. It is a recognition of conditions constitutive in that fulfillment. Its force is to unmask sophistic pretensions, whether melancholy or triumphal, romantic or rationalistic, to the effect that individuals can reach fulfillment through (or only through) violation of their sociality and that societies can reach fulfillment through (or only through) the exploitation (violation of the personhood) of their members or of others—or through the suppression of civility or the degradation of the non-human environment, on which our being depends, in still more basic if less elevated ways.

God's judgment that the world is good becomes normative when His creatures are commanded to flourish, to be fruitful and multiply, making the earth abound and the sea teem with life. The imperative becomes yet more explicit and directive when God tells His human creatures: "Choose life!" (Deut. 30:19) This is not just a slogan on an anti-abortion T-shirt, although it is not out of place there. It is an affirmation of value and a counsel against defeatism. It arrays itself against a seductive appeal that the Hebrew prophets discover and combat in ancient Egyptian culture and that persists in ours, the fascinated expectation that death is somehow morally or spiritually the matter of ultimate concern. Biblically, light and life are what is blessed—good in themselves and good in what they will achieve. The transcendence of the Holy is linked not with death or violence but with life, love, and generosity. Far from being a static facticity, existence here is a good that points beyond itself, toward the Absolute. Through the goodness of finitude, Mosaic naturalism glimpses the timeless, infinite goodness of its Source.

Monotheism is based on recognition of the goodness of being.[33] Indeed, it is a mistake, and I think a grave one, to describe religion in general as a source of meaning in human lives. On the contrary, I think of religion as one way of giving expression to the meaning we find. For just this sort of reason, I do not seek to derive the deserts of creatures from the will of their Creator, or the mere affirmation of our dependence on Him. Rhetorically, we can say, with Malachi (2:10), "Have we not all one Father?" But the question has power only with those who already believe that we have one Father and who have already accepted the moral nisus of that fact. The more fundamental, indeed foundational, move is from the recognition of the worth of beings and the moral power of their claims to the acknowledgment of God as the source of their being, beauty, and worth. This is the logically prior turning—the reasoning of Genesis—that founds and funds the religious impulse, when that impulse is morally and intellectually channeled into monotheism, powering Malachi's prophetic rhetoric—and that of others in turn. We do not hold being dear simply because it is what God made. Rather, we see the act and grace of God in the goodness and intrinsic worth of being. God is the absolute Goodness in terms of which relative goodness is recognized, gauged, celebrated, and acknowledged. The argument can move in either direction: from God to nature, or from nature to God. But the inference that involves an act of discovery is the apprehension of nature *as* creation, and that discovery is mediated, as is every recognition of holiness in experience, by our encounter with the relative perfection, the imperfect beauty of *things*, the fleeting but precious moments of transcendence that we glimpse within and just beyond the dance of being.

Just as Plato, in his task of uniting all values by acknowledging their complementarity, recognized that what is fairest and best must be most real, so the Torah discovers that what is most real, what is divine, must be not only absolute but fair and good. Accordingly, when Abraham confronts God, he equates divine power with unswerving justice, asking rhetorically, "Will not the Judge of all the earth do justice!" (Gen. 18:25). Saadiah Gaon makes the underlying reasoning explicit: God rules *because* He is just; the combination of rule with caprice would be possible, he argues, only through a power struggle.[34] But God did not come to power in some pagan theomachy. He rules eternally. Goodness is constitutive in the very idea of God. Thus, when we read that God's throne is firm and everlasting (Ps. 45:7; cf. 9:5, 8; 47:9), we understand not only God's ontic stability but His legitimacy, the stability that only justice brings (see Ps. 93). God stands at the summit of a series in which goodness and reality go hand in hand.

5. Zekhut

The Torah rarely speaks in sheer metaphysical language—although there is the stunning exception (Exod. 3:14) in which God names Himself I AM THAT I AM. Yet we can discern a metaphysical grounding in the morals that the Torah teaches. That kind of insight enables us clearly to thematize the Torah's legislative intent and mark the nisus of its prescriptions, as elaborated in the prophetic and rabbinic tradition and in the work of philosophers sensitive to that tradition, from Philo and Saadiah to Maimonides, Spinoza, and beyond. It is here that we trace the outlines of our idea of desert. It is grounded in the Mosaic conception of the goodness of creation and the medieval conceptualization of reality as a perfection.

The rabbinic term for desert is *zekhut*, a legal and moral term rooted etymologically in one of the key biblical words for purity. Thus Exodus (27:20) speaks of *shemen zayit zakh katit la-ma'or*, "pure olive oil beaten for lighting" (cf. Lev. 24:2, Exod. 30:34).[35] The idea of clarity and purity underlies the ancient appropriation of a cognate root[36] in the Hebrew word for glass (*zekhukhit*), first found in a single reference to rock crystal in the Book of Job (28:17). But, as is typical with the biblical repertoire of terms for purity,[37] the word *zakh* takes on a moral sense. Thus Proverbs (20:11; cf. 16:2, 21:8) speaks of whether a boy's doings are pure (*zakh*) and straight. Job (33:9; cf. 8:6, 11:4), protesting his innocence, urges that he is "clear" (*zakh*) and without sin. The English word 'innocent' draws etymologically on the denial of harm or wrong, whereas the moral force of the term *zakh* stems from the more positive image of purity and clarity. Thus when the word is taken over by the Rabbis as their favored term for juridical innocence, it does not mean "not guilty" but connotes "meritorious". Similarly the root, *tz-d-k* (e.g., in *yitzdak*, Ps. 143:2), means "right," "true," "righteous," even saintly—not just vindicated but worthy of being vindicated. There is no original sin. Merit—that is, positive desert—is the base or resting state; but nothing in nature, of course, is at rest.

The rabbinic understanding of *zekhut*, desert, in terms of merit (see B. Berakhot 7b, Bava Metzia 107b) shows up vividly in Avot (5.18 in *Mishnah*, ed. Danby; 5.21 in Hertz). The text argues that one is protected from sin who "leads many to virtue" (Danby) or "causes many to be righteous" (Hertz)—*mezakkeh et harabbim*. As the passage explains: "Moses was pure (*zakkah*) and made pure (*zikkah*) the many. Their purity redounded to him, as it is said, 'He wrought God's justice and His ordinances with Israel' (Deut. 33:21)."[38] Israel acquired merit through the actions of Moses—not by osmosis, but by habituation in the mores of the Law, which enhanced the ethos of the people, collectively and individually. That purity in turn safeguarded Moses himself from sin, since he took part with his people in the virtue that the new law instilled.

Through the core idea of merit, the term *zekhut* acquires the sense of earned desert, privilege, advantage, success, even ownership (B. Eruvin 7.11; Yevamot 63a, Y. Kiddushin 60a); but it never departs from the core idea of a status that merits favor. R. Eleazar b. Azariah confesses, in a passage well known in the Passover Haggadah, that until he heard Ben Zoma, he was never privileged (*lo' zakhiti*), to understand how it is that the story of the Exodus is recited at night. In courtly piety and modesty, the sage sees himself as having lacked the merit, until that time, to grasp the small but subtle point that interests him and that Ben Zoma explained. All blessings and benefits are acts of grace or responses to desert.

The pious often humbly disclaim their own merit and appeal to that of their ancestors, or to the grace of God, asking Him to act not for their own sake (or merit) but for that of their ancestors,[39] or for His name's sake. Such courtly rhetoric does not obscure the fundamental presumption of the preciousness of creation, which undergirds the juridical presumption of innocence and which is articulated in the biblical *mitzvot* of love and charity and in the biblical theology of mercy, grace, and favor. The Sages dramatize the nexus of this theology, with its ethical and legal expressions, in their frequent conceits of a heavenly court. Relying on the iridescence of midrashic imagery, they hyperbolically voice the precedence of merit to guilt by saying that if only one angel in a thousand pleads in a man's behalf, a favorable decision will result (B. Shabbat 32a; Y. Kiddushin 22b). They picture the scales of justice with two pans, one for sin and the other for merit, "and the Holy One, blessed be He, tilts the balance, favoring the pan of merit (*le-khaf zekhut*"—Pesikta Rabbati, Ki Tissa 10.9, p. 185.)

The idea that merit can be stored up and preserved transgenerationally is as ancient as the poetic visions of Jeremiah (2:2), in which God urges the prophet to proclaim to Jerusalem: "I remember in thy favor the devotion of thy youth, thy love as a bride, when thou didst follow after me in the wilderness, in a land unsown." The words are recalled and repeated on the Day of Atonement, when Israel humbly seeks forgiveness for God's name's sake and for the sake of her own past sufferings and sacrifices. But it is wrong to suggest that *zekhut* is simply "supernatural favor" or that its presence is sheerly a matter of national belonging or communal inheritance. The idea of communal desert is also applied prospectively, in the affirmation that God's saving acts were performed for the sake of later generations, or for the sake of the Torah. And general desert is ascribed not only to Israel but to humanity at large (Gen. Rabbah 100.6; B. Nazir 23b; B. Sotah 42b; B. Sanhedrin 94a; Gen. Rabbah 29.5) and even to inarticulate creatures (Y. Bava Metzia 8b).

While emphasizing the communal locus and supernatural basis of *zekhut*,[40] Neusner is careful to argue that *zekhut* has a moral origin (in self or in others) and that it need not be inherited or vicarious. Yet he rejects the idea of translating *zekhut* in terms of merit and favors a definition in terms of "heritage" and "the protecting influence of good conduct." To understand *zekhut* as a heritage preserves the connection to grace, and to speak of good conduct preserves the moral weight of the acts (or sufferings) through which *zekhut* is acquired. But taken together, the two paraphrases tend to collapse the effect or implication into the cause or ground from which it is expected to spring, as though prayers were made for protection on the grounds of past protection.

A. Marmorstein showed many years ago, rather exhaustively, that in rabbinic usage *zekhut* may be either inherited or earned.[41] Many of the Sages held that those who lacked adequate deserts must rely on the favor of God, who keeps, as it were, a treasury in behalf of those who lack merit of their own (see, e.g., Exod. Rabbah 45.6). Emphasizing the solidarity and integration of Israel as a people, many of the Rabbis thought of the merit of ancestors as a source of free grace for later generations. R. Judan, for example, said of King Solomon: "An ox, before its sinews are cut, can be hung on any one of them. After they are cut, how many strings and nails are needed to hang it! The same with Solomon. Before he sinned he could rely on his own merits. After he sinned he had to depend on the merits of his ancestors" (Eccl. Rabbah 1.2). Rival emphases, one ascribing *zekhut* to the actions of the living individual or community (Jewish or non-Jewish) and the other ascribing it to the works or the trust of ancestors, are traced traditionally to the teachings of Avtalyon and Shemaya respectively. A parallel division is found between R. Joshua and R. Eleazar of Modiim.[42] A synthesis, traditionally credited to the statesmanship of Hillel, compromised by invoking an elaborate and structurally balanced interplay of earned and inherited deserts: He who relies on his own merits, it is said, is heard for the merits of his fathers; he who relies on the merits of his fathers is heard for his own merits (B. Berakhot 10b).

It was natural for some to take rather literally the pictorial imagery of a storehouse of deserts. And in the context of persecutions and diatribes claiming that Israel was forsaken by God, it was natural for some to take comfort in the magic of inherited deserts.[43] But the moral nisus of the idea of deserts continually reasserts itself. Thus, if offspring suffer for the sins of the fathers, we are reminded that it is by taking part in the same sins that they become vulnerable (B. Berakhot 7a). Correspondingly, wherever the merit of ancestors avails, it is through their teaching and example. Glossing Hillel's famous words "If I am not for myself, who will be?" *Avot de R. Nathan* (ed. Schechter, p. 54; trans. Saldarini, p. 158, *ad* Avot 1.14) thus argues that even the merit of Abraham could not save Ishmael, and even the merit of Isaac and Jacob could not save Esau. Fathers and brothers might change a person's character, but in the end that character is what determines desert. *Ethos anthropo daimon.* Thus, glossing Hillel's words "If I am for myself alone, what am I?" we see an acknowledgment that merit can be gleaned from the past; but if the moral and communal arguments are to be balanced and not just left to jar against each other, we must recognize that even the *zekhut* streaming from the past is that of a heritage appropriated, not a passively received genetic endowment or a paradoxically unearned moral legacy.

Returning the idea of *zekhut avot*, the merit of the ancestors, to the moral aegis from which it springs does not exclude the free imparting of desert by an act of grace, which is, after all, the heart of creation. For when God creates, He does not bring mere existence out of non-existence but imparts natures that pursue their needs and elaborate their goals. Creation, then, is the imparting of deserts; and God's grace is displayed in the capabilities that beings gain of pursuing those deserts. When we call creation an act of grace, we mean in part that there was no prior desert to which it answered. But we also mean that in the act of creation came both the purposiveness that makes all creatures loci of desert and the powers to act which prevent that purposiveness from being wholly in vain. Midrashically, desert may be articulated in vignettes of judgment, but underlying those vignettes and the juridical context from which they spring, we find an ontological concept that is worthy of philosophical articulation: Earned desert is a special case of ontic desert, which beings acquire in their histories, building on their divinely imparted capabilities for existence, bestowed as a free gift in the act of creation.

The idea of creation as an act of grace, then, is not so much the warrant as the equivalent of our core claim, identifying the being with the desert of things. For being is an expression of divine creativity manifested in, and upon, the recipients of grace. It was in keeping with such a conception that the school of R. Ishmael framed their question about the purpose of the world's existence as a quest for deserts: For whose sake — "for whose merit does the world exist?" Why does God bother, why create or sustain the world? Their answer: "For the merit of the righteous" (Midrash ha-Gadol, Gen. 3, ll. 11–13; cf. B. Shabbat 119b; B. Yoma 38b, glossing Gen. 1:4). Or, generalizing: For the good that it contains, for the sake of the beings, which is to say, for God's glory.

To state our theory of desert in its sheer simplicity: The good or worth or value of any thing is its being, where being is construed dynamically and conatively. Beings make claims, and these constitute their essence, their identity or nature, their prima facie interests and entitlements. It is because desert is the very reality of things that it is universal and positive in all beings — although, of course, beings may overstep, and the equilibration of deserts in a multifarious universe will never simply serve the unqualified or unreflective claims of a single crude conatus.

Universal deserts are bespoken in the biblical protection of the trees of a besieged city (Deut. 20:19–20), the land that needs its sabbaths (Lev. 25:8; 26:34, 43; 2 Chron. 36:21, with Jer. 25:11), the ass in the story of Balaam (Num. 22:28), the human person, and even the human form, which must not be desecrated or exposed, even after the execution of a criminal (Deut. 21:23), nor mutilated, even in the service of God (Lev. 21:5). The values sketched here are systematized in the Mishnah's broad rule against wanton destructiveness (*bal tashḥit*) and in the phased measures taken against a *rodef* or aggressor in hot pursuit;[44] and, accordingly, in the phased measures taken against a fetus in those rare cases where it becomes a *rodef* but still merits recognition as a being on the threshold of human life. Biblical humanism is not the rival but the culmination of this general recognition of deserts. Thus cattle must be milked on the sabbath, to prevent the suffering of living beings. A fortiori does Sabbath rest give way in the face of threats to human life or health. The principle of *pikuaḥ nefesh* rests on the reasoning that the Sabbath is created for us, not we for the Sabbath — and so with all the commandments: "You shall live by them" — not die for them (B. Yoma 82a–85b). Life is the aim, but a certain kind of life, not any sort at all costs. Life is good, being is good, worthy of sustenance, capable and deserving of nurture.

The humanism articulated in the Mosaic norms, mounted in the larger fabric of love of life and being, provides the grand thematic of the Gemara. Marking that humanism, Ben Azzai locates the great principle of the Torah in the words of Genesis (5:1–2): "This is the book of the generations of man: In the day that God created man, in the image of God He made him; male and female did He create them, and he blessed them and named them Man on the day of their creation."

6. Community and Desert

Society does not create justice. Rather, justice creates society. How so? My argument centers on the notion of community. A community is a group whose members depend on one another. Persons are capable of community in a unique sense. Human beings, of course, rely on one another for their survival and well-being. They depend on one another, and on a host of other sorts of beings, in a variety of ways, for their realization as human beings. But, beyond this elemental form of interdependence, it is only through community that the real worth of human beings, as subjects, can be acknowledged explicitly, recognized pragmatically, and given scope to flourish.

At its base, my argument is biological. We are a social species. That is what Aristotle meant by the phrase *zoon politikon*, a civil animal: We live in communities and depend on one another for the character of our existence. From an evolutionary standpoint, we can go further: Communities long antedate any formal social undertakings; they afford the basis of our humanization, biologically as well as culturally. Consider the obstetric problem of the human head. Human evolution depended on the growth of cranial capacity. But the birth canal can expand only so far, so human beings are born immature compared with other animals. That fact, the fact of neoteny, accentuates the importance of the social division of labor, the two-parent family (as with birds, only more so), and the relevance of culture. Hume put it well: "The long and helpless infancy of man requires the combination of parents for the subsistence of their young."[45] The value of culture in turn places yet greater adaptive significance on cranial capacity and further heightens the import of the social division of labor. In this sense we can say with confidence that community antedates not only formal, societal rules and undertakings but the emergence of humanity itself.

A community (gemeinschaft), as distinguished from a societal organization, is informal. It derives its legitimacy from the goods it serves, and it may indeed be abandoned if it fails to serve as expected. In this sense it is a voluntary association. But it is not, as other voluntary associations may be, the mere product of a compact, contract, or other formal undertaking. Many communities are natural groups. We might move into a neighborhood, but we are born into a nation, culture, family, or tribe. And our dependence on our communities is often prior, temporally or ontically, to any choices we may make—as is also the case with the gift of language. Our communal obligations stem not from any formal undertaking or equivalence of goods received to services returned or sufferings and risks undergone, but from human interdependence. We are not atomic isolates and cannot survive as such. Still less can we thrive in isolation, that is, develop or express ourselves in full measure—intellectually, spiritually, culturally, morally, even physically, as, say, the institutions of medical research and practice make abundantly clear. The obligations legitimately imposed by any community stem ultimately from the worth of individuals and from the power of a community to foster their interests and promote the emergence and recognition of subjecthood. That is the heart of the usefulness of any community, and the source not just of its power but of its legitimacy.

A society (gesellschaft) relies on arrangements and reciprocities that are formal and explicit. Communal relations, by contrast, are informal and implicit. The metaphor of a social contract has a different meaning in each case. Societally, it refers to our engagement in a system of relations marked by agreements and overt rules. Communally, it refers to our existential interdependence, tacit understandings, and bonds of commitment. Roles rather than rules matter most in a community.

We should not be romantic about community. Formal, legal relationships are needed to regulate the often oppressive or disproportionate demands that communal links can impose. But we cannot ignore the priority of the communal. Communities create societies and survive within them, around them, and above them — as neighborhoods exist within a city, nations embrace a state, and humanity itself senses its rarely exercised but still crucial role as the community above all states and nations.

Natural communities such as the family, the nation, and humanity are prior to societal institutions such as the state, the firm, and the union — ontically and in legitimacy. They underwrite our societal undertakings by establishing the bonds of trust and extended identity that ground the more explicit versions of a social contract. For example, the economic trust that makes trade possible and a monetary system feasible and the political trust that makes civil life secure and military and police protection practicable when that security is threatened are communal bonds of cooperation that express our interdependence and thus address the underlying claims of personhood. Even so delicate a modality as courtesy, as I argued in *On Justice*, is not an adornment to social or economic relations but foundational to them, a prerequisite to what superficially might seem the most elementary transactions. It is because we find ourselves in a community, *ab initio*, that we are capable — morally, intellectually, even physically — of making the commitments to one another out of which our societal arrangements arise.

If Socrates is right in the *Crito* to argue that the laws are our parents, then the demand the laws make is not simply a return of benefits received. That is rarely what parents ask for. Parents and children make demands on one another, not by virtue of a contract, but by virtue of interdependency: Parents depend on their children to carry forward the project of their lives; children, on their parents for the launching of their own project. Similarly, it is only in the most tenuous way that allegiance to the laws can be construed as somehow reciprocating the protections received under the law. The demands of obedience to legal authority extend far beyond an undertaking to refrain from harm. The underlying reference of the argument is not to promises made or debts repaid but to an engagement that in some measure demands that we take one another's interests as our own. In any effectual community, this means mutual recognition of worth and dignity, a practical expression of regard that binds us to concrete obligations — even including obligations to risk our lives for one another's sake. The foundations of obligation here are existential, not formal; they are rooted in the worth of human beings.

The biblical idea of a covenant, similarly, symbolizes a more than merely formal consent, by picturing to us an oath whose parties are God and a host of persons most of whom were not yet born at the time represented. The bond envisioned reaches into past, present, and future — through a shared history, situation, and destiny. It is on the basis of these commonalities that the new, formal agreement is predicated. Beyond the boundaries of neighborhood or peoplehood, where the relationships of interdependence are enacted more impersonally than in a family yet far more intimately than in a club or firm, humanity at large has a common history, situation, and destiny which link us with one another in bonds of mutual obligation and legitimate expectation.

All relationships, from those of a business contract or a simple sale or trade of goods to those of a state or a union of states, rest on and presuppose informal relationships of trust, civility, understanding, and even the constantly renegotiated significances of communication. Language and the conventions it supports in a community of language users ground a complex network of obligations and expectations without which there would be little scope for formal undertakings, and none at all for law. Formal contracts are dependent, then, not just historically but ontically, and for legitimacy, upon the informal and implicit compacts that the members of a community (or a community of communities) hold with one another. The normative foundation of such informal compacts in turn is the recognition due to individuals, among whom persons come first but do not stand alone.

7. Synthesis

This chapter began with allusions to the unseemly struggle between church and state, society and the individual, over the control of human acts, priorities, and choices. This struggle is so characteristic of the epoch or the mind-set of modernity that one can almost characterize the thought of individuals as modern or traditional by the extent to which they presume a schism along such lines to be an inevitable feature of the human condition. But note that the terms of the polarity — church and state, "the" individual and "the" collectivity — are all abstractions. There is no universal individual or universal conscience, but only you and I, your conscience and mine. The state and church, Israel and the nations, do not exist without the particular individuals who are their members. And there is no nation or state per se, but only Britain or America, Australia or Poland. It may stick in the craw of some moderns to say it, but there are no societies — no states, municipalities, counties, corporations — without communities, that is, nations, neighborhoods, families, clans, and tribes. There is no society without the particularity and rootedness in time and place and human history, water and blood, of some community or community of communities. And there are no human individuals without communities, functional or dysfunctional, familial at the base, and never wholly impersonal.

I pronounce these home truths not because I think they are unknown but because I think they are known well enough to serve as axioms on which to mount a stronger claim, from which we can start to see how to pull back together the raveled elements of human identity and sensibility and thereby replait the strands of obligation and responsibility that have grown so frayed in a world out of focus, where our responsibilities to ourselves, to one another, to God, to human laws and institutions, seem so often at variance, and where alienation frequently projects the image of an isolated, indeed titanic self, battling or confronting or merely standing cowed before a hostile or indifferent world, an absent God, an impersonal rule, an uncaring, dehumanized, or deracinated society, or a vast and largely empty and unechoing cosmos.

We can begin to piece together our world by mending the false conflict between God and nature. This is part of the message to us of the Book of Genesis: Nature is God's nature, His work, His attribute — the way in which the Infinite is made manifest ("expressed" is Spinoza's word[46]) in all the determinacy and particularity of finite being, not just to us or for us, but to reality and for itself. It was such thoughts that the Kabbalists had in mind when they noted that the numerical value of the letters of *Elohim*, the Divine, is identical with that of *ha-teva*, nature.

What our minds apprehend of the goodness and wisdom of nature is a direct expression of the goodness and wisdom of God. The law of nature is, in that sense, although in no reductive sense, God's law. It is this that we reflect upon when we speak of laws of life — laws that give us life through our adherence to them. The idea is double edged, voicing not only the hypothetical imperative: Follow these laws "that ye may live" (Deut. 5:30, 8:1, 12:1, 16:20, 30:16, 30:19), but also the more categorical, "Choose life."[47] Nature makes a value of life; and evolution, culture, and experience assign ever richer meanings to that value. Nature does not call on us to choose between the right and the good[48] but sets before us an open chapbook full of lessons on the content that goodness can give to rightness and the guidance that righteousness can give to goodness — a chapbook in the sense that we too are called upon to write in it.

The well-framed laws of man, like those of nature, are not at odds with and not a thing apart from the laws of God. It is only by artifice or perversity that human laws affront the laws of nature or assign to them a sense at variance with the laws of conscience. Human laws are in fact, as the Stoics taught, a part of nature, and their proper function is to give circumstantial specificity to the universal dictates of the laws of nature. This is the particularizing function without which laws would not be laws or would be such only in a remote or metaphoric sense, the sense in which principles that are not lived by remain inchoate, because they are uninstituted and thus uninstantiated.

The task of imparting particularity to principles is the function that Maimonides assigns to the divine will, as distinguished from the divine wisdom manifest in the universal (and thus abstract) dictates of natural law or individual conscience. The ascription of the laws of Israel to a divine legislator in such a context as this is thus no mere rhetorical device. For it intends an authority not just behind the moral core but behind the necessary element of positivity as well. Both will and wisdom, particularity and principle, are expressions of divinity, and neither is complete in itself. What would we call a law that did not serve the common good, and what would we do with a law that did not specify a proper course in formal, uniform, and discernible terms? A good and just law draws its material content from the universal law of nature and brings to bear its formal content in behalf of concrete and particular concerns. These two facts—that wisdom in the law serves the particular, that concrete interests and deserts are addressed by way of principles so universal as to seem almost Pythagorean in their formalism, and that such formalism is relieved not by arbitrariness but by love, which enspirits the generalities of sheer law with concern for the welfare of all beings—point sharply to the unity of will and wisdom in God. For they show us that divine wisdom is not empty mathematism and that divine love is neither capricious nor indiscriminate, but attuned to the deserts of beings.

Beyond glimpsing the intentions of the Creator and catching the theme of goodness through the translucency of creation, there is a moral point to be drawn from our aspiration to the divine: that for us too love must not be blind and wisdom can never be wisdom while it comes empty handed, empty headed, or empty hearted. From here we can see our way back to our original, jurisprudential point. The idea that God's law would be somehow alien to what human love or conscience consciously and conscientiously commands is a product not of mere neutral analysis but of dissociation and alienation, the Nietzschean sundering of 'Thou shalt' from 'I will' that results from the misappropriation by arbitrary authority of the divine 'Thou shalt' and that leads inexorably to the misprision of the 'I will'—its transformation into a mere expression of alienated and rebellious willfulness.

If man indeed aspires to divinity, then he will aspire to the love and grace and wisdom of divinity, not merely to the divine aseity that is already mirrored in human subjecthood. And if man indeed desires autonomy, he will find the freedom he seeks by building a self that has strong moorings in its natural and social environment, to render it capable of freedom and of the self-integration that enables the integrated personality to find its own choices choiceworthy and worthy of acknowledgment as its own. It is by such means that we find, as the well-known phrase from the Book of Proverbs (3:4) puts it, "grace and good sense in the eyes of God and man": A genuinely autonomous self is one that is not at variance with itself. For that very reason it is not at variance with its fellows, with the good it finds in its surroundings, or with the commands of God. It recognizes in all things the intrinsic worth enunciated in their entitative claims. So it seeks not just to exploit but also to sustain those beings in the measure of their worth. It recognizes in the subjecthood of other selves a desert not lesser than its own. So it seeks not merely to profit from them but to enhance their dignity. And it recognizes in God a perfection which it seeks to emulate and share. So it seeks to serve God not by slavish submission to an alien other nor by the blind self-assertion that chases after negations of human finitude, but by appropriation of the human virtues that are the hallmark of the perfection by which alone God is recognized as divine.

2

Judaism and Human Rights

It is widely supposed that human rights are a modern invention,[1] and if rights are defined narrowly enough, I'm sure that illusion can be preserved. Ancient societies, after all, held slaves, regulated prices, persecuted religious non-conformists, subordinated women, criminalized sexual deviance, and typically espoused norms that set the interests of the community ahead of individual needs. Medieval societies were somehow worse. They burned witches—who were, we are assured, simply early feminists—organized religious crusades and holy wars, and locked up some of their brightest people in monastic orders, where they could not pass on a fair share of their genes.[2] It would be an arduous task to sift truth from propaganda in such seasoned charges, but I think we can recognize that just as excesses were perpetrated in the name of liberty during the Enlightenment, so were there conceptual and normative advances in behalf of liberty in the Middle Ages.[3] The founding texts to which medieval authors looked with studious, constant, and creative reverence anchored and energized such advances. The idea of rights, as I will argue, is not a modern conception in any but a question-begging sense. Indeed, we almost stumble over the impressive metaphysical roots given to that idea in two of the great Jewish rationalists of the Middle Ages, Saadiah Gaon (882–942) and Moses Maimonides (1138–1204).

It is in the moral person, valued as an individual and not merely as a member of society, that rights reside. First visible in classical literature and in biblical institutions, the moral subject gains definition in the medieval period. For the conceptual resources of formal metaphysics, made available to medieval thinkers by the translation of Greek works into Arabic, allow thinkers like Saadiah and Maimonides to give shape and ontic standing to the moral personality. And the cosmopolitan humanism of Saadiah and Maimonides fuses with the biblical and rabbinic ideal complementary notions from the Islamic philosophers—Kindī and Rāzī among Saadiah's predecessors; al-Fārābī, Avicenna, Ibn Bājjah, and Ibn Ṭufayl among the predecessors of Maimonides. The staunch loyalty of both men to their people and to its rabbinic tradition is not unusual. But the biblicism they share is striking among committed talmudists. It expresses a philosophical zest for work at the conceptual roots of the issues while not neglecting the practical branches.

Both Saadiah and Maimonides were polymaths—at once philosophers and jurists of distinction. Maimonides was a working physician, the author of ten medical works in addition to his philosophical masterpiece, the *Guide to the Perplexed*. His three great legal works included *The Book of the Commandments*, ordering the traditional 613 precepts of the Mosaic Law; *The Book of the Lamp*, a multivolume commentary on the *Mishnah*; and the authoritative fourteen-volume code of rabbinic law, the *Mishneh Torah*, familiarly called the *Yad Ḥazakah*.[4] Saadiah was the first systematic Hebrew lexicographer, grammarian, liturgist, and chronographer, and the author of rabbinic commentaries and thematic treatises on Jewish law.[5] His *Book of Critically Selected Beliefs and Convictions*,[6] was the first thematically organized and systematic Jewish philosophic treatise. His Arabic translations and commentaries on books of the Hebrew Bible laid a solid philological foundation for his elicitation of biblical themes; they remain indispensable for Bible scholars to the present day. Scripture, Saadiah believed, must often be read figuratively, but never capriciously. To guide his exegesis, he deployed a disciplined hermeneutic similar to the inductive method of the Arabic grammarians and the Hebrew jurists. Every sense imputed to an expression, Saadiah held, must be warranted in canonical usage. Whenever the apparent sense of a scriptural expression diverges from another biblical text, from sound tradition, or from the findings of reason or natural science, some appropriate alternative sense must be found that can be shown by textual parallels to be an accepted usage in the language of the text.[7]

Before examining the metaphysical foundations of the idea of rights in the philosophies of Saadiah and Maimonides, I want to reflect on the backgrounds—Greco-Roman, biblical, and rabbinic—and on the larger context of medieval thinking about rights, in order to set the stage and provide a standard of comparison. Then we will examine the metaphysics of rights in the light of the biblical and rabbinic ideas. Doing so will enable us to assess the contributions of Saadiah and Maimonides and help to clear up some of the confusions about the premodern ideas of rights, from which our modern ideas of rights take their departure.

1. Ancient and Medieval Ideas about Rights

The roots of the idea of human rights run back to Hebrew Scripture and to Greek and Roman antiquity. Although we find no formal catalog of rights in classical antiquity, Pamela Huby[8] has shown how the Greek idea of the free man fostered normative expectations that were often reflected in law. The polarity of liberty and slavery and, at Athens in particular, the practice of free speech (*parrhesia*), bolstered such expectations.[9] Aristotle founds his political and social philosophy on the distinction of the free from the enslaved. At the core of that distinction stand his valuations of public deliberation, consultation, and participation (*Politics* I, 2, 3, 7). Susan Ford Wiltshire, like Huby, cites Thucydides' account (2.40.2) of Pericles' funeral oration for the Athenian pride in free speech and quotes Demosthenes' explication (3.11–12) of the full extent of that freedom.[10] Socrates did not exercise this freedom with impunity. But the right was recognized, and its suppression was one of the offenses of the Oligarchy of 400 (Thucydides 8.66).

As Huby's argument suggests, we can gauge Greek sentiment toward the protection of private persons against the aggressive intentions of the powerful if we follow the normative development of the familiar Greek idea of *hubris*. Hippodamas, the city planner and legislative reformer, according to Aristotle (*Politics* II, 8, 1267b 37), identified three types of grievance in lawsuits: killing, injury, and *hubris*. Aristotle himself, a bit further on, ascribes such aggression specifically to kings. *Hubris*, then, was not simply the tragic pride that goeth before a fall. It was often the characterization given to an actionable offense against recognized rights, and it was attributable to any powerful person, including a ruler. The idea is preserved in Maimonides. Like his biblical, Platonic and Fārābian models, he describes illegitimate exercise of governmental authority in terms of rapacity. He lists suspension of the human penchant for wrongdoing and overreaching (*rafᶜ al-ẓulm wa-ʾl-taghālub*) among the minimal objectives of any system of law, be it human or divine (*Guide* II, 40).

As evidence for the legal enforceability of positive rights at ancient Athens, Huby points to the case that foregrounds the *Euthyphro*—despite Plato's sympathy with the accused and evident scorn for the notion that there could be piety in a son's bringing murder charges against his father in the death of a servant who was himself a homicide.[11] The charges were not dismissed; and conventional wisdom would see their basis, although hardly approving a son's stepping forward as the self-appointed "pursuer." Noting Plato's "remarkably complicated" argument that justice should improve (not harm) those it affects (*Republic* I, 335), Huby ascribes Plato's obliquity to his attempt to anchor basic rights without a suppositious appeal to social conventions: Plato looks not to the deserts of persons (here guilty *ex hypothesi*) but to the internal or thematic consistency of the idea of justice. It was from the idea that justice has its own nature or form that Plato drew what he voices as a radical idea of human rights, problematizing punishment at large.[12] Conventional thinking, however, would clearly focus on the rights of the workman who had been left to die.

The idea of rights both rests on and supports the idea of individual worth. For Aristotle this value was articulated politically in participatory institutions. Although somewhat romanticized and exaggerated for the sake of contrast with the practice of the "barbarian" societies that served as his foil, Aristotle's ideal of civic participation had a counterpart in social reality. Mogens Hansen finds that some 6,000 of the 30,000 to 40,000 Athenians eligible to sit in the popular assembly (*ecclesia*) regularly attended.[13] Citing this work, Wiltshire also notes the Roman legal protection against double jeopardy and against compelling the accused, or their relations or dependents, to testify against themselves. Such immunities bias the law in favor of the accused. That bias is justified only by the presumed worth of the individual. It anchors what we must call a right, if the term is to have any conceptual consistency—a protection of human dignity against even the exigent demands of justice.

In all, as one of her colleagues remarks, Wiltshire has shown that "virtually every one of the numerous rights affirmed in the U.S. Bill of Rights has ample precedent in terms of legal protections in ancient Greek or Roman law."[14] Some rights, even if recognized by law, were difficult to enforce in antiquity. But that difficulty most often reflects the inefficiencies of premodern governments rather than any conceptual weakness among the ancients, whose confusions about rights seem not much greater or lesser than our own. We may cast centralized governments in the role of threats to human liberties; but such governments make rights effectual and operative, even as the powers they deploy in behalf of those rights pose new threats to the maintenance of rights.

In the Hellenistic period, Stoic notions of natural law fostered the idea of natural rights.[15] Thus Cicero, writing in a Stoic vein in *De Officiis* (I, 7), preserves what seems to be the earliest extant reference to natural rights, a denial that there is any natural right to private property, since all things were made for humanity at large, and men, to serve and help each other. Stoics again pronounce our first attributed criticisms of slavery as an institution. Aristotle mentions earlier criticisms. He himself recognized that slavery negates the human telos, but he accepted the institution as a necessity of civilization (*Politics* I, 5). It was the Stoic Rufus Musonius who argued against slavery as an institution, despite the Stoic contention that we find happiness in integrity alone, regardless of external circumstances.

The *Politics* was the only Aristotelian treatise not translated into Arabic. But its central theme, that the state exists for the sake of the individual—to provide for the moral education of its members and to open up the possibility of their spiritual growth and intellectual enlightenment—had been highly developed in Plato's *Republic*, a work well known to Saadiah and Maimonides and the Arabic philosophical tradition that nourished them. This doctrine—and not any notion, say, of the equal capacity of human beings to harm one another—is the classic foundation of medieval appeals for legal recognition of individual rights. But besides what philosophers like Saadiah and Maimonides could learn from Plato and Aristotle and kindred Greek traditions (including texts of Galen that preserve Stoic, Epicurean, and other philosophical ideas about norms), the idea of rights is well founded in the tradition that Jewish philosophers inherit as their own.

The Torah sharply distinguishes the law of persons from the law of property and never makes property crimes capital.[16] It extends its laws to the stranger, making God's sovereignty the warrant of the repeated injunction, "One law shall there be for ye, homeborn and sojourner alike" (Num. 15:15–16; cf. 15:29–30; Exod. 12: 49; Lev. 16:29, 18:26, 24:22). It insists on the right of the accused to a hearing before impartial judges (Lev. 19:15; Deut. 1:17)[17] and demands two eyewitnesses to the overt act in capital cases (Num. 35:30; Deut. 19:15).[18] It casts a wide net of protection over strangers, widows, orphans, and the poor, and it forbids the taking of interest from Israelites.[19] It prohibits the permanent alienation of their land (Lev. 25:8–13) and blocks their permanent involuntary debt servitude (Exod. 21:1–6; Deut. 23:17–17). It demands that day workers' pay not be withheld overnight (Lev. 19:13), bans keeping millstones in pawn (Deut. 24:26) or garments beyond sunset (Exod. 22:26). It bars creditors from entering a debtor's house to retrieve collateral (Deut. 24:10–11),[20] reserves the produce of the corners of the field and the fallen or forgotten sheaves and ears as the portion of the poor (Lev. 19:9–10; 23:22; Deut. 24:19–22), and allows wayfarers and passersby to help themselves to the produce of a field, requiring only that they not use baskets or vessels to take away more than their immediate needs (Deut. 23:25). It affords freemen, slaves, even animals one day of rest in seven, remits debts in the seventh year (Deut. 14:1–2), and affords the land too a sabbath, as we have noted, one year in seven, in which what grows is the portion of the poor (Exod. 23:10–11; Lev. 25:1–7). These are rights,[21] and the Talmud, in its work of harmonizing and systematizing, tends to enlarge them in scope and formalize them in practice, for the rabbinic technique of making a fence (*seyag*) or margin around the Law holds humane concerns uppermost among its interests.[22]

In denying the presence of the idea of rights in ancient and medieval sources, some argue that premodern rights were material and positive rather than formal and universal like modern civil rights. Others seek entitlements to positive goods. Still others demand that rights be construed subjectively, as ego's desiderata. Since premodern rights involved the discharge of responsibilities, doing what was right, and giving to each "his due," rights in the older sources, it is sometimes argued, could include the "right" of a parricide in Roman law to be tied up in a sack of vipers and cast into the Tiber. But jarringly "objective" notions of rights are not confined to antiquity. No less a bastion of the Enlightenment than Immanuel Kant insists that human dignity and ownership of our own actions mean that persons deserve retribution for their misdeeds. Unlike Plato, Kant does not flinch at saying that such retribution entails harm. He goes out of his way to name the natural law punishment of a rapist as castration: *per quod quis peccat, per idem punitur et idem.*[23]

Medieval thinkers, for their part, like moderns, are diverse in their thinking. They do not uniformly eschew subjective notions of right. Thus the French legal historian Michel Villey, for example, singled out William of Ockham's (ca. 1285 – 1349) development of a distinctively subjective idea of rights as the exercise of some power to attain a good. But, as A. S. McGrade shows, Thomas and others uphold a conception of natural rights that is entirely congenial to the idea of rights as claims. The approach is clearly in play when sixteenth-century thinkers like Francisco de Vitoria and Alonso de la Vera Cruz appeal to the text of Thomas in behalf of the rights of the Indians of the New World. These Spanish advocates of the Indians were seeking, among other things, to protect them, against excessive taxation. That is a claim about rights.[24]

The very difficulties of enforcement that give color to the notion that there was no idea of rights in antiquity show that biblical rights, typified in the Torah's immunities against certain forms of search and seizure, were claims: Workers could be expected to claim their wage, debtors to demand return of their cloak, the kin of homicide victims to seek their two witnesses, and the accused to demand their hearing. Indeed the prophetic admonition *shiftu yatom, rīvu 'almanah* — "uphold the rights of the orphan and champion the cause of the widow" (Isa. 1: 17)[25] — shows that such claims were not alien to ancient Israel. That is why Isaiah can charge those who "frame iniquitous laws and legislate mischief (*ha-hokekim hikekei 'aven u-mekhatvim 'amal*)" with "deviating from the rights of the helpless (*hatot mi-din dalim*)" (Is. 10:1–2). Among the abuses inveighed against, he specifies the despoiling of widows and plundering of orphans.

Addressing our focal concern, the metaphysical foundations of rights, Mc-Grade highlights:

> Thomas's campaign for the individuality of the agent intellect [or Active Intellect, as it is also called] in each person and his parallel contention that God's promulgation of the natural law is not through an illumination above the mind but by the creation in each of us of a capacity for practical reasoning in virtue of which we ourselves may *come up with* dictates for decent, responsible, and personally fulfilling conduct. In making the agent intellect a power of the individual and making the precepts of natural law into dictates of an ontologically individualized reason, Aquinas, it seems to me, makes us the sort of creatures who are natural bearers of subjective rights, natural rights in the modern sense of the term.

Pertinently, McGrade adds, "Following John Dunn, I don't accept that Locke's natural rights-based political theory was an ideological mask for early capitalism." "Subjective rights" are not subjectivized rights; their affirmation is not tantamount to their skeptical or relativistic reduction to mere claims or mere fictions.[26]

Ancient and medieval norms, like many modern ones, do not always sharply distinguish negative from positive liberties—entitlements from freedoms. As Martin Golding notes, the idea of rights in the older sources is typically couched in the language of desert: "The root notion is that of an interest or, more generally, welfare. The basic idea is that of entitlement to a good rather than freedom."[27] Paradigmatically, Ulpian (third century), in the famous opening line of Justinian's *Institutes*, defines justice in terms of right, but even in so doing, conceives rights as entitlements: *iustitia est constans et perpetua voluntas ius suum cuique tribuens.* That is, glossing *iustitia* in terms of *ius*, right, "justice is the permanent and unwavering intent to render unto each his own right." This sense of right as one's due survives at least until Bracton (d. 1268), who explains *ius suum*, one's own right, as *meritum*, "one's own desert."[28]

If we grant that medieval and classical rights pursue a good, the objection then becomes that absolute liberties from interference were not affirmed until modern times. But how great a step is it from thinking of one's deserts to thinking of one's due as interests that are vested or established—thus as liberties not to be interfered with? This, clearly, is what the barons had in mind when they stipulated, vis-à-vis the Crown in the Magna Carta (1215), that "the English Church shall be free and have its rights unimpaired"—*habeat iura sua integra.* So we can hardly *exclude* liberties in the sense of "freedoms from" among at least some premodern ideas of rights. These might involve unmolested use of property that is one's own, as when Abraham in Genesis calls the holding he wishes to acquire for Sarah's burial *'ahuzat kever,* that is, *possessio monumenti,* as the Vetus Latina renders the expression, or *ius sepulchri,* as Jerome's Vulgate sensitively renders the Hebrew.[29]

In Ockham we find the idea of a right as a power to be exercised—lest one imagine that rights might be real without being effectual, existing perhaps only in theory or on paper. Here, I think, we do see the upper portions of the root of a notion later familiar to us from the reductive and ghost-chasing language of Bentham, who regards rights as nothing more than effectual claims.[30] But, as McGrade and Tierney showed, Ockham's political realism (and metaphysical nominalism) did not lead him to a subjectivist, relativistic, or skeptical idea of rights, and the subjective conceptualization of rights as claims to a good was in widespread use for at least two centuries before Ockham. It can be traced back to Roman law, and, I suggest, perhaps to Stoic ideas about the law of nature.

Suarez (1548–1617), who does not share Bentham's (or Ockham's) anxieties about fictive beings, is perhaps more respectful of the intensionality of rights. He recognizes that rights are effectual claims, but only when those claims are also legitimate. Thus, where Ockham classifies a right as *potestas*, a power, Suarez has *facultas quaedam moralis*, "a certain moral capability," and adds "which every man has, either over his own property or with respect to what is due him."[31] McGrade, accordingly, seems more than justified in concluding: "Both in the particularities of scriptural revelation and in the general conception of the relationship between God and natural human reason, there is considerable support in the age of faith for resolute theoretical affirmation and practical defense of human rights."[32]

2. Biblical Rights and the Idea of Deserts

Premodern rights do not hang in the air. They are elements of a larger scheme of natural justice, which situates humanity in creation vis-à-vis God's law, as articulated in Scripture and as implicit in the human frame and condition. Thus the twelfth-century jurist Placentius will write that rights derive from justice *tanquam ex fonte rivuli*, "as rivulets from a spring."[33] Biblically rights are construed in just this way. Indeed, the imagery is biblical, harking back to the symbolic "river whose streams make glad the city of God" (Ps. 46:4). Conceptually, we find a case in point with the Torah's legislation for all Israelites' undisturbed possession of their ancestral land: The communal right to the land God promised the nation, through their earliest ancestor, is institutionalized as a right of possession by all Israelites and their heirs, severally (Gen. 15:7, 15:18, 24:7; Exod. 6:4, 34:24; Lev. 25:18, 25:23–38). In the vignettes of the Prophets, that right is transmuted into an arcadian vision paradigmatic of the reign of universal justice, when "nation shall not take up sword against nation . . . but every man shall sit, unmolested under his own vine or fig tree" (Micah 4:3–4).

Biblical rights are not confined to matters of property. They include the right to an exemption from military duties for men who are newly married or who have a new home or vineyard, and even for those who are fearful or fainthearted (*yare'*; *rakh ruaḥ*, Deut. 20:5–9). They also include the right to a bill of divorcement (Deut. 24:1), designed to clear up any ambiguities about a divorced woman's status that might impede her right to remarry. But property rights are prominent among the "rivulets," reflecting elemental and universal needs and the dependence of other dignities on these. Thus the day worker's wage becomes a paradigm of biblical rights. As David Novak writes:

If one looks at the very beginnings of Jewish law, in Scripture itself, one notices that the original prohibition of robbery (*gezel*) is presented in this context: "You shall not exploit your neighbor and you shall not rob (*lo tigzol*); you shall not let the hired laborer's pay remain overnight with you until morning" (Lev. 19:13). Note that the juxtaposed prohibitions are all concerned with individual subjects and individual objects. The "you' who is not to exploit, rob, or delay the payment of wages is in singular form. "Your neighbor" (*re'akha*) does not refer to any collective object. . . . But we have no explicit source for individual rights against those of the community in the Pentateuch. When we look to the Prophets, however, we come across one of the best known and most dramatic incidents in Scripture, in the incident of the vineyard of Naboth being appropriated by King Ahab: ". . . The king spoke to Naboth saying, 'Give me your vineyard to become a vegetable garden for me, since it is near my house, and I will give you in its stead a better vineyard, or if you please, its price in money.' But Naboth said, 'It is forbidden to me from the Lord himself to give my ancestral inheritance (*nahalat avotai*) to you' " (1 Kings 21:1–3).[34]

As Novak explains, Elijah prophesies against Ahab and Jezebel and pronounces their doom for framing Naboth and having him killed to gain possession of the coveted vineyard. Samuel had warned that monarchs would demand of Israel the best of their fields, vineyards, and olive groves (1 Sam. 8:11–14). In a corrupt monarchy, the machinery for enforcing one's rights against the monarch would be especially problematic. But one can hardly compound the crimes against poor Naboth by pretending that he does not know his rights under the Mosaic Law. Even as regards institutional support, Novak astutely asks, "Why did Jezebel have to resort to the crime of framing Naboth for the crime of blasphemy in order for Ahab to take what was lawfully his to take?"[35]

Nor should we presume that ancient law relied exclusively on self-help, like that of the *go'el ha-dam* in cases of homicide. The injunction against false witness (Exod. 20:13; Deut. 5:17), for example, is enforced by the subjection of perjurers to the same penalty that the accused would have suffered (Deut. 19:19). The right of protection against perjury here is not only presumed but enforced.[36]

If the argument is made that Ahab might legally have expropriated Naboth's vineyard for *public* use, one still has acknowledged the operation of some form of process and procedure, and some form of restriction on the invasion of a subject's ancestral lands. Even if the claim is made that the conflict was between an older, tribal idea of property and a newer, commercial notion, the idea of rights inherent in a vested interest (and enshrined in the Mosaic Law) remains. Thus, R. Yohanan, responding to the biblical condemnation of the generation of Noah, argues that "judgment against them was not sealed until . . . *the earth was filled with lawlessness*" (B. Sanhedrin 108a). Seeking a sense for this notion of universal criminality, the rabbinic Sages understood the "lawlessness" (*hamas*, commonly rendered 'violence') of the generation of the Flood as socially sanctioned larceny: "each one stole a negligible amount, so as to make none of them liable individually" (Gen. Rabbah 31.5). Nahmanides, accordingly, following Rashi and the Midrash, interprets the crime of the antedeluvians as institutional complicity and social acquiescence in the ultimately ruinous practice of (mutual and universal) exploitation and expropriation—practices whose wrongfulness was evident to reason, without need of any explicit or revealed prohibition.[37] In the light of these reflections, to say that there was no idea of rights in biblical times amounts to saying that there were no property, no laws, and no courts. In other words, it is a romantic claim.

If the syntax and semantics of rights do not stand out in biblical and post-biblical legislation as we might like to see them articulated, in the familiar form of a table of constitutional guarantees—ten rights like those of the American Bill of Rights, balancing or perhaps replacing the Ten Commandments—that may be so because the Mosaic and rabbinic system envisions as its goal an integrated community, in which favorable treatment is expected to emerge from inclination as much as it is demanded by right. For the system is moral as well as legal in the narrow sense. It aims to promote a certain kind of character in those who live by its provisions, although it does not, as a utopian law would, presume upon the predominance of that ethos as a precondition of the Law's operation.[38] Guarantees we do have, their effectiveness limited (like those of any law) only by the effectiveness of government and the good will of those who govern, which here, as in any constitutional system, rests on the compliance of the governed.

What I take to be essential in the idea of rights is the ascription to individuals of positive deserts that are in some sense categorical, concrete, enforceable, and determinate. I have been urging that all beings have their share of deserts in virtue of the projects through which they constitute themselves as beings. But deserts that are only relative are not rights. Rights are the legitimate claims that persons make in virtue of their subjecthood. Deserts that cannot be recognized without the violation of equal or greater deserts are not rights. Deserts that are vague or nebulous in their conception are not rights, because they lack the determinacy needed to transform them into recognized norms in a moral, social, or legal setting.

I do not think that rights need to be recognized or instituted before they can exist. If that were so, it would be impossible or incoherent to call for the establishment or implementation of specific rights, as the biblical prophets do from the time of Moses on, and as many legislators and advocates of legislation and moral reform have done since. Nor is enforcement part of the definition of rights, or it would be illogical to complain against the authorities for failure to enforce our rights—the retort would be all too ready that we have no rights if none are being enforced. Enforceability is the standard; enforcement, the demand.

Yet a right not articulated concretely and determinately cannot be accorded the social recognition that alone would render it effectual or availing. Thus an unrecognized right is like an unrealized talent: of practical interest only insofar as its recognition is feasible. It is because the evolving institutions of society can enlarge the effectual recognition of deserts that the realm of rights can grow. This does not mean that morals change, but rather that our capacity to enjoy our rights, and indeed to enhance the humanity that is the basis of our claim to rights, is a product (one of the most important) of that human creativity and cooperation which it is the mission of society and civilization to serve. Let me offer an example.

The Pentateuch (Num. 35) identifies for homicides who did not kill with malice aforethought, a right to security from being hunted down by a patron or advocate or surrogate deputed to that purpose (*go'el ha-dam*). It renders this right effectual by mandating the establishment of Cities of Refuge and setting a term — a statute of limitations — to the very interest of the "blood redeemer" in the fate of such a homicide, rendering the homicide immune after the death of the High Priest. In time, when blood vengeance is no longer the expected vehicle of deterrence, the institution will either lose its meaning or change its function. But that function, in the first instance, is to provide the support necessary to render effectual a specific right, the right to a continued peaceful life of one who commits homicide but not murder. Law and practice render rights operational, sculpting the boundaries of desert — here by setting out the criteria governing admission of a fugitive to a city of refuge. Civil society acquires a new level of security, and civil rights are accordingly ratcheted up a notch, when homicides and their victims' family and friends need no longer confront one another — like Cain and the descendants of Abel — and, indeed, cannot for a period of years.

I think it is tautologous to say that every right entails some duty (if anyone exists to recognize it). But I do not believe that rights exist only when their possessors recognize correlative obligations toward others. For a criminal has rights even when he does not recognize correlative rights in others, an infant has rights although in no position to reciprocate their recognition, and a person in a far-off corner of the globe has rights (regarding my use of this aerosol can) even if he is wholly unaware of what I may take to be his responsibility, say, to abandon swidden agriculture or opium poppy cultivation.

Equality has a long and legitimate connection with the idea of rights, but I do not believe that all human beings are equal in all ways. They are in their basic human rights. But many human rights rest on the achievements of a highly integrated social system and can be withdrawn in response to the defeasance of the civil or social presumptions on which they were founded; others can be modulated in respect of the specific roles that individuals may play. Thus the criminal's rights are not the same as those of other citizens, a soldier's rights are not the same as a civilian's, and strangers do not have the same right to your paycheck as you do.

We learn much about the standards a society sets when we examine comparatively the dimensions of entitlement in which equality is normative. Thus, in the rabbinic sources, it is argued that all Israelites may lead congregational prayers and that each may pray individually or with the community.[39] This was a right. An early Jewish legal ruling sought to proportion the damages due in cases of an affront to personal dignity in the measure of the rank or status of the party affronted. But this notion was opposed and overruled by Rabbi Akiva, who argued that all Israelites deserve the same respect. Even the poorest and lowliest, he insisted, must be treated the same as any free person, since all Israelites are the offspring of Abraham, Isaac, and Jacob. Rabbi Akiva was challenged in this ruling by a defendant contesting the fine for loosing a woman's hair in the public street. The respondent devised a means of proving that the complainant herself did not value her dignity as highly as the rabbi's ruling: Watching for her in a public place, he spilled a small amount of oil in front of her and had observers standing by to see how the poor woman scooped up the oil and put it on her hair, oblivious of propriety. Even this evidence did not move Rabbi Akiva. The respondent, he argued, had proved nothing: The woman had wronged herself, but in this case that action was not legally culpable; the injury to her by another was, and the standard was not the value she may have placed on the indignity but rather the objective worth of her dignity, which was the same for any subject of the Law (Mishnah, Bava Kamma 8.6).[40]

It is not my purpose here to show at length how the Torah and the Prophets identify specific rights or how the Rabbis continue that task and the related one of rendering effectual a system for the recognition of rights that aims to humanize and enhance our lives with one another by maximizing that recognition. That point has been argued elsewhere at some length,[41] and it would take us far afield to course that hare. The period in which Jewish ideas of rights were laid down was ancient, and the idiom of articulation was first mythic and cosmogonic, then juridical, then allegoric and parabolic. The language was not predominantly or in the first instance conceptual and theoretical.

But the frequent claim that there is no word for rights in any ancient or medieval language does need to be addressed. Biblical morality and law do favor a language of duties. But post-Enlightenment codes too, from Kant to the traffic code, use the language of imperatives and prescriptions. It would surely be false reasoning to conclude that such laws know nothing of rights, when the Bill of Rights itself is couched in the format of "Congress shall make no law. . . ."

It is untrue, however, that premodern discourse has no word for rights — although the claim is so well repeated that it is widely thought a truism. Thus al-Ghazālī (1058–1111) writes at length in his forty-book pietist summa, the *Ihyā ʿUlūm al-Dīn* or *Revival of Religious Sciences*, of the rights and duties of friends or brethren, using the the standard Arabic term *ḥuqūq* to designate both rights and duties. He writes, for example: "Your brother," that is, your comrade, "has rights in your regard in terms of money, your person, your tongue, and your heart." Al-Ghazālī goes on to detail these in each case.[42] We have already noted the use of the term *din* with the sense of right in Isaiah (10:2), and we have seen the imperative *shiftu* (Isa. 1:17) used with the same force — for we get only incoherence if we try to render the phrase "judge the widow" and sheer nonsense if we take it to mean "vindicate the widow" — as if the rights and wrongs of the matter had no bearing on the prophet's admonition. Relying on the same root, the Torah often uses the term *'mishpat'* with the sense and force of *'right.'*[43] It speaks, for example, of the right (*mishpat*) of the firstborn (Deut. 21:17), the right to redeem ancestral land (Jer. 32:7–8), and the rights of the Levites (Deut. 18:1–2), the king (1 Sam. 8:9–11), the stranger, the orphan, the widow, and the poor (Exod. 23:6; Deut. 24:17). The terms *tzedek*, *ḥok*, and *torah* often have the same force. But since we have a conceptual definition of rights, we are perfectly capable of identifying rights where we find them without the use (or ambiguity) of any particular term.[44]

When modern scholars fail to find rights in biblical or rabbinic sources, the reason is often that they set their sights on levels of absoluteness or universality that they do not expect to find in any ancient document, or that they do not find in Scripture the specific and detailed rights that they most prize. But no realizable system of social norms can render every liberty absolute. Claims must be modulated, shaped, and reconciled — to be made real — and the social or societal recognition of rights, ideally or in practice, can be categorical without the contouring of those rights precisely as we might fancy. Different societies often treat different cases similarly and similar cases differently. The resultant "anomalies" reflect differences in social agendas. Modern, "egalitarian" commercial codes, for example, may make no restrictions like the Torah's against the pawning of essential articles like a millstone (Deut. 24:6) or keeping a coat overnight (Exod. 22:25–27). Yet they do permit bankruptcy and often preserve a debtor's domicile and basic income.

In the Torah, the levirate law imputes rights to a widow. She has a right to marriage with her husband's surviving brother. We can see that the right is hers, because the shift in priorities that brings the law into disuse is already underway when the biblical legislation is recorded: When marriage to her brother-in-law is not feasible, she is called upon to waive her right, with suitable symbolic acknowledgement of her entitlements (Deut. 25:4–10; cf. Gen. 38:8). Again, the Torah gives a female war captive the right to mourn her parents for a month before she may be married and insists that she if is espoused, it can only be as a wife, not as a mere concubine. She may be divorced but not sold, "because thou hast humbled her" (Deut. 21:10–14; Exod. 21:8). This is not the Geneva convention, but the law of the "fair captive" is a far cry from Homeric values. The captive has rights, and she has them by virtue of her personhood.

Uriah the Hittite has rights, which David has violated by sending him to the front in order to take Bathsheba for himself (2 Sam. 11–12). True, the Torah typically voices its norms as God's imperatives, but these mark out rights no less for being framed prescriptively than does Nathan's criticism of David for being expressed by courtly indirection, through a parable. Parents have rights in the Torah, including a right to press for the execution of an incorrigible offspring (Deut. 21: 18–21). This is not children's liberation, but neither is it the Roman ideal of *patria potestas*. The parental right is determinate. It is not a right of abuse. Fathers may not slay their offspring out of hand or secretly. That would be murder. Parents must bring the offending recalcitrant before the public assembly and declare his offense—which the accused may deny or recant. The law here is centuries out of use by rabbinic times, and there is no active movement for its restoration today, but it does articulate clearly the Torah's broad abhorrence for abuse of parents by their offspring (Exod. 21:15, 17, Lev. 20:9), and it does impute rights both to the children and to the parents who face the extremes of filial rebelliousness. In time the Rabbis will declare, "The rebellious son never was and never will be!" (B. Sanhedrin 37b). This law, they will argue in effect, was just a regulative idea, perhaps a means of warning potential incorrigibles and so ensuring that their numbers would be few—or none. Be that as it may, the Rabbis, by their characteristic methods, have expanded the sphere of acknowledged rights from the procedures laid out in Deuteronomy to the presumptions more familiar and acceptable to them and to us. Yet the alienness of the Deuteronomic law to our desire for gentler standards should not obscure the fact that even here, in the procedures provided, there were rights.

3. The Metaphysical Foundations: Saadiah and Maimonides

Turning now from rights to their foundation, I call attention to the concept of personhood that supports or legitimates the rights ascribed to persons in the Mosaic code. I have argued that deserts are grounded in the worth of all beings in general and of human beings specifically. That grounding is the basis of the biblical idea of rights. But neither the written Torah nor the canon that the Rabbis call the Oral Torah articulates its theory of the human person in Socratic, conceptual terms. Biblical norms are elucidated through narrative *(aggadah)*, not analysis; biblical ideals are expressed in vignettes and tableaux—the vine and the fig tree— not analytic formulations like 'rational animal.' The rabbinic idea of personhood is expressed more elusively still, in a dialectical discourse that relies on parable and allegory, not thematic exposition. The Rabbis typically avoid second-order abstractions like 'equality'; they prefer striking dialectical challenges: "How do you know that your blood is redder than his? Perhaps his blood is redder than yours!" (B. Pesaḥim 25b, Sanhedrin 74a, Yoma 82b). We can still hear the ironic tones of the generation of Moses: "Weren't there any graves in Egypt. . . ." But now the subject is our human stake in life. " 'Jerusalem was destroyed because its people judged according to the Torah.' 'What then, should they have followed the law of the Magians?' 'No, but they judged strictly by the Law and did not go beyond its sentence *(lifnim mi-shurat ha-din)'* " (B. Bava Metzia 30b). Words like 'super-erorogation' are out of place here, but the ideas are vividly marked.

It is the work of philosophers like Saadiah and Maimonides, using the conceptual vocabulary of Aristotelian philosophy, to articulate the theory of personhood upon which the Mosaic normative system rests. In so doing, both men are doing original philosophic work. They are filling in and rendering systematic moral insights and legal imperatives which, in the absence of a theoretical framework, might have been read (by an alien spirit or alienated one) as fragmented positive prescriptions. Yet the work of the philosophers here is that of translators, not sheer originators, for the norms they speak for are not of their own invention. They are the biblical norms, rendered thematic by the conceptual articulation of the idea of the person.

Neither Maimonides nor Saadiah writes an ethic of duties. When Saadiah thematizes the biblical ethos, he chooses thirteen aims of human life, which he elicits from Scripture and from his own warm appreciation of human nature, arguing that the life prescribed by the Torah provides the optimal mix among these multiple goods, any one of which, pursued in isolation from the rest, would become a self-destructive monomania. Maimonides goes further, finding a virtue ethic and a more organic eudaimonism in the Torah.[45] He groups the traditional 613 commandments and the entire corpus of rabbinic law under fourteen rubrics, which resolve to three central aims that any divine law must serve: (1) the regulation of human social relations to restrain force and fraud (overreaching, *taghālub;* cf. the Greek idea of *hubris*), provide civil security, and promote economic and social cooperation and well-being, (2) the improvement of human character, through the institution of behaviors designed to instill the moral virtues—for example, the mitigation of irascibility by such biblical ordinances as the requirement to aid an enemy in righting and reloading his fallen ass (Exod. 23:5),[46] and (3) the opening up of avenues for human intellectual and spiritual perfection, by the use of symbols and stories that draw out our intellectual potential and so help us to realize our affinity with God. But although Saadiah and Maimonides bring the apparatus of Greek virtue theory and eudaimonism to the analysis of biblical and rabbinic norms, neither philosopher is using a method foreign to the tradition and its canon when he thematizes individual commandments as general moral principles with broader behavioral applications than the cases called forth in the biblical vignettes. The ancient Rabbis do the same. For example, they read the biblical commandment against putting a stumbling block before the blind (Lev. 19: 14) as entailing, *inter alia*, a prohibition against tempting a Nazirite to drink wine, and against administering corporal punishment to a grown offspring, tempting him to turn in violence against his parent (B. Pesaḥim 22b, Mo'ed Katan 17a; cf. *Sifra* ad loc.). Nor does either philosopher need to derive the idea of rights from Greek sources. On the contrary, in view of the willingness of both Plato and Aristotle to compromise principle to prudence, Saadiah and Maimonides need to supply some of the rigor of the idea of rights from the scriptural side.

i. Saadiah's Metaphysic of Rights

Three interlocking themes underlie Saadiah's political and moral humanism: (1) his qualified naturalism—for he believes that sufferings are genuine evils and that pleasures are genuine goods, although not the ultimate goods and evils; (2) his belief that man is the adequate judge of moral issues, of life itself, of his own character and actions, and even of God—here Saadiah's conception of the individual as a moral judge wholly undermines any merely pietist or quietist attitude of resignation and is essential to the integrity of his acceptance of life; (3) his affirmation of human moral freedom and concomitant conception of the authenticity of human existence. Let me detail each of these three themes and then go on to consider Maimonides's position.

1. Saadiah accepts from the freethinking Muslim physician and philosopher Muḥammad ibn Zakariyā' al-Rāzī (d. 925 or 932) the view that pains and sufferings outweigh pleasures in this life. This is an Epicurean view, and Saadiah supports it with Rāzī's Epicurean line of argument: It is because pleasures are bound up (*maqrūna*) inextricably with pain and hurt that we can be certain physiologically that a modest equilibrium is, on average, the best that can be hoped for in this world. Even that, of course, cannot last. The exposure of our bodies to the vicissitudes of nature ensures that death will overwhelm us in the end; and, for many, sufferings overbalance joys long before surcease is reached. Saadiah does not draw a pessimistic or rebellious conclusion from his observations and the theory that supports them. He takes them, along with the unshakable premise of God's goodness, as clear proof that there is another life, and he confirms this conclusion by the observation of unrequited evils and the not unrelated alienation of all people from this life—even those who have reached exalted positions in it.[47] Life in this world is simply not good enough, Saadiah argues; it is inconceivable that God, in His wisdom and generosity, would not have reserved better for us. Indeed, Saadiah

can reason confidently (*ED* III, 10) that if innocent animals have suffered more through their use in sacrifices than they would have through a natural death, even they will be requited. God Himself will recognize human rights.

The otherworldly conclusion Saadiah draws from the facts of pain and suffering does not lead him away from the worldliness that was its source. He rejects asceticism as unwholesome and condemns the anchorite ideal for the misanthropy it engenders and the bitterness it expresses and exacerbates (*ED* X, 4). Although finding this world's life inadequate and internally unfair—the true object of the world-weariness of Ecclesiastes—Saadiah denies that God is ignorant, impotent or unconcerned. He does not find fault with the act of creation, as does al-Rāzī, who holds that God only countenanced and sustained it but did not directly cause or choose it.[48] Rather, Saadiah revels in life, finding sufficient good in this world to allow him to infer its creation by the infinite largesse of a transcendent God (*ED* I). All existence is a blessing, and the afterlife portended by the unfulfilled promises of this world is not the negation but the consummation of our present flickering joys.

2. Saadiah's worldliness and affirmation of life find expression in his expectation of a this-worldly restoration for the people of Israel, vindicating their historic mission and requiting their long endured sufferings (*ED* VIII). But Saadiah's humanism is perhaps most vividly seen when contrasted with the views prominent among his Muslim contemporaries. Some might hold that each human being's fortunes exactly mirror his deserts. This is the posture Saadiah finds adopted by Job's friends, whose intended words of comfort rapidly turn cold when they advise him that he must have deserved all that has befallen him. Job's own position, before his enlightenment by God's speech from the storm wind, is that God's doings are inscrutable. This is the view held by many of our own contemporaries, who are perhaps attracted by its irrationalism and almost delightedly take the idea that "there is no answer" as the message of the Book of Job. Saadiah recognizes in such views a perennial response to the problem of evil, a response represented in his time by the theodicy of his Muslim contemporary al-Ashʿarī, whose position, a reaction against the seeming pollyana-ism of the Muʿtazilite theologians of Islam, would in time become central to Islamic orthodoxy.[49] Ashʿarism held that God has no obligations to a chattel. What is right is for the creature to obey God's commands; what is wrong is to disobey them. But our notions of right and wrong do not apply to God, who issues the commands. We must simply accept without question.[50] As later Ashʿarites argued, even to praise God's creation as an act of consummate perfection is an act of hubris, suggesting that the Omnipotent could have done no better, had He pleased, and that human judgment is adequate to gauge the worth of creation.[51]

The adequacy of human reason and of moral knowledge in particular, is precisely the claim from which Saadiah does not flinch. We know right from wrong, good from evil, without the direction of authority. Like the Muʿtazilite theologians, Saadiah believes that if we are to be punished or rewarded, it is for actions over which we can exercise responsibility. Like the Muʿtazilites, he knows that the suffering of innocents and prospering of evildoers are wrongs that must be righted. And, like the Muʿtazilites, and Plato long before, he will find powerful leverage in the idea that the Divine is perfect. Echoing the Muʿtazilite phraseology, Saadiah reasons that it would be unseemly, "impermissible," to ascribe any suffering to God's agency, unless that suffering had some purpose — in disciplining the wayward, requiting past wrongs, or justifying an enlarged recompense in the hereafter, in keeping with the rabbinic doctrine of the sufferings of love. God here is the pivot of the argument, but man is the judge. The world is not created for our pleasure, but it is created in our interest. If we looked, as it were, into God's ledger books, Saadiah writes, we would find ourselves more than satisfied with our allotment.[52]

From Plato no less than from Scripture, Saadiah draws the idea that God is absolute Perfection. In a few verses of the Book of Job (34) he finds no less than seven arguments against the elements of the Epicurean dilemma. The verses, as Saadiah renders them:

> (12) True it is, too, that the Almighty wrongeth not, and the Allsufficing wresteth not judgment (13) of him to whom He gave charge over the earth, and on whose account He set out the whole world below. . . . (17) How can he who hateth justice prevail in his own affairs? Or wilt thou overrule Him who is great in justice? (18) Is 'scoundrel' said unto the king, or 'unfair' to the openhanded, (19) who favoreth not princes and sustaineth not lavishness in the presence of the poor, since they are all His work?

Saadiah's comment:

> Elihu now adduces seven arguments against Job, refuting the notion of divine injustice. Three are basic, and four are subsidiary. The central three he unites in a single verse, in the words (19) *Who favoreth not princes and doth not regard munificence before the poor. For the work of His hands are they all* [Saadiah here quotes the Hebrew, and I translate to reflect the unglossed text].
>
> These words capture the three proofs monotheists use. For a judge rules wrongly only for one of three sorts of reasons. First, under the heading of intimidation. . . . But since the Creator fears no one, it is absurd to claim that He is unjust; of this Elihu says, *who favoreth not princes*. Second, under the heading of venality. . . . But since He needs nothing from His creation, it is again absurd that He do injustice; of this Elihu says, *doth not regard opulence in the face of the poor*, mentioning lavishness strictly to allude to venality. The third heading is that of ignorance . . . of the facts or the rightful way of dealing with them. But He is the Legislator and Executor of the requirements of justice; of this Elihu says, *for they are all His work.*

So God's sovereignty bespeaks not his transcendence of human ideas of justice but His responsibility. Saadiah continues:

> The four other arguments. . . . First, *Doth one who hateth justice prevail?* (v. 17). This means that when a man is unjust and hates just rule, his own affairs are not well ordered or successful, as it says, *A man is not established by iniquity* (Prov. 12:3). But He, whose concerns run in perpetual order and stability, is on a plane which precludes His being unjust.
>
> Second, *Or wilt thou condemn Him who is the great in justice?* (v. 17). This means that the doings of the Creator cannot be impugned and His judgment overruled by some denier. For it is absurd to impugn the Truth Itself.

Third is his saying, *Is 'scoundrel' to be said unto the king?* (v. 18). Here Elihu makes clear that the king deserves to rule only for his justice. So it is absurd that He be a rightful king and yet be vicious. Such a thing could occur only among humans, through a struggle for power.

Fourth, *'unfair' to the openhanded?* For munificence means bestowing more than is deserved. One does not call a giver lavish if he retains anything that ought rightfully to have been given. Munificence begins where fairness leaves off. Hence, since it is established that His bounty surpasses the lesser level, it goes without saying that He is fair.

So much for the exposition of the seven points which Elihu employs as proofs in behalf of theodicy. And as stated they do prove his conclusion, as he claims.[53]

The exegesis is muscular. Saadiah knows it is a *tour de force*. But the three arguments meant to blunt the prongs of the Epicurean dilemma are the easy points. The so-called subsidiary arguments are the crucial ones metaphysically. For it is here that Saadiah finds vindicated in explicit terms the biblical conception that God's power rests on His goodness and justice.

The sequence of the argument is critical: We know that God is just from the order and regularity of nature. We see that order in nature's stability and infer the perfection of its cause, since we know that wrong produces not stability but disorder. The argument is Platonic, and the Platonism grows more explicit when God is called Truth itself, so that it becomes incoherent to deny His justice — given the biblical and rabbinic synonymy of justice with truth. In effect, God is *eminently* just.[54] Again note the sequence: We know the justice of God's acts because God is Truth itself. We do not argue that we must call whatever occurs justice because it is God's act. We accept as God's doing only what comports with the pure idea of justice. God is not the author of every criminal act (*ED* IV, 6), nor can we regard God as the author in the primary intention of every natural accident that results from the general operation of the laws of nature. All events are part of God's wisdom, but not all sufferings are punishments or even warnings. Some are simply — or, perhaps not so simply — trials.[55]

So, in the third argument, we are called upon to see that injustice is incompatible with the very idea of God. A theistic subjectivist might also have said that what God does is just a priori, because it is what He chooses. Saadiah relies on an absolute idea of justice, to which we humans have access, and he holds God to the standard set by His own perfection. Ultimately, there is the appeal to the bounty and generosity of creation. In bestowing existence on what was not, creation answers to no prior desert; it is an absolute act of grace.[56] But the assumption, once again, is that creation is a good (albeit not a perfect one), and a good that we can recognize for ourselves, by its own merit, not simply by its provenance. Grace, being absolute, exceeds and presupposes fairness. And grace is what we see in creation, for we can recognize goodness when we see it.

Critical to Saadiah's view that man is an adequate judge of the fairness or unfairness of this world and the next is his thesis that one can know one's own innocence. This pietists often deny. They hold that even constant self-scrutiny cannot vouch for the integrity of one's motives, which God knows better than the individual. The notion is well suited to the Christian doctrine of original sin, by which one who is innocent in his own eyes has not even set his foot on the first rung of the ladder of redemption. But Saadiah accepts the biblical premise that Job knew his own innocence. He rejects the flailing about of midrashic charges that Job (of all biblical figures!) is somehow guilty of bad faith.[57] Job's self-knowledge contrasts dramatically with the complacency of his would-be comforters. Their bad faith (*ma'al*) finds comfort in a false piety that assumes Job must deserve punishment, when they know that he does not.[58] Job's truer piety finds an existential discomfort in the dissonance between his awareness of his own innocence and his knowledge of God's justice.

The deep humanism of Saadiah's theodicy, his uncompromising hold on human standards of worth and judgment, on human fairness and sensibilities, spring from a moral center anchored in the humanism of the Mosaic and rabbinic sources. Clearly, any form of theistic subjectivism or legal positivism would put a jurist and rabbinic legislator like Saadiah in a quandary, forcing him to elaborate a tradition without access to its moral intensionalities, allowing the law that he must shape and channel to twist and turn in his hands, ungovernably and without hope of any adequate interpretation or application. Knowing God's intentions, Saadiah, as a Rabbanite, can confidently expand and shape the Torah's norms. Knowing that human dignity and desert lie at the heart of the Torah's intent, he will read the Law with a view to sustaining human rights. This matter of rights was not just a point of theory for Saadiah. He broke with the Exilarch David Ben Zakkai and endured deposition from his judicial office, slander, abuse, and humiliation over a period of years (before his ultimate reconciliation with this leader of Iraqi Jewry) over his insistence that judges and civil authorities may not exact a fee from the proceeds of cases they decide.

3. Freedom is the core of the moral personality for Saadiah. It is as a theater for the exercise of human freedom that he thinks the world was created. It is freedom that renders human beings capable of the transcendent acts of goodness or evil that ensure their immortality and make them susceptible to eternal requital. The light that is "sown for the righteous" (Ps. 97:11) is the same as the fire that consumes the wicked.[59] This supernal light affects the good and the evil differentially because of the enduring, indeed ineradicable, significance of what they have made of themselves. That is why the Sages say, "Fairer is one hour of penitence and good deeds in this world than the whole life of the world to come, and better one hour of peace in the world to come than the whole life of this world" (Avot 4.22). For in this world there is no peace, but in the other, no repentance.[60]

Saadiah's thesis, that moral authenticity is found only in the exercise of freedom, is pointedly spelled out in a fascinating gloss of his, based on a curious chiasma that he notes between the self-knowledge, say, of Job, and the self-deception of evildoers. Saadiah believes that God characteristically warns wrongdoers to correct their course, through the imposition of sufferings. So the first thing one must do who undergoes some suffering is to examine his ways to find if he is guilty of some wrong[61] and correct the fault before it overmasters him. If one finds no warrant for one's sufferings, then one must know that they are a trial and that their outcome will be the recompense reserved for those chosen for the sufferings of love. But in this case there is no confirmation, for that would trivialize the trial. We must live, in other words, in doubt and trust. That is human condition, the full measure of the fact that we are created, given an existence of our own, and not simply clutched unborn within God's bosom. This authenticity is the clearest mark of human dignity, for it means that our acts, even our trust and doubts, are inextricably our own.

God might simply have granted us His bounty. But Saadiah agrees with Kant[62] that the theme of creation is not bliss but freedom. The object of creation was not that we should enjoy bliss but that we should deserve it, so that God might exercise His justice by requiting us. Thus, in his commentary on Job, Saadiah elicits the rabbinic idea of the sufferings of love from the speech of Elihu, who makes it very clear (Job 33:6) that he speaks as a mortal. But the higher idea that emerges from God's speech from the storm wind, as Saadiah analyzes its themes, points to the value of authenticity. For if one asks, pointedly, whether the innocents who suffer might have preferred never to undergo their trials and might rather have foregone both their suffering and its reward, Saadiah's answer is that "wisdom is not identical with what creatures yearn for." One might naturally shun birth itself, given the choice—but out of ignorance, not out of wisdom. "The proper object of concern is not whether the decrees of the Allwise gladden His creatures or grieve them. For what is agreeable to them is not the standard of His wisdom. Rather His wisdom is the standard for them."[63]

This life is valued not for its comforts and still less for its security, but for the fact that in it, and in it alone, we can act. We have an identity of our own and the opportunity to choose—once in each moment, not multiply—wisely or unwisely. That is a gift we may underrate, especially if we slight its transcendent dimension. We may picture immortality as a mere continuation of our personal lives. But in God's terms, transcendence is perhaps far more compact with our choices themselves, since each choice impinges not just on time but on eternity. It is this thought that demands of us that we confront the fact of creation and that makes creation the appropriate theme of God's speech from the storm wind. For when God gives existence, He also gives sustenance, an environment, and a nature to each being—wisdom and design, not externally imposed but implicit, as in the metiers of all creatures, or explicit, as in the consciousness and conscience of human beings.[64] Our measure of independence is the emblem of the authenticity of our existence; human sufferings are not the mark of some inveterate primal sin but the price of authenticity.

What this means, in moral terms, is that authenticity—freedom in the human case—gives meaning to our vulnerability. Suffering and loss would not matter were it not for the preciousness of what is lost. Our mortality is assured, in the language it knows best, that all unwarranted losses will be made good in a supernatural moral calculus. But on a higher plane, we are told that creatures matter and persons matter supremely, not because of what God has in store for them, but because of the reality and the freedom God gives them.

ii. Maimonides's Reworking of the Foundations

Maimonides takes exception to much that Saadiah did. He does not believe that the world exists for man's sake, and he rejects the notion that evils outweigh goods in this life. He sees the Epicurean premises of the latter view, and he condemns the anthropocentrism of the former (*Guide* III, 12, 13; cf. *ED* IV, Exordium). Yet he knows that pains are real evils, and when he seeks broader ground than the view that "all things exist for man, and man that he might worship God," he turns not toward theocentrism but to the Neoplatonic doctrine that all things exist for their own sakes. Here, as we have seen, he finds the true meaning of the biblical dictum (Isa. 43:7) that God created all things for His glory.

Maimonides is markedly uninterested in the idea that the wicked are tormented in the hereafter. He holds to a Platonizing account of immortality that owes much to Avicenna and Ibn Bājjah's modified monopsychism.[65] By such an account, the wicked would dissolve with the dissolution of their bodies, never having realized the inner affinity of the rational soul for the divine. Their eternal alienation from their Source is their damnation — only figuratively called suffering. For there is no state lower than non-being. As for the blessed, their intellectuality places them in intimate contact with the Divine, even while they live. Thus Saadiah's theory of God's created glory, so important to his soteriology and his account of theophany, is indulged by Maimonides as acceptable but rather naive.[66] For prophets, like philosophers, need not behold any overt object. They have the real light of God within them. The intellect that is fulfilled in them is the very image of God. In prophecy this intellectual light overspills the rational intellect to inform the prepared imagination with concrete images and symbols that body forth the pure ideas of philosophic inspiration in laws, rituals, myths, and institutions that are accessible to ordinary human beings and that foster not only sound practices but the beliefs that will nurture good character and will invite a higher level of apprehension, directed toward the Truth Itself.

1. Maimonides does not think that life is a test. He does not believe that God is obligated to requite anyone. He rejects the rabbinic, midrashic idea of the sufferings of love as unbiblical and untrue. Nowhere in the Torah is this doctrine stated, he says. Nowhere is it even hinted, except in the binding of Isaac (Gen. 22), where the notion has been read into the text quite improperly "that God causes injuries to descend upon a person who has not previously sinned in order to increase that person's reward." Many of the Rabbis, Maimonides explains, rejected this idea of the sufferings of love; and rightly so, for the doctrine is incompatible with God's justice (*Guide* III, 17, 24). On the contrary, "The biblical principle is diametrically opposite to this view and is enunciated in His words: 'A God of faithfulness and without injustice' (Deut. 32:4)."

But God's justice is the great constant uniting the Rambam's thought to Saadiah's. When Maimonides reflects on the predestinarianism so widely held among monotheists, he knows that the Torah gives as much foundation for such views as does the Qur'ān. In the biblical idiom every event is called an act of God (*Guide* III, 17.5). And not only the dynamic of the idea of God's power, but the problematic of theodicy militates in favor of predestination. For the natural response to the sufferings of innocents is to say not that they were deserved but that God does as He will. Maimonides respects the seriousness of purpose that brought the Ash'arites to this conclusion (*Guide* III, 17.4), but he rejects the conclusion and the reasoning that led to it, because it violates the implicit humanism that he, like Saadiah, imbibes from the canonical sources:

> The third view is . . . held by those who believe that nothing occurs by chance; indeed everything is intended, willed and controlled. . . . This is the doctrine of the Ash'arite party in Islam. Their view entails a number of outrageous consequences, which they recognize and accept. . . . it is not the wind that causes leaves to fall, rather each one falls at the decree of God, and it is He who ordains when they fall and where. That they should fall earlier or later or anywhere else is impossible, for all this is predestined from eternity.
>
> In consequence of this opinion, they must accept the foreordainment of all animal motions and rests and the powerlessness of any to do or refrain from doing anything. . . . Another consequence which follows necessarily from their view is that the message of revelation is of no use whatever, since man, for whose sake every revelation has been given, can do nothing to fulfill what he is commanded, nor to avoid what is forbidden. . . . it follows that God's actions need have no object or purpose.
>
> They bear the burden of all these impossible consequences in order to save their dogma. Even when we see someone congenitally blind or leprous, of whom we cannot say that by his prior sins he deserves what has befallen him, we still should say, "So it pleased God"; and when we see a good and pious man killed in the midst of worship, we should say, "So it pleased God to do." And there is no injustice in this; for it is perfectly permissible according to them for God to punish the innocent and reward the sinful. Their pronouncements on these matters are well known. (*Guide* III, 17.3)

Maimonides condemns the Ash'arites for abandoning the naturalism and the concomitant doctrine of free will that would have made sense of God's creation. He understands God's providence as acting through, rather than despite the laws of nature, and he finds special providence in the nexus of each human mind to the Reality of God. When I speak of humanism in his view, I am referring to his staunch rejection of the idea that man must simply accept all events as the particular acts of God even when we find them unintelligible or unjust. It is as true for Maimonides as for other monotheists that God is the cause of all that is. But God's determinations are often general, and we need not truckle, in the manner of Job's friends or the unenlightened Job himself, as Saadiah reads the book, to find justice or the sheer will of God in every particular determination. The Ash'arite idea that man is simply God's chattel, to be used or abused as God pleases, is a detriment to human dignity and, for that very reason, inconsistent with God's honor. Maimonides's insistence that divine justice be understood in terms accessible to human understanding and commensurate with human values is an expression of his humanism; it is a forthright rejection of authoritarianism, even when the authority is God.

> It is an axiom of our teacher Moses and all who follow him that man does have the power of action absolutely, by which I mean that whatever he does

within the compass of human action, he does through his own character and by his own free will and choice, without [as in Ash'arite theory] any sort of ad hoc capacity being created for him. Likewise all species of animal move by their own volition. So God willed it from eternity: that all animals would move by their own free will and that man would have the power of doing whatever he chose to do, so long as he was able to do it. No denial of this axiom has ever been heard in our religion, thank God. (*Guide* III, 17.5)

The heartfelt "thank God" is spoken with one eye on the heavy burden of predestinarianism that Ash'arite theology loaded into the saddlebags of Islamic orthodoxy, and the other, gratefully turned in the direction of Saadiah, whose clear understanding of the implications of predestination assured that the equilibrium between divine omnipotence and human freedom would be struck quite differently in Judaism than it was by Saadiah's Muslim contemporaries, allowing Jewish scholars to interpret the rabbinic dictum "Everything is in the hands of Heaven except for the fear of Heaven" not as a paradox but as a bestowal of freedom, exempting *all* human choices from the absolute control of the divine decree.

It might be imagined that "metaphysical freedom" and political freedom are unrelated. But that would be a mistake. If free choices are unavailable to us in the nature of the case, then opportunities for the exercise of choice will not be the first but the last priority of governments. Besides, fatalism is a common refuge of tyranny, whose apologists sincerely or insincerely plead the divine decree (or, from Thrasymachus to Marx and beyond, the laws of nature) in behalf of acquiescence. Revulsion with political extremism and discomfort with political criticism put wind in the sails of Islamic predestinarianism and many another doctrine of resignation.[67] Maimonides normatively *expects* a different attitude. Moses, at the moment of his call by God, still standing before the burning bush, is pictured in the Torah as raising a question about the God who has summoned him: "They shall say to me, 'What is His name?' " (Exod. 3:13). Maimonides interprets this as a courtly request for some proof to offer the questioning Israelites of the authenticity of his mission:

> What was it in the situation that made it necessary that they would ask this question, so that he must seek some answer to it? He says, "They will not believe me or hearken to my voice, but they will say, 'The Lord hath not appeared to you' " (Exod. 4:1)—for it is quite obvious that this is just what should be said to anyone who claims to be a prophet, until he offers proof. (*Guide* I, 63)

Maimonides approves the critical stance that the leaders of enslaved Israel are expected to adopt. What Moses is given as a response, Maimonides argues, is no mere name but a compact argument for God's necessary existence, based on His absoluteness. For a name, if familiar, would prove nothing, and if unfamiliar, would only sound like gibberish. But the Tetragrammaton, made up of the letters of the verb 'to be,' encapsulates God's epiphany I AM THAT I AM, offering a miniature or cameo of what we now would call the ontological argument.

Note Maimonides's expectations, however: The elders of Israel will comprehend the argument, its cogency will be essential in establishing Moses's authority, and Moses himself, with all his courtly deference to God, will not approach his people with a claim to authority that he cannot himself believe. What is crucial to us here, at the foundation of the idea of human rights, is Maimonides's normative expectation of critical thinking. This will be echoed in Aquinas's idea of the immediacy and particularity of the Active Intellect, but it is an articulation in normative and epistemic terms of the ancient biblical (Deut. 13) and rabbinic criterion for distinguishing true from false prophets: True prophets are those who tell the truth.

It is not only natural, Maimonides insists, but normative *(yajibu)* that the Israelites should respond skeptically to a prophetic claim to authority and that they should be satisfied only when Moses can present what the wisest among them (the legitimate leaders) will recognize as a sound argument. Saadiah renders the same line of thinking very concrete: A would-be prophet who commands us to commit adultery, he argues, should be rejected as decisively as if he had commanded us to accept falsehood and reject truth *(ED* III, 8). Saadiah's epistemic assumption that we can know the truth independently of claims to revelation and his appeal to a moral case to exemplify the kind of truth that we can know independently of prophecy show clearly that the responsibility he locates in the biblical ordinance about false prophets is rooted in freedom and subtends a right of refusal even (or especially) of prophetic pretensions. We see here a vivid precedent for what McGrade finds in Ockham and calls "still to the best of my knowledge the first defense of what might be called the right to a reasonable explanation in matters of religion."[68]

Ockham's approach is precedented, as McGrade shows, in Thomas's qualifications of the claims of authority, arguing, for example, that since all human beings are equal in regard to bodily sustenance and procreative capacity, all should be free to contract marriage or vow virginity; again, quoting Seneca, that the mind, in making choices, is a law unto itself, even before God; and again, that non-Christian captives must be allowed to decide for themselves whether or not they wish to accept Christianity.[69] These "scattered texts" as McGrade calls them, display the nexus between individuality and freedom as metaphysical doctrines and between individuality and free choice as political values. That is the nexus we find still earlier in Saadiah and Maimonides—not surprisingly, since the metaphysics reflects the normative thinking as well as guiding it. Both the norms and the outlook are rooted in biblical and classical antiquity.

2. For Maimonides, as for Saadiah—and Aristotle before them—the law exists for the sake of human beings. Its aim is to enhance human life, not only materially but morally and intellectually, enabling us to reach the plane at which our innate likeness to God is realized. The same humanism that sparks Maimonides's rejection of predestination is voiced in his claim that all revelation is for the sake of man. "There are among mankind," he writes, "certain people who regard the giving of grounds for any of the laws as something dreadful." But the alternative is to believe that God acts to no purpose, "as though . . . man were higher than his Creator, for it is man who speaks and acts purposively while the Deity does not but simply orders us to do things of no good to us and forbids us to do things of no harm to us" *(Guide* III, 31). Such legal positivism destroys not just God's wisdom but His grace.

But if revelation does serve human needs and does offer us means toward our fulfillment, we can interpret, and (as was the rabbinic charge) enlarge the Law—not *ad libitum*, but faithfully to the purposes that are its authentic themes. It is in keeping with this mandate that Maimonides reads not only the biblical but the talmudic text that is the proximate matter of his Code. I do not wish to suggest that Maimonides as a jurist is anything but a strict constructionist. Worries that he may have invested his jurisprudence with conclusions derived from his rationalist philosophy or his personal predilections have proved illusory. His legal rulings are well grounded in precedent; and he does not need to import any humanism of his own into the rabbinic canon, since such humanism, is, as we have seen, already well established there, both in the Mosaic and prophetic foundations and in the talmudic elaboration. But reason does provide an overarching structure to Maimonidean jurisprudence, and reason in Maimonides, as in Saadiah, is substantive, not merely formal. For it is understood in a Platonic vein as a recognition of fundamental values, including the existential worth and dignity of the human person. It would take us far beyond the scope of this book to explore fully the ramifications of this theme in Maimonides' legal work, but I would like to single out one area of public law where the impact of his approach is striking: the conception of constitutional monarchy enunciated in the final volume of the *Mishneh Torah*.

Monarchy was established under protest in ancient Israel. Yet it was not imposed on the people but demanded by them, in response to the anarchic situation graphically described in the Book of Judges, when "there was no king in Israel, and every man did what was right in his own eyes" (Judg. 21:25). The idea of simply waiting for some new Deborah, Jephthah, or Gideon to arise and champion the people's cause was ineffectual and dangerous. Not only was it passive, but it offered no rules to regulate the choice of such self-selected champions or to govern their actions. The Judges, after all, were neither elected magistrates nor hereditary lords, but charismatic warriors. Both the prophet Samuel (1 Sam. 8:4–22) and the Book of Deuteronomy (17:16–17) warn of the dangers of a monarchical government: the amassing of wealth, wives, and horses—not necessarily in that order. Samuel's warning, issued at the express command of God, is the more explicit:

> This will be the practice of the king who will rule over you: He will take your sons and appoint them as his charioteers and horsemen, and they will serve as outrunners for his chariots. He will appoint them as his chiefs of thousands and of fifties; or they will have to plow his fields, reap his harvest, and make his weapons and the equipment for his chariots. He will take your daughters as perfumers, cooks and bakers. He will seize your choice fields, vineyards and olive groves, and give them to his courtiers. He will take a tenth part of your grain and vintage and give it to his eunuchs and courtiers. He will take your male and female slaves, your choice young men, and your asses and put them to work for him. He will take a tenth part of your flocks, and you shall become his slaves. The day will come when you will cry out because of the king whom yourselves have chosen.[70]

God calls the people's desire for monarchy a rejection of His own direct rule, softening Samuel's sense of personal rejection. Yet God instructs the prophet to honor the people's request.[71] And the reason is not hard to see. It is stated openly to Samuel by the elders of Israel: "You have grown old, and your sons have not followed in your ways. Therefore, appoint a king for us, to govern us like all other nations" (1 Sam. 8:5). Even before Samuel first encounters Saul, it is revealed to the prophet how he will identify the man God has chosen to be king, and the attributes for which Saul is chosen are telegraphed in the prophetic narrative earlier still: We learn of Saul's piety (and its intellectual level) from his seeking some divine purpose in the seeming wild goose chase he has been led on after his father's strayed asses; further, he is the son of a man of heroic might (*gibbor ḥayil*) and himself a fine young man (*baḥūr va-tov*), the best in all Israel, head and shoulders above all his fellow Israelites in stature (1 Sam. 9:1–14). These are the reasons God has made Saul his "designee (*nagīd*) over My people Israel" — his task, to "save My people from the hand of the Philistines. For I have seen My people, and their cry has reached Me" (1 Sam. 9:16).[72]

Maimonides, seeing his people in historical straits as dire as those that faced the ancient Israelites, speaks unequivocally for the people: Without a king, or, more pointedly, without a central government, how will Israel survive and reestablish herself on her ancient soil? Thus, where Deuteronomy, like Samuel, voices only a permission, hedged with conditions — that the king must be an Israelite and must not (as Solomon would do) collect (foreign) wives, after whom his heart (drawing with it his religious loyalties) will stray — Maimonides finds a positive commandment ordaining establishment of a monarchy. He glosses Samuel's and God's displeasure with the people's demand for a king as a rebuke only to the querulous spirit in which the request was made, not a critique of the institution of monarchy itself (*MT* XIV, ii, 1.2); and in his *Sefer ha-Mitzvot*, cataloging the commandments, he lists the imperative to establish a monarchy as the 173rd of the positive commandments. His reading, disputed by many another exegete and jurist, is precedented in the authoritative commentary of *Sifre*. But it is also given a clear rationale: The king "will bring together our whole nation and act as our leader."

From *Sifre* (Piska 157 to Deut. 17:15; cf. B. Kiddushin 32b) Maimonides learns that the king must be honored; and from the Talmud (B. Horayot 13a), that among his contemporaries a monarch of Israel takes precedence even to a prophet; disobedience to his authority is a capital offense. Here Maimonides reasons as he does with regard to punishment: "There is no more fatuous fool than those who claim that the abrogation of all punishment would be a kindness to mankind. It would be the utmost cruelty to men in fact and the ruin of civil order. What is compassionate is what God commanded (Deut. 16:18): 'Establish judges and magistrates in all your precincts' " (*Guide* III, 35). It is by the presence or absence of order and respect for persons and their needs that we can judge whether any place has a government, and the effectiveness of government is perhaps most readily seen in the presence or absence of the fear of punishment among those who might think they have no reason beyond the fear of sanctions to adhere to a law or respect the interests that laws seek to protect (*Guide* I, 46).

But although the Rambam supports the institution of kingship, he understands it as an office, not an inherited prerogative — still less a divine privilege. Only the full Sanhedrin, acting in concert with a prophet, can establish a dynasty (*MT* XIV, ii, 1.3). The first duty of a king, as the biblical sources make clear (1 Sam. 15:1, 3, cited at *MT* XIV, ii, 1.2), is the conduct of war. So a regency is required if the king is a minor (7). The Davidic monarchy is the historic ideal, but any Israelite king's legitimacy can be judged by his adherence to the Torah and his fighting the battles of the Lord. Thus anointing does not make a king; in the case of a son's succession to his father's throne, it is not even performed, unless the succession is contested, and then only to underscore symbolically the legitimacy of a prince's claim.

Kings are subject to a variety of restrictions designed to protect their dignity among the people. For example (despite David's dancing naked before the ark), no one must see the king naked, and he must have his hair trimmed daily. But the biblical ordinance against "multiplying horses" is understood globally as a rejection of all empty pomp. The Mishnah (Sanhedrin 2.4) reasons that it means that Israelite kings may ride only with as many horses as they need to draw their chariot. Maimonides explains that a king of Israel "is forbidden to add even a single idle horse to run before him, as other kings do." Otherwise he is flogged (*MT* XIV, ii, 3.3)! Nor may the king get drunk (5, citing Prov. 31:4) or overindulge sexually (6).[73]

Where the exigency of the hour demands, kings may impose a kind of martial law, suspending the biblical rules of evidence (10). But they may not sequester the property of those who are punished, nor may they punish someone who gives precedence to a religious obligation over obedience to a royal edict. For the king's command is not law. The High Priest does not bow to him, and the king must honor Scholars of the Torah, rising before the Sages of the Sanhedrin, if they visit him in the privacy of his home, and showing deference even to the students of the learned. He must cultivate humility and execute justice graciously and compassionately, pursuing the interests and protecting the honor "even of the lowliest," and addressing the public gently, as their servant, in accordance with the model set forth in the 1 Kings (12:7, cited at *MT* XIV, ii, 2.6). The sin of Moses that barred him from entry to the Promised Land, Maimonides writes, was in allowing his character to reach such a state that he could address his people in anger, despite their provocation:

> Moses himself, as you know, the master not only of Antiquity but also of Posterity (peace be upon him), was told by God, "because you did not trust Me to sanctify Me" (Num. 20:12), "because you disobeyed me at Meribah water" (Num. 20:24). . . . All this! And his sin—that he inclined slightly away from the mean with respect to one particular virtue of character, namely patience, and toward spiteful anger when he exclaimed, "Hear me, rebels," etc. (Num. 20:10).
>
> God was strict with him because for a man like him to be angry before the whole congregation of Israel in a situation that did not call for anger was, relative to such a man, tantamount to blasphemy. For they all modeled their actions upon his and studied his every word in hopes thereby of finding fulfillment in this world and the next. How then could anger be seemly in him, when it is, as we have made clear, a bad mode of behavior and has only bad psychological effects? . . . Moses was not addressing a nation of fools nor a nation that lacked

virtue but a people the least woman of whom, as the Sages put it [*Mekhilta* to Exod. 15:2, ed. Lauterbach, 2.24], was on a par with the Prophet Ezekiel. Everything Moses said was scrutinized by them. Thus, when they saw him angry, they said, 'He has no faults of character; unless he knew that God is angry at us for asking for water and that we have angered Him by so doing, he would not have gotten angry.' But we do not find that God (blessed be He) was angry in speaking to Moses about this matter. He simply said, "Take thy staff . . . and give water to the congregation and their cattle" (Num. 20:8). ("Eight Chapters," 4)

Like Plato, Maimonides understands the role of the ruler as one of responsibility toward his people, and for them. He emphasizes that Moses was a role model whose every word was scrutinized by the people, doubtless with the Muslim *sunna* in mind, that is, the practice of treating the example of the Prophet as normative. Although careful to show that the standard God applied to Moses was stricter than would normally apply to a lesser leader, Maimonides does not vitiate the moral he draws: that leaders, who stand in a position analogous to that of Moses, must provide for the needs of their people with humility and respect. The classic image of kingly responsibility is that of a shepherd, attested as early as Homer among Greek writers. The Psalms (78:71) expect the king "to be shepherd over Jacob his people," as the Rambam notes. But, as in the contretemps between Thrasymachus and Socrates, the question naturally arises whether the shepherd is to care for the sheep or fleece them. Maimonides finds his answer, which is the same as Plato's, unequivocally stated in Isaiah (40:11). He writes: "The way in which a shepherd is to act is spelled out in the prophetic text: 'Even as a shepherd that feedeth his flock, that gathereth the lambs in his arms, and carrieth them in his bosom and gently leadeth those that give suck.'" Plato provides some argument in support of this conclusion (*Republic* I, 343–47). But for the Rambam's juridical purposes, the prophetic text is more valued here: It makes responsibility toward his people part of the very meaning of the biblical ordinance of kingship.

The biblical requirement that a king must write out a scroll of the Law and read it all the days of his life (Deut. 17:19) is the bastion of what we must call a constitutional conception of monarchy. The Maimonidean king must commence to fulfill this commandment as soon as he ascends the throne. Once the scroll he has written has been corrected by the Sanhedrin, he must keep it with him at all times — even in the field of battle. As for the scroll he has inherited from his father, he must keep it in his treasury. If he has inherited none, he must write two, one for constant use and another for the archive.

Kings may levy taxes and customs imposts. Their authority to do so is discovered in the very warning that Samuel issued: "And ye shall be his servants." The complaint becomes definitional, and the definition, normative! The same is true with the levying of troops and ordnance, officers, concubines, and palace attendants. Goods and services may be requisitioned, as may fields, vineyards, and orchards needed for the quartering and supply of troops. But all these must be paid for. Otherwise the king is guilty of theft.[74] As each warning is transformed into a norm, it is regulated and restricted. Nothing is arbitrary. For monarchy is a means to an end and is judged by its effectiveness in achieving that end: "The prime reason for appointing a king was that he execute judgment and wage war,"

Maimonides reminds his readers, citing 1 Samuel (8:20). So a king's "sole aim and thought should be to uplift the true religion, to fill the world with righteousness, to break the arm of the wicked, and fight the battles of the Lord" (*MT* XIV, ii, 4.10).

Democrats may dislike the pomp that Maimonides allows the kings of Israel, and liberals will chafe at his compromising some of the categorical protections of biblical and rabbinic law. Maimonides does ride the rabbinic exemption of the "exigencies of the hour" a good way back in the direction of the broad discretionary powers that Plato gives the philosopher king.[75] He does not go so far as Machiavelli or Hobbes will, but he clearly seeks a compromise with practicality as he understands it. The political institutions of his Egyptian surroundings and his Andalusian and Maghribī youth were not designed by the ACLU. Pomp, of course, is not of the essence. As Maimonides himself remarks: It is simple country folk who spot a ruler by the panoply that surrounds him; the more urbane observers focus on the unseen relations of authority (*Guide* I, 46). But, as Maimonides would be the first to note, symbolism can create a reality. That likelihood, surely, is the reason for the stress he lays on the outward trappings of majesty. These shore up and sustain its inner power. And it is for the sake of power that kings are made.

Political authority for Maimonides represents a rather small but still essential portion of the apparatus of the Law, the portion that Maimonides designates by the term *sultān*, government.[76] He takes this term in the broadest sense, as a lowest common denominator, meaning magistracy, civil authority. Halakhically the monarch derives legitimacy as a chief magistrate through the biblical ordinance to establish "judges and magistrates in all your settlements" (Deut. 16:18, cited at *MT, Hilkhot Sanhedrin* 1.1).[77] Maimonides's notion that monarchy is biblically ordained is thus an application of the command to establish a government, applying to Israel in its particularity the sole positive ordinance of the Noahidic commandments, the obligation to institute courts and magistracies. The Maimonidean monarch is not a legislator or sovereign, since those roles in their primary sense belong to God. Nor is he an interpreter of the Law. That role is reserved for the Sanhedrin. But ideally he is an administrator, executor, and, in fact, a reformer of the Law. For he sees to its application in concrete circumstances, as in the conduct of war, the implementation of policy, the levying of taxes, and the oversight of courts. The notion that an administrator makes no policy is an illusion. [78]

Max Radin remarked half a century ago how remarkable it was (he begged strict Austinians to note) that Maimonides wrote a comprehensive code of Jewish law—including his impressive laws of judges and kings—at a time when Jews lacked the institutional machinery to effectuate that law.[79] Talmudic discourse tends to create a world of virtuality, self-contained and self-sufficient, which, like its epochal predecessor, prophetic discourse, is impatient of brute facts. Prophecy may speak with reference to the past, future, or present, but it does not speak *of* those times but rather of the values it projects onto facticity, in promise, warning, or critique. Talmudic discourse, in effect, is the analysis of those values, so it too creates a world of virtuality, whose geography is Halakhah. What was radical in the idea of *Talmud Torah* was that it refocused Jewish life from the give and take of civil, economic, and intellectual activity toward a largely academic plane. Judaism transformed itself from a comprehensive system of concrete practical norms into a comprehensive system of ideals, whose realization was projected onto the past or deferred to the future, but whose present and fullest reality was interior — in the mind of the scholar and the private, familial, and synagogal realms of ritual practice, custom, meditation, and devotion.

Against this background, Maimonides is a remarkably political thinker. He does not explore the academic niceties of the Law in the classic manner, making their study an end sufficient in itself. His interest is profoundly practical. It is in this spirit that he speaks of mathematics as an intellectual discipline, not simply as training for the mind but as conceptual preparation for thinking, say, about infinity — allowing the mind to come closer to the idea of God.[80] As a jurist, Maimonides wrote no comprehensive commentary on the Talmud but an elucidation — literally, "illumination" (*sirāj*) — of the Mishnah. His global treatment of the Law is a practical code. He puts *pilpul*, or logic chopping, for its own sake on a par with such other negativities (in his estimation) as fasting and asceticism for their own sakes.[81] The closest he comes to a purely academic interest in the Law is in his remarkable scholarly discussions of the Temple cult, where his overriding interest, insofar as it is academic, is anthropological. He wishes to explain how such a system could have arisen and what its functional value was — a valuable and interesting approach but hardly in the spirit of the *yeshivot*. For Maimonides, the Law is not an academic document or a mere mode of thought: It is the blueprint for a way of life. His practical treatment of it is the most impressive testimony to the confidence with which he looked forward to the historic conditions that would make possible its restoration and, in the context of a new level of social vitality, its renewed reform. For him, the political institution represented by a head of state was critical in that process of restoration and in the inauguration of the renewed and robust national life that would follow.

If we ask why Maimonides is generous with the powers of kings, then, despite the long prophetic and rabbinic tradition of protest against royal power and its trappings, and despite the even longer Jewish experience of the abuse of royal authority, the answer is given clearly in terms of the work Maimonides expects the kings of Israel to do. He expects no less of them than the rebuilding of the Israelite nation and, ultimately, the establishment of universal peace and justice. This they will do, he insists (*MT* XIV, ii, 12), not by conquering the nations of the world, but (in a more Platonic mode) by ruling Israel so wisely, justly, and well that the nations of the world will flock to follow Israel's example. The kings of Israel will rule effectively, but justice, as in Saadiah's Platonizing model and as in the promises of the ancient prophets, will be the basis of their power (Jer. 23: 5–6). What Maimonides envisions here is something like an ideal of the modern nation–state: central authority, made effectual by the rule of law; efficient, beneficent administration within the parameters of what we would call a constitution. Thus, even the ad hoc provisions for conditions of war and emergency do not abrogate the basic commandments (and guarantees) of the Law. The ruler is still an officer, and his acts are judged by their conformance to the Law and their effectiveness in the realization of its aims.

We cannot say that the Maimonidean monarch is a prime minister, responsible to his Sanhedrin. He is not *elected* in our now familiar sense, and he does not seem to be deposed in any routine fashion, in the manner that parliamentary government has now made familiar (but that even a Thomas Jefferson did not perfectly envision). Yet neither is the Maimonidean ruler the "absolute" monarch of stereotypic "oriental" fable and fantasy, for the extremes and even the cruelty of such rulers were often the reflex of attempts, prudent or hysterical, panicked or calculating, to maximize the impact of what little practical power medieval monarchs typically could wield.[82]

Following up on Plato's, and Saadiah's, theme, that justice is a source of power and that arbitrary violence is a mark of weakness, not of strength, Maimonides leavens Plato's discretionary model of monarchy with the legalism of the Rabbis and the categorical *"thou shalt"* and *"thou shalt not"* of the Mosaic Torah. The effect is to place constitutional constraints on the monarch, even as his powers are buttressed for the task he must confront. The faith behind that mixed message is the biblical, Platonic, and, as we might add, Lockean, faith that even constraints are a source of strength when justice is their basis. For just rule wins the arm and the voice of a free populace and expresses more clearly than any declaration of rights, trust in the inherent power of goodness.

3

Abortion and the Emergence of Life

I have already intimated that our theory of deserts bears entailments with regard to the issue of abortion. What are those entailments? If beings deserve to be treated in accordance with what they are, does a human fetus deserve treatment as a full-fledged person, or does its empiric status limit its deserts? After all, no one urges the vote or the right to hold office for the as-yet unborn. I would argue that our approach yields something like the middle ground that many have been seeking between the polarized extremes of the ongoing abortion struggle. The desire for such a middle ground is expressed in calls for tolerance and the avoidance of extreme and inflammatory rhetoric on all sides of the dispute. Such irenic postures are hard come by in a polemic that pits the absolute claims of individual freedom and protection from the threat of an "alien" or "invading" organism against the claims of fetal personhood and the myth of instantaneous ensoulment. The Jewish sources, speaking as they always do in many voices, envision a more gradual emergence of personhood. They thus suggest an emergence of deserts, phased to reflect the emergently entitative claims of the unborn. They respect a prospective mother's prior claims to life and well-being and take seriously any threats to her welfare. But they do not treat either choice or incipient humanity as absolutes. Nor do they accept as universal or even typical the radical isolation or alienation of a prospective mother's claims from those of her unborn child. If we follow the mishnaic doctrine, as incisively understood by Maimonides and as modulated in the tradition that follows in his wake, we find a juridical approach that contours the deserts of the fetus to its changing ontic standing.[1] This approach warrants neither the labeling of abortion as murder nor the dismissal of fetal deserts as nugatory.

1. The Ontic Standing of the Fetus

Arguing in behalf of a biblical idea of creation, Maimonides speaks of how hard it would be even to imagine our own development if we had only reason and limited experience to guide us:

Everything that comes to be for the first time—even if it originates in matter that already exists and just sheds one form and puts on another—has a different nature after coming to be, once it is ready and settled, than it had while developing and emerging from potency to act—different too from its nature before starting out towards realization.

The female seed, for instance, has a different nature as blood in the blood vessels than at conception, on meeting the male seed and starting to develop. And its nature is different at this stage from that of a maturing animal already born. There is no way of inferring from the nature of the stable, finished product to the condition of that same thing while it was developing, nor from the developmental state to what preceded the start of development. When you err in this way and try to infer from the nature of the thing that has reached completion to the prior potentiality, you are liable to fall into grave difficulties, mistaking necessities for delusions and impossibilities for necessities.

Suppose, in our example, that a person of consummate ability were born and that his mother died after nursing him only a few months, leaving only men to finish raising him on an isolated island, so that he grew up and was educated and learned to reason without ever seeing a woman or any other female animal. Now he asks one of the men with whom he lives: "How did we come to be and in what manner did we develop?"

The other would answer: "Each of us developed entirely inside the belly of another of our kind, like us but 'female'—having such and such a form. Each had a tiny body that lived inside the womb, moving, taking nourishment, growing little by little, until reaching a certain size. Then a portal was opened for him on the underside of the body, from which he was extruded and came forth. He continued to grow until he became as you see us now."

The orphan then would have to ask: "This miniature of ourselves, when it was in the womb, living, moving, and growing—did it eat and drink, and breathe through its mouth and nose? Did it defecate?"

"No," he would be told, and he would doubtless lose no time in judging the entire account a lie and disprove all these facts, inferring their impossibility from the character of the mature and independent being.

He would argue: "Any one of us deprived of breath for even a few moments would die. All his movements would be stilled. How then is it conceivable that one of our number could exist enveloped in a heavy sac inside the body's cavity for months and yet remain alive and motile? If one of us swallowed a sparrow, it would die as soon as it reached the stomach, let alone the abdomen! Every one of us who does not take food by mouth and drink water would perish in a few days, without a doubt, so how could a person stay alive for months without eating or drinking? Every one of us who takes in nourishment and does not defecate would die within a few days in dire pain. How then could *this* survive for months without evacuating? And if the belly of any one of us is pierced, he would die within days. So how can it be claimed that this "fetus" is open at the naval? Or that it does not open its eyes or spread out its hands, or stretch out its feet, if all its limbs are sound and unimpaired, as you claim?"

In this way he would press the analogy, to show that a man cannot develop in the fashion described. (*Guide* II, 17, Munk, 35ab)

The world for Maimonides, as for most medieval philosophers, is a macrocosm, a single, integrated organism, with limbs, soul, and living spirit.[2] For Maimonides, unlike strict Aristotelians, this organism has a linear rather than a cyclical history. It grew and developed, like a fetus in the womb, and had a different nature while developing from the one we observe and study today. It was not subject before it began to develop—still less before it existed—to the same necessities that naturalists would find in a mature adult. The fetus, then, is the type of the developing cosmos, as the man is the type of the settled and invariant cosmos in which we live and to which the classical natural scientist directed his attention. Maimonides's interest, in the passage just quoted, is the disparity between the embryo and the mature, free living adult: The world at large does not allow of inferences like those made by philosophers of Neoplatonic/Aristotelian stamp, from the present, settled order to the formative stages of nature. But the illustration also casts light on Maimonides's idea of the fetus—in part because it resonates with echoes.

The notion of a perfect man growing up motherless on an isolated island harks back to Ibn Tufayl's classic story of Ḥayy ibn Yaqzān.[3] Although the naturally inquiring orphan philosopher of Maimonides's illustration does not originate quite as spectacularly as the hero of Ibn Tufayl's philosophic romance, both figures model the human condition. Both originate in ways that might seem incredible. On the scientific account, Ḥayy ibn Yaqzān develops by spontaneous generation. On a more mythic account, he is born in dramatic circumstances, concealed in a little ark, and wafted by a providential current to the island where a doe nurses him through infancy. The scientists emphasize the proper preparedness of the matter that was to receive the human form; the fabulists stress the elements of pathos and particularity. But both versions of the story find indispensable the divine afflatus that guides Ḥayy's fortunes or gives life to his clay.

Maimonides does not introduce any special appeal to the supernatural in his account of the fetus—quite the contrary. He sees God as acting through nature rather than despite it. But the spirited incredulity of his too purely rationalistic young philosopher stumbles at the same issue that fascinates Ibn Tufayl: the emergence of one nature from another. This brings us to our second echo.

Arguing in behalf of prophecy, miracles, and a kind of religious empiricism, al-Ghazālī, whose *Incoherence of the Philosophers* is an important backdrop to the work of both Maimonides and Ibn Tufayl, urges in his spiritual autobiography, *Rescue from Error*,[4] that without experience one would never admit that something no larger than a grain could devour an entire town and then itself. Yet fire has such a nature. Rationalist philosophers ascribe the effects of opium to its coldness and claim that earth and water are the cold elements. Yet pounds of water and earth have not the effect of a single dram of opium. Experience is the key to knowledge. Human reason has not the power to legislate the course of nature but must await discovery of God's plan. As Maimonides puts it: Man can learn the workings of a water clock by taking it apart and following the sequence of its motions. But God, like the clock's inventor, knows the workings of nature prior to its being. Indeed God's understanding is its cause (*Guide* III, 21).

For al-Ghazālī, as for Maimonides, the fetus is emblematic of nature. In criticizing the rationalist philosophers' account of causality and defending the scriptural idea of miracles, al-Ghazālī is particularly concerned with the imparting of life and consciousness to what is otherwise inert matter.[5] Here is a clear instance of the sort of transformation that aprioristic philosophers would deny.

Prior to al-Ghazālī, Muslim practitioners of *kalām* addressed the problem of the imparting of life and consciousness to non-living matter rather frontally, almost by invoking the divine creative word. *Mutakallimūn ("loquentes")* of occasionalist persuasion devised a rather ad hoc but still powerful cosmological atomism, founded in turn upon a stringent logical atomism which enabled them to treat no fact in nature as dependent on any other[6] but required that all be dependent, without mediation, upon God: This atom, given by God, exists here and now, not again or elsewhere unless God so pleases. This accident (it could be life or consciousness in an atom) is present because God so willed.[7] Consciousness and life, some argued, must be predicable of an atom, because no predicate is applicable to an aggregate unless applicable to its parts. Moreover, consciousness does not require the presence of life. Each thing and each accident is what it is, and its presence does not require or entail the presence of any other. Thus there are no causal dispositions or capacities, but each thing and state of affairs is uniquely and directly created by God and re-created, or allowed to vanish at His pleasure.

A straightforward argument from Aristotle, whose works were being translated when *kalām* was in its heyday,[8] severely undercut this occasionalist line of thinking: If natural or voluntary agents lack the capacity to act, their action is impossible and will not take place (*Metaphysics*, Theta 3, esp. 1047a, 10; cf. Delta 12, 1019b3). Al-Ashʿarī, the great systematizer of *kalām*, provides a shrewd response to this argument, which Aristotle used originally against the Megarians: Things have capacities by which they act, but the capacities are not their own. They are imparted by God and compass no future event and no bivalency but only the immediate action which is at that very instant performed. Turning the tables on the Aristotelian reasoning, al-Ashʿarī insists: If the requisite capacity is present and nothing is lacking for action, then the action must take place.[9] No capacity governs the future. Al-Ashʿarī thus preserves the force of the Qurʾanic (8:17, 18:39) dicta: "When you shot, it was not you who shot but God"; "There is no power but in God."

Al-Ghazālī went much further in his concessions to naturalism and thus offered a more sophisticated version of the idea of divinely imparted powers than did al-Ashʿarī. His treatment creates a subtler gloss of the scriptural principle that all powers stem from God. Pressing the point that causal relations are not matters of logic (since "this is this and that is that," and there is no logical incongruity in affirming the one while denying the other),[10] Al-Ghazālī concedes that in certain respects causal relations *are* matters of logic: One cannot simultaneously and univocally affirm and deny the same predicate of the same thing or affirm the particular while denying the general that it falls under. One cannot, for example, ascribe consciousness to non-living matter, for conscious beings are a subclass of living ones, and the specific presupposes the generic. Even God cannot do the impossible.[11] Accordingly, there are natural prerequisites for natural changes and events. God performs miracles not by contradicting the natures of things but by providing the necessary sequence of material and formal causes. "For matter can receive any form," and God can impart to bodies the form He desires:

Earth and the other elements can become a plant; the plant, when eaten by an animal, can become blood; the blood, sperm; and the sperm, implanted in the womb, can be formed into an animal. Familiarly this involves an extended temporal sequence. But our adversary cannot debar it from God's power for matter to cycle through these phases more rapidly than usual. (*TF* 200–1 = *TT* 533–34)

Al-Ghazālī quietly adopts the hylomorphism of "the Philosophers" and drops the atomism of the occasionalist *kalām*. He allows the necessity, in any developmental transformation, of suitable matter and predisposing forms, exactly as required by the scientific account. He insists only that God may miraculously initiate or accelerate the natural sequences. Similarly, he may even allow the bivalence of human volitional dispositions, that is, the assumption that men act voluntarily and at their discretion in the normal case. For the bivalency of human volition is the model Al-Ghazālī uses to establish the credibility of divine volition, on which hinges his (and Maimonides's) account of the credibility of creation.[12] But al-Ghazālī's paradigmatic demand is that divine volition can intervene in nature to produce motion in a corpse (*TF*, 204 = *TT*, 537). For in a way, by al-Ghazālī's account, that is just what God does in producing dispositions in us or any active "forms" in matter.

The image of the fetus and allied images related to the imparting of life, consciousness, and ordered movement to what is in itself non-living, not conscious, not animate at all, recur repeatedly in al-Ghazālī's analysis of nature: the rod transformed into a serpent, the corpse that God causes to sit and write with an orderly movement, above all the embryo emergent in the womb. Al-Ghazālī's concern is not simply with "the miracles that disrupt the accustomed course of nature," but with the more familiar and in a way even more mysterious miracles of birth, conception, and development. Al-Ghazālī follows the lead of the Qur'ān in founding his conception of the miraculous upon his conception of the natural order. For in the Qur'ān God instructs Muḥammad to argue dialectically for the plausibility of resurrection from the established given of creation: "Does not man see that We formed him from a drop of sperm? . . . He says 'Who shall give life to these bones when they are rotted?' Say: 'He will give them life who raised them up at the first. He knows the formation of every creature! The same who gave you fire from the green tree. . . . Has not He who made heaven and earth power to create their like again? Indeed He has. He is the all-knowing Creator. When He commands a thing, He has only to tell it 'BE' and it is.' "[13]

Saadiah too links the rise of human life with the re-creation of man at the resurrection: "Job's words 'I am mindful, O Lord that Thou didst form me. . . . Didst Thou not pour me out like milk and curdle me like cheese? In skin and flesh dost Thou clothe me, and in bone and sinews dost Thou shelter me' allude to the three modes of generation by which God gives being to men at three different junctures: The first is His creation of Adam from dust. . . . The second is procreation, by which God creates man through the mediation of two persons, as Job says, *Didst Thou not pour me out as milk?* which is the second mode of generation, namely, from semen, which develops like a clot [cf. Qur'ān 22:5, 23: 14]. The third is the resurrection . . . generation not, as in the first two cases, out of dust or semen, but beginning with flesh and bones, sinews and skin, as Ezekiel

(37:8) says, *I looked, and lo there were sinews on them, and flesh and blood came upon them, and skin covered them over.*"[14]

For al-Ghazālī, as for Saadiah before him and for Maimonides after him, sexual reproduction is a paradigm case of a miracle. It is also al-Ghazālī's model for creation and resurrection. By his account, even the most dramatic miracles ascribed to the action or anticipation of scriptural prophets, those that seem to disrupt the course of nature, are no different in ultimate structure (but only in speed and outward appearance) from natural events. In all natural events God acts by providing matter and forms. Embryogenesis is the paradigm case, emblematic of the human condition at large. Indeed, the embryo metamorphoses to a kind of ideal. For Al-Ghazālī argues in *Reviving the Religious Sciences* — that reliance upon God consists initially in simply trusting in providence, but at a higher stage the devotee depends on God like an infant on its mother: "For the infant knows only her, turns only to her for support, and relies on none but her." At its most sublime, trust means placing oneself in God's hands "like the corpse in the hands of the washer."[15] Mediating between the two images — of the child at its mother's breast and the corpse in the hands of the washer — is the image of the fetus, not yet born nor yet dead, wholly dependent on the sustenance it receives, as all things depend on matter and form, which stem ultimately from God.

Maimonides does not adopt fetus, infant, or corpse as an ideal. Nor does he share al-Ghazālī's suspicion that reliance on the powers of natural or volitional causes is a subtle form of idolatry.[16] In fact, as we have seen, Maimonides criticizes fatalists, occasionalists, predestinarians and even theologians who maintain (like Saadiah) that all things exist for man, and man that he might worship God. Such thinkers, he argues, by making God's means unnecessary to his ends, render God's acts futile or vain and ignore the aim of creation, which is not merely the attainment of God's ends but the attainment of those ends by these means, omitting no step from the natural sequence. For each being in creation serves a subtle purpose — as milk nourishes an infant and the womb shelters an embryo — and each being exists for its own sake and not just for the sake of all the rest.[17]

Maimonides accepts a hybrid naturalism that mediates between the logicism of the Aristotelian neoplatonists, who think of causes as ideas, and the scriptural voluntarism that seems to assign all natural and human acts to God. But this Maimonidean naturalism is an adaptation and extension of the position pioneered by al-Ghazālī, and the image of the fetus remains prominent in its exposition, as though to attest the kinship. Arguing that biblical and rabbinic angels are in fact natural forms and forces, Maimonides urges:

> If you told one of those men who purport to be the Sages of Israel that the Deity sends an angel who enters the womb of a woman and then forms the fetus, that would impress him and he would accept it as an expression of God's greatness and power and an instance of His wisdom — although still convinced that an angel is a body of flaming fire one third the size of the entire world — supposing that all this was perfectly possible for God. But if you told him that God placed a formative power in the semen, by which the limbs and organs are shaped and demarcated, and that this is the angel, or if you told him that the forms of all things are the work of the Active Intellect and that this is the angel constantly

mentioned by the Sages as the magistrate of the world, he would bolt at such a view. For he does not understand the real meaning of greatness and power. (*Guide* II, 6, Munk 17ab)

The "Magistrate" (*Sar*) given charge over the world, the Active Intellect, imparts from itself the intelligent and intelligible forms of all things. It thus stands forth at all levels of nature, manifest in the spiritual or intellectual aspect of reality. Its work is manifest in the forms that differentiate elemental matter and give all things their specific character and inner form or design. This manifestation of God (which had been called God's word or wisdom by Jewish thinkers from Philo to Halevi) is most prominent in the living, conscious, choosing souls of rational beings, whose intelligence, liveliness and volition mirror the self-constituting self-sufficiency of the living God.

For Maimonides there is really only one great problem of nature and grace — thus, ultimately, only one great miracle, of which all others are instances: the problem and the miracle of theophany, the finite and particularized manifestation of God's infinite perfection. Reverting to the words of the rabbinic sages, Maimonides meditates on the two mysteries which they withheld from common, public study: the scriptural account of creation (*maaseh bereshit*, the account of Genesis) and that of theophany (*maaseh merkavah*, the account of the chariot — Ezekiel's vision of God in creaturely lineaments). These, Maimonides reasons, correspond, as areas of inquiry, to the philosophical explorations of physics (that is, cosmology) and metaphysics (first philosophy or theology, as Aristotle called it). Physics asks after the ultimate character and constitution of nature. For a scriptural monotheist, that means the principles of its creation. Metaphysics asks after reality at large — being as such. It is for that reason that metaphysics must ask what, if anything, transcends the natural world. The two areas of inquiry are linked by the metaphysical question which for centuries inflamed relations between philosopher theologians of the Aristotelian and Neoplatonic tradition on the one hand and those of the Mosaic tradition on the other: 'Can the world have originated? How can a God that transcends time be manifest on a temporal scale?' But that question is just a special case of the larger one that affects all philosophical theists, creationist and eternalist alike: the question of the nexus between the finite particularity of natural beings and God's infinity and transcendence. The great problem of theology was not so much how to reach God from our finite knowledge: The contingency of being, the determinacy of things, the life and beauty — indeed the existence of the cosmos — all bespeak a transcendent Cause. But how could a God who is infinite and absolute be related to this cosmos? The problem of creation, the problem of revelation, the related issues about physical resurrection and spiritual immortality, even the problem of evil, were all special cases of this issue of divine condescension or contraction, the emergence of the temporal and bounded from the Timeless and Boundless.[18]

Maimonides's approach to a solution relies heavily on the Philosophers' idea of emanation. He takes the Philosophers to task for their apparent loss of nerve in not following through on Plato's original conception by which matter would not be an independent (thus eternal) and radically recalcitrant (thus evil) Thing

(*Guide* III, 16). Matter, Maimonides argues, is not (like the natural forms and forces) a "son of God" but a mere principle of otherness and receptivity, itself given definiteness (thus existence) by forms,[19] as Aristotle's metaphysics requires. The formation of a fetus, then, like the informing of a mind, is an achievement of order and organization. It is the imparting of form, conceived in Aristotelian terms as the pattern and plan that make each thing a member of its kind, and so impart the definiteness that is a hallmark of being.

The vehicle that imparts being in this sense, miraculously breaching the chasm that separates the finite from the Infinite, is intellectual. For being, conceived in terms of its specificity or definiteness, is intellectual. That is why it can be shared, as Plotinus explained, without division or loss in its Source. Form traverses the gulf between the finite and the infinite as light radiates from the sun—although, in Maimonides's view, not so mechanically and automatically, but volitionally and by grace. For there is no prior entitlement to existence in beings that do not yet exist. That is why the bestowal of matter, which allows existence to finite beings, differentiated from the all-encompassing infiniteness of God, is understood as an act of grace. It is in this sense that Maimonides reads the words of the Psalmist (89:3), "the world is built by grace" (*Guide* III, 53, Munk 131b). As the matter that God bestows meets and gains its suchness from the form that flows from divine intelligence, God imparts to each being its goal-directedness, and each pursues the Good by seeking the good defined for it by nature. It is in this sense, as we have seen, that Maimonides interprets the dictum that God created all things for His glory as meaning that God created each thing and kind for its own sake (*Guide* III, 13, 25).

Commonly miracles are thought of as disruptions in the causal fabric. But clearly, in the "settled order of nature" established by Maimonidean naturalism, there will be little room for such miracles. Maimonides leaves the door ajar by citing the midrashic dictum (Avot 5.9) that ten miraculous things were made in the twilight of the sixth day: the mouth of the earth that swallowed Koraḥ (Num. 16:32), the mouth of the well (that in legend accompanied the Israelites, Num. 21: 16), the mouth of Balaam's ass (Num. 22:28), Noah's rainbow (Gen. 9:13), the manna (Exod. 16:14), Moses's rod (Exod. 4:17), the *shamir* (the fabulous worm that cleft the rocks for Solomon's Temple, to form it with no iron tool; see Josh. 8:31), and the tablets, stylus, and script of the Ten Commandments. The list includes the script on the tablets, Maimonides urges, to show us "that the writing on the Tablets was like any other act of creation"—the writing was part of nature (*Guide* I, 66 ad fin.).[20]

Just as the Rabbis (Gen. Rabbah 5.5) picture God as stipulating at the creation that the sea must part to let the Israelites pass; the sun and moon stand still for Joshua; the ravens feed Elijah; the fire not harm Ḥananiah, Mishael, and Azariah; the lions not maul Daniel; and the fish spew out Jonah (thus incorporating these miracles into the fabric of nature rather than treating them as violations of God's covenant with nature), so Maimonides can argue that the fish was moved by its own volition. For God does not literally speak to fish, making prophets of them.[21] Following al-Ghazālī's adaptation of Neoplatonic emanationism, Maimonides can reason that God, at the creation, imparts to man the sort of matter that will make him capable of life and consciousness and (at the creation of the individual) even the particular material constitution that will make one person incapable of prophecy, no matter how high his intellectual apprehensions may rise. For imagination is necessary to prophecy, and imagination depends on matter.[22]

The human embryo, on the Maimonidean model, then, is a natural miracle, a paradigm case of the miraculous imparting of form to matter that is the heart of the divine creative act. All the matter that we find in nature is constituted as a particular receptivity by the initial creative imparting of form. But with human beings matter is raised to a far higher pitch than customary, making possible the emergence of what is alive and conscious from what is in itself non-living and non-conscious — what is in itself ultimately nothing at all.

Having set out the ontic status of the human fetus in Maimonidean metaphysics, we might now attempt some moral determinations. The ontic appraisal seems robust in the sense that it outlasts the hylomorphic categories in which it is framed. It fairly enunciates, even celebrates, the critical junctures between matter and mechanism on the one hand and a living, potentially thinking and choosing person on the other. And, in matters of right and valuation, as I have been arguing, our practical responses should reflect our recognition of the reality of the beings we encounter. For, as we have urged, deserts are nothing distinct from the ontic claims made by each being in its own behalf — the claims that constitute its essence — duly qualified by the purtenant claims of others. Applying that thesis to the present case, we can argue that deserts belong to a human embryo as such from the moment it makes entitative claims — in implantation, for example. Deserts grow *pari passu* with the growth of the embryo toward humanity. Jewish reflections and norms about abortion have consistently followed this line of thought. In so doing, they articulate a pattern of practice that gives far clearer guidance to our current moral quandaries and legislative debates than is likely to emerge from continued polarized litigiousness and politicized jurisprudence.

2. The Halakhic Status of the Fetus

Biblically abortion was conceived as a tort, an assault upon a woman. The injury was not manslaughter, because the fetus was not yet born: "If men struggle together and one of them pushes a pregnant woman, causing a miscarriage, but no other harm ensue, he shall pay damages imposed by the woman's husband, according to the reckoning" (Exod. 21:22). Rashi, following the *Mekhilta* (to Nezikin 8), explains that "no other harm" here means no fatal injury to the woman. The Rabbis gloss "according to the reckoning" as an allusion to the role of judicial authority in determining the damages: the matter is not left to the discretion of the parties.[23]

But the Exodus text is rather elliptical. How do we know that "no other harm" refers only to mortal injury to the woman? The *Mekhilta* admits to having no direct evidence for the inference that only fatal harm is intended. But it offers a parallel use of the word for harm (*'ason* in Gen. 42:38), to show that fatal injury is intended. It relies on the immediate sequel (Exod. 21:23) to show that the woman is the victim the law seeks to protect, since it treats that case as one of homicide;

any lesser injuries have already been addressed as tort damages. The *Mekhilta* argues informatively: "Scripture comes to teach you about one who, aiming to kill his enemy, kills his friend" (ed. Lauterbach, vol. 3, 63–69). Thus we have a clear division between homicide, which falls within the biblical law of persons, and aborticide, which is treated as a tort.

External evidence confirms the authoritative reading of the *Mekhilta*. In the Code of Hammurabi compensation for an abortion of the type described in Exodus is dependent on the status of the parties, and the death of the woman is punished by the execution of the offender's *daughter*.[24] The moral thrust of the Mosaic law stands out vividly against this contrasting background. Here we see the expectant mother identified explicitly as the potential victim in the law's concern. Treatment of feticide as a homicide emerges as precisely the kind of disproportion (see Gen. 4:23) that the biblical law seeks to correct (Exod. 21:20, 26; etc.) when it provides that damages shall be proportioned to the gravity of injuries sustained (Exod. 21: 23–25), and not the status of the parties (Deut. 1:17), that homicide belongs in a separate and restricted category of offense (Lev. 24:17, Exod. 21:12–14), and that "Parents shall not be put to death for children, nor children for parents, but each individual for his own offense" (Deut. 24:16; cf. Exod. 21:28, Lev. 4:3, etc., Num. 9:13, 12:11, 16:22).[25]

The Pentateuch does not directly consider intentionally induced abortions. As Stephen Ricks writes, "With the exception of the Middle Assyrian Laws (ca. 1600 B.C.), the earliest Near Eastern law codes do not deal with the willful destruction of the fetus with the consent of the mother."[26] That an Israelite parent might consider intentionally aborting a fetus seems almost beyond the moral horizon of the Torah's original audience. For in the moral environment where the law was first received, the memory of genocide and infanticide was still fresh (Exod. 1:16);[27] every birth was precious. The Torah vividly articulates the ideals of patriarchal times and the vision of national destiny embedded in those ideals when it voices the loftiest and most sublime blessing to a patriarchal or matriarchal figure in God's promise: "I shall indeed bless thee, making thy seed as numerous as the stars of the heavens and as the sand on the shore of the sea" (Gen. 22:17; cf. Gen. 21:13). Against this backdrop, the solitary and oblique reference to abortion in Exodus is all the more striking, for it clearly shows that aborticide, even through an assault, is not biblically deemed a homicide — although fatal injury to the expectant mother in such an incident would be.

In the Hellenistic period contact of Jews with the ideas and practices of other nations regarding abortion and infanticide put the matter in a different light. As Tarn writes:

> The prevalence of infanticide in Greece has been strenuously asserted from the literary texts and as strenuously denied; but for the late third and the second centuries (B.C.) the inscriptions are conclusive. . . . Of some thousand families from Greece who received Milesian citizenship *c*. 228–220, details of 79, with their children remain; these brought 118 sons and 28 daughters, many being minors; no natural causes can account for these proportions . . . more than one daughter was practically never reared, bearing out Poseidippus' statement that "even a rich man always exposes a daughter." Of 600 families from Delphic

inscriptions, second century, just 1 per cent reared 2 daughters. . . . The general conclusion from *c.* 230 onwards seems certain: the one-child family was commonest, but there was a certain desire for two sons (to allow for death in war); families of four or five were very rare; more than one daughter was very seldom reared; and infanticide on a considerable scale, particularly of girls, is not in doubt.[28]

In this Hellenistic environment, which in so many ways anticipates the commercialism and individualism of our own era, the humanism of the Judaic ethos asserts itself in a fashion that the allied natalism of the same tradition had not found necessary. Thus the Septuagint renders the verse from Exodus:

> If two men strive and smite a woman with child, and her child issueth imperfectly formed, he (sc. the assailant who struck the blow) shall be forced to pay a penalty: as the woman's husband may lay upon him, he shall pay with a valuation. But if it be perfectly formed, he shall give life for life . . .[29]

Here the Greek glosses the Hebrew with a clear nisus toward finding an authority for the sanctity of human life, even before birth. It dissolves the mention of "other harm" into a disjunctive reference to a formed or unformed fetus rather than to the mother, whose interests it presumes to be already covered by the laws of assault, homicide, and injury.[30]

Philo's exposition and paraphrase make clear what a Jewish reader in a Hellenistic milieu saw to be at stake in the Exodus passage,[31] and why the Septuagint translators brought to it the animus that they did:

> If a man comes to blows with a pregnant woman [he writes, cutting away from the biblical *mise en scene*, where the assault is presumed incidental to a fight between two men] and strikes her on the belly [agreeing with the *Mekhilta*, here, that not just any blow is relevant], and she miscarries, then, if the result of the miscarriage is unshaped and undeveloped, he must be fined, both for the outrage [of striking a pregnant woman upon the womb] and for obstructing the artist Nature in her creative work of bringing into life the fairest of living creatures. [Here the values underlying natalism are made explicit.] But if the offspring is already shaped and all the limbs have their proper qualities and places in the system, he must die, for that which answers to this description is a human being, which he has destroyed in the workshop of nature, who judges that the hour has not yet come for bringing it out into the light, like a statue lying in a studio requiring nothing more than to be brought outside and released from confinement.[32]

The Septuagint knows nothing of Hammurabi but is clearly alarmed by the indiscriminate practice of abortion and infanticide. By the time of the Roman Empire the textual evidence has become unequivocal: The teacher of Epictetus and of Dio Chrysostom, Rufus Musonius, the first-century Stoic philosopher exiled by Nero, a pacifist moralist who bears the distinction of having condemned slavery, the sexual double standard, and concubinage even when legal, also condemned abortion. Seneca, the tutor of Nero, later forced to commit suicide after being named a conspirator against the emperor, pays tribute to his mother for never "crushing the hope of the children nurtured in her body" (*Ad Helviam, De Con-*

solatione, 16.3). And Juvenal bitingly comments that giving birth seems to have become one of the toils of the lower classes (*Satires* 2, 29–35). Tacitus reveals the more widely held values of his day when he ascribes the Jewish prohibition of infanticide to Jews' "passion for propagating their race" and desire to "provide for the increase in their numbers." What seemed humane to Jews seemed extreme to pagan detractors and a good example of the "perversity" Tacitus found in Jewish institutions.[33] Against this background Philo, a contemporary of Caligula, explains the law he finds in the Septuagint:

> This ordinance carries with it the prohibition of something else more important, the exposure of infants, a sacrilegious practice which among many other nations, through their ingrained inhumanity, has come to be regarded with complacence. For if on behalf of the child not yet brought to birth by the appointed conclusion of the regular period thought has to be taken to save it from disaster at the hands of the evil-minded, surely still more true is this of the full-born.[34]

Philo does not confuse abortion with infanticide; but he sees the same ethos in the acceptance of either, an ethos that he describes as hedonistic, cruel, selfish, and misanthropic—narcissistic, as we might put it. The fetus, like the infant, he argues, is innocent and helpless, and if fully formed is no less human than an adult. Philo's intent, consistent with the Septuagint, is to find a middle ground between treating the fetus as a mere appanage of the mother's body and treating it as a full legal person. The Septuagint's sharp distinction between a formed and an unformed fetus allows him to assimilate late abortion to infanticide and thus bring the formed fetus under the penumbra of the Torah's protection of persons. But the distinction between a fetus and a child is preserved. Philo argues, "the Law is not concerned with ages, but with a breach of faith to the race"[35]—the race, not the person. For in the physiology of Philo's day the fetus is deemed part of its mother; and in Jewish law, as Philo knows, abortion is not categorically prohibited or even rhetorically equated with murder.

The Mishnah recognizes that a woman may need to abort her fetus: "If a woman is in hard travail, the embryo is dismembered within her and brought out limb by limb. For her life takes precedence over its life. But once its head has emerged, it may not be touched, since we do not set aside one person's life for another" (Ohalot 7.6). The full claims of humanity are acknowledged in the prohibition against preferring the claims of one life to another. "How do you know," the Talmud demands rhetorically, in enunciating the general principle which we have encountered already, "that your blood is redder than his?" (B. Sanhedrin 45b). As Maimonides sums up the law, whose formulation still preserves the odor of the Roman Imperium: "If the heathen said to them, 'Give us one of your company and we shall kill him, otherwise we kill all of you,' let them all be killed but do not deliver a single soul of Israel!" Only a named criminal whose life was forfeit *de jure* could be given up—even to save many lives.[36]

The great exception to this rule is in the case of an aggressor, the Talmudic *rodef* (pursuer), where the demands of protection for the innocent and prevention of the gravest mortal sins (B. Sanhedrin 87) suspend the presumed inviolability of human lives. Maimonides explains the Sages' willingness to set aside the deserts of the fetus as due to their treatment of the fetus itself as like a *rodef*:[37]

> It is a negative commandment (Deut. 25:12) not to have pity for the life of an aggressor *(rodef)*. That is why the Sages ruled that if a woman is in hard travail the embryo is removed, either by drugs or surgery: because it is regarded as one pursuing her and trying to kill her. But once its head has appeared, it must not be touched. For we may not set aside one person's life to save another, and what is happening is the course of nature.[38]

Later authorities are puzzled that Maimonides resorts to the law of hot pursuit to justify embryotomy, since the Mishnah seems to find sufficient warrant for its ruling in the precedence of a mother's life to that of her fetus—a precedence explained by Rabbi Israel Lipschutz on the grounds of the unestablished viability of the as yet unborn.[39] Indeed, in addressing the case of a woman condemned to death by a court unaware of her pregnant state, the Talmud remarks of the fetus: "Of course, it is part of her body" (Arakhin 7a).[40] The Jerusalem Talmud (Y. Shabbat 14, trans. Neusner, p. 398) explains further: Once the babe has begun to emerge into the open air, we can no longer say who is a threat to whom. But prior to that event, as David Novak puts it, the mother's is clearly "the more proximate life."[41]

Rashi uses the Mishnah's reasoning to draw a clear line between the fetus and the deserts of personhood. As he observes, when the Mishnah says that we do not set aside one person's life *(nefesh)* for another, it plainly does not consider the fetus a person *(nefesh)*. Accordingly Rashi states the normative view of the status of the fetus: "As long as it has not emerged into the air it is not a person" (ad Sanhedrin 72b, *dibbur ha-maskil: "yatza ro'sho"*). It is for this reason that there can be sufficient grounds to warrant some abortions. The Sages warrant their exclusion of abortion from the category of homicide by the wording of the law against homicide: "He that smiteth a man so that he dieth" (Exod. 21:12): "a man," not a fetus (B. Sanhedrin 84b).

Why then does Maimonides have recourse to the negative commandment (see Deut. 25:11–12) to have no pity on a pursuer, an appeal normally used to obviate charges of homicide? Clearly the impact is to lay narrow grounds for the permission of abortion. What warrant has Maimonides to do so? To begin with, there is the situational context evoked by the Mishnaic law itself: Without "hard travail," the feticide would not be acceptable. But why not? What values is the Mishnah protecting? The Mishnah distinguishes abortion from homicide when it categorically prohibits touching the infant once born. And Maimonides agrees: He is a prime exponent of the talmudic principle that we may not sacrifice one human life to save another. Yet, like the Mishnah, he does not extend this protection to the fetus.

Isser Yehudah Unterman, the former Ashkenazi chief rabbi of Israel, explains the basis of the Rambam's stance: Apart from the prohibition of homicide, there is an obligation to preserve fetal life.[42] Novak grounds this obligation in the general prohibition of destructiveness *(bal tashḥit)*, much as Philo points up the value in question by calling the human fetus the fairest of nature's artistic creations, giving it a special precedence among the things one is forbidden to destroy. It is this value that explains the classic rulings that permit violation of the Sabbath to save a fetus or enhance its chances of survival (B. Arakhin 7a):[43] The fetus enters the penumbra of personhood, although it is not a person. One may not arbitrarily or wantonly destroy it. As Novak explains, "This is why Maimonides emphasized that the fetus is 'like' a pursuer"[44]—not that it literally *is* an aggressor, with the deserts of a person, but because it has material deserts of its own, which approach those of personhood and ultimately reach those of personhood at the point of birth.

The commandment against destructiveness places the fetus on a scale of deserts with other living beings whose claims to life advance with their claims to being. The ontic orientation of that scale is clearly articulated by Spinoza: "Nam cum posse existere potentia sit, sequitur, quo plus realitatis alicuius rei naturae competit, eo plus virium a se habere, ut existat": "For since it is a power to be able to exist, it follows that the more reality pertains to the nature of a thing, the more powers it has to exist of itself" (*Ethics* I, Prop 11, Scholium).

The sharp line drawn by the law, then, is between such relative claims and the absolute deserts of personhood. Some authorities, like Rabbi Yair Ḥayyim Bacharach (1638–1701),[45] derive the prohibition against fetal destruction from the prohibition against wasting the male seed. But the argument is a weak one, since it assimilates abortion to contraception. It was criticized powerfully on those grounds by R. Unterman. R. Bacharach, known for his general opposition to casuistry, strikes closer to the Torah's theme when he relates the law on feticide to biblical pro-natalism by citing Isaiah (45:18): "He created it not a waste but formed it to be inhabited." Yet pro-natalism alone and the general commandment to be fruitful and multiply again are too weak to govern here. For the Law does not allow one who has fulfilled his obligation to be fruitful to abort his offspring arbitrarily. Nor may one conceive offspring and abort them, say, to use fetal brain tissue in the therapy of Parkinson's or Alzheimer's disease, no matter how many living children one already has and no matter how many lives might potentially be saved. Here the life of the fetus becomes "more proximate."

We are brought back inexorably to the entitative claims of the fetus, spoken for by the command against wanton destruction: Fetal claims are ontically grounded, as are the more absolute claims of personhood. These claims increasingly approach those of personhood as the fetus matures. Thus Maimonides's reliance on the case-narrowing appeal to the *rodef*: For a *rodef* has deserts that must be set aside before we can act against him, even in defense of human life. Specifically, we must scale our response to the imminence of the danger. We block a blow or cut off a hand, if we must and can, before we may place even an aggressor's life at risk (B. Sanhedrin 72b-73a; thus: *bekhol davar she-yakhol*). And if the danger is brought about unintentionally—perhaps the *rodef* is a mere human missile or somnambulist—we may cause that person no harm, because we may not sacrifice one (innocent) person's life to save another. Like a *rodef*, the fetus makes claims to life that are not yet absolute. So when it threatens maternal life, its claims are overthrown. But only a grave threat could outweigh the entitative claims it does make—not because we seek to populate the earth but because a human life is precious, and a human fetus stands upon and advances along the path toward personhood.

Philo, the Septuagint, and the Mishnah are justified, accordingly, in assigning the fetus lesser deserts in the early stages of pregnancy and progressively greater deserts in the later stages. Human deserts emerge *pari passu* with the claims of the fetus as an organism, and we can understand Philo's appropriation of the rule he found in the Septuagint, that a perfectly formed fetus does not differ in principle from a newborn infant.[46] The Zohar vividly explicates what is at stake, in language that all but echoes Philo's: "One who kills the fetus in his wife's womb desecrates what was built by the Holy One and mars His craftsmanship." The ethos of Israel, the Zohar argues in effect, is to respect that craftsmanship, which is in fact the human image. When Pharaoh decreed, "every son that is born shall ye cast into the Nile" (Exod. 1:22), "not a single Israelite was found who would kill the fetus in the womb — let alone the newborn after birth. It was through this merit," the Zohar urges, "that Israel went forth from bondage" (Warsaw, ed., 3b). Aggadah here underscores the values that ground the *Halakhah*: At every stage of embryogenesis there are real deserts: We must dismiss the rhetorical claim that the fetus is just the exuviae of the mother with the same rigor that we must dismiss the equally rhetorical claim that abortion is tantamount to murder. The Talmud artfully grounds the value to be protected in a midrashic glossing of the biblical text to yield the thesis that while a fetus is not a man, it is a virtual man, "a man within a man."[47]

Maimonides accordingly sets the authority of his Code behind a strict reading of the mishnaic permission — or rather, mandate, for the authorities are in clear agreement that when a fetus threatens its mother's life, abortion is not optional but required: Absent such a threat, the requirement to preserve the fetus prohibits abortion. The subsequent authorities follow, differing only as to the seriousness of the threat that would justify a decision to abort. R. Ḥayyim Soloveichik (d. 1918), for example, read the Mishnah as restricting abortion to cases of an imminent and direct threat to maternal life.[48] R. Israel Mizraḥi in the 19th century, heeding Naḥmanides's treatment of insanity as a threat to life, allows abortion to prevent mental illness.[49] R. Joseph Trani (1568–1639) permits abortions to preserve maternal health, rather than only life itself.[50] R. Jacob Emden (1697–1776) sanctions abortions even up to the onset of labor (fetal "disengagement") to end severe pain or (by the hand of the mother) to prevent the grave stigma of biblical bastardy resulting from adulterous or incestuous unions.[51] We can see an analogy here to the permissions widely discussed today for cases of rape and incest, although the analogy is not drawn by R. Immanuel Jakobovits.[52]

R. Judah Eiyush and others even allow abortions to preserve the life of a nursing sib.[53] The background: R. Ḥisda (B. Yevamot 69b), in a context not directly related to abortion, treats the human embryo up to forty days as "mere water"; and the Mishnah (Niddah 3.7) does not discover the impurity of childbirth prior to that term. In specific talmudically enumerated cases, R. Meir Dan Plocki (1867–1928) therefore allows a woman's use of an abortifacient pessary in the first forty days of pregnancy. For the Talmud (B. Yevamot 12b) allows the use of a contraceptive pessary by pubescent wives, pregnant women, and nursing mothers. If there is "mere water" for forty days after conception, R. Plocki reasons, abortion during that period is not to be more restricted than is contraception. He treats the two as equivalent—as was typical in recent years with family planning information about intrauterine devices. R. Eliezer Yehudah Waldenberg extends the period of permission and the acceptable grounds to include evidence that a deformed or abnormal child might be born, but few Orthodox rabbis concur with him.[54]

The limits placed by all these rulings and the varied but real gravity of the threats they address clearly reflect Maimonides's principle, which is grounded in turn, as we have seen, in a biblical and rabbinic reverence for the emergent life and virtual personhood of the human fetus. There are disagreements among the authorities as to the exact conditions that may warrant abortion. But these are in many ways matters of detail, comparable to the slight differences among the talmudic rabbis about the exact point at which the newborn emerges into the open air—when the head or the main body mass or any part breaches the birth canal (Mishnah Ohalot 7.6; cf. B. Sanhedrin 72b, Y. Sanhedrin 8 ad fin., and Tosefta Yevamot 9). The normative stance of the tradition is remarkably stable thematically over the ages and across diverse shadings of opinion and constituency. Indeed, abortion is one issue on which we find the roots of a genuine Judeo-Christian consensus,[55] an outlook that led to critiques of both religions by ancient pagan authors. Among the rabbis, the Noahidic law against bloodshed was traditionally interpreted as forbidding abortion. A fortiori, it was argued, should abortion be restricted for Jews, lest the Torah seem more lax than the general laws of civilized humanity (B. Sanhedrin 58b, citing Gen 9:5; and Tosafot ad 59a, s.v. *leika*). R. Bacharach urged that a common Judeo-Christian morality should inform halakhic decisions in such areas as this,[56] and David Novak argues today that the common moral commitment to humane and humanizing norms that is exemplified in a shared repugnance for abortion offers a valid starting place in common concerns for the ongoing dialogue among Christians and Jews.[57]

All of this does not settle the detailed and casuistical questions that bedevil today's abortion controversy. But the moral weight and moral concord of the Judaic tradition and the extent of its harmony with other moral and religious traditions should not be obscured by the insistent and often shrill demands that surround the issue and tend to submerge both the niceties of bioethical detail and the broader issues of humane concern. As Novak remarks, fewer than one percent of the abortions performed in the United States in recent years have been for reasons of a direct threat to maternal life.[58] A high proportion are performed for convenience and on demand. Judaic values cry out against such excess: Rabbi David Feldman sums up their central theme: "Although it is warrantable under some circumstances, abortion . . . remains a last resort in the Jewish view. . . . Potential life has the sanctity of its potential—casual abortion is accordingly abhorrent . . . abortion for reasons such as 'population control' is repugnant to the Jewish mind. Abortion for economic reasons is also not admissible."[59] Rabbi Laura Geller similarly collates the sources and the values they articulate: "1. In the case of a conflict between maternal and fetal life, the mother's life must take precedence. 2. Abortion is not murder, but it is a serious loss. 3. There can be no casual use of abortion as implied by the rhetoric of 'abortion on demand.' 4. The notion that a woman has a right to control her own body is not acceptable; no one has the right to harm himself/herself or to commit suicide. Issues of life and death are in God's hands, not ours."[60] In the same spirit, Rabbi Novak reads the prohibition against destructiveness *(bal tashḥit)* in the light of its special case, the prohibition against self-mutilation, so that even if the fetus is simply a part of the mother's body, no blanket permission of abortion is entailed.[61]

The claims of the fetus are not diminished by its dependence on the mother. Otherwise, all human beings would be vulnerable in the same way. We are all dependant on one another. The presumptive deserts of the fetus are powerful and positive. In the Judaic sources, as in nature, they are scaled to its ontic standing, from "mere water" to the onset of labor, and are suspended, prior to birth, virtually never, unless the presence of the fetus represents a clear threat to maternal welfare. Formalizing the moral concerns, as is the function of law, Halakhah draws a sharp line: Once the birth canal is breached, any threat must be ascribed to God — heaven is now the pursuer, as the Talmud expresses it (B. Sanhedrin 72b). That is, as Maimonides explains, the danger confronted now is part of the course of nature, a risk that must be borne, since no human being has the right to place one human life before another.

The nisus of the Rambam's resort to the theory of pursuit, then, comes in the fact that the Law's treatment of the fetus as less than a full person does not set its deserts at nullity. If the claims of the fetus can be recognized without threat to the mother's life, those claims are to be met. Thus the nuance drawn from Maimonides's text by R. Isaac Schorr (d. 1776): When Maimonides specifies that the threatening fetus may be eliminated by drugs or surgery, he intimates a preference for the least violent and violative means available — the same phased approach that is applied in the case of a *rodef*. Deadly force may not be used where lesser measures would suffice.

R. Ḥayyim Soloveichik caps the discussion by explaining that it is not the principle of saving human lives (for which the laws of the Torah may be set aside almost en bloc) that determines the Mishnah in favor of abortion to save a mother's life. That principle *(pikuah nefesh)* might have been pled in behalf of the fetus. Rather it is the fact that the fetus is the aggressor.[62] Soloveichik here overstates the case somewhat, since the fetus is not literally a person *(nefesh)* in Jewish law and does not enjoy the full protections of a person. But the presumption in favor of the deserts of the fetus and the need for a clear danger if these are to be overthrown are the values that Soloveichik, like the Mishnah itself, underscores: One need not assign full personhood to the fetus to recognize the strength of the argument. For a *rodef* need not be a person or a moral agent. Even excess baggage on a ship can pose the same threat. Property rights in a life-threatening emergency literally go by the board.[63] The entitative, conative considerations that give a fetus deserts qualify its deserts when it becomes a threat to another. But it is not the case that the fetus has no deserts. It has the powerful deserts of its virtuality as a person, undercut in rare cases by the threat it poses to its mother. Were it not human, its claims would be all but nugatory. Were it not a threat, they would be the near equal of any other human claims.

Throughout the Jewish discussion we see the signature of the Rambam in the assignment of narrow grounds for warranting abortion and in the recognition of constitutive deserts on the part of the developing fetus. Maimonides's ruling is informed by the recognition that sacred work is underway when lifeless matter is making its way toward the air in which it will have thought and life. But it is not the case that the Rambam simply "reads into" the ancient canon the findings of the science of his day or the opinions of his own philosophy. On the contrary, that science and the philosophy that interprets it only heighten his sensitivity to the values bespoken by the biblical and rabbinic texts. Rather than competing with the revealed law, the pronouncements of reason complement and inform it. They allow coherence to emerge from the dialectic of the sources and a single, powerful theme to stand forth as the underlying message of the canon and ethical nerve of the culture it informs: the sanctity of human life.

The rabbinic discussion does not hinge on theories of ensoulment and so does not seek an instant where the biblical right to life springs from nullity to absoluteness. Rather, with the gradual emergence of form in the "shapeless mass" of which the Psalmist speaks (139:16), the developing fetus moves toward the shores of life and gradually acquires heightened moral standing. Full moral personhood is not acquired, de facto, until well after birth. Some of us may never acquire it. But even prior to the emergence of a real moral person, the Law extends the dignity of humanity, out of deference to what will unfold, spreading its protections to life and limb ("he may not be touched") up to the portals of light; and, even prior to that point, recognizing gradually emergent, distinctively human[64] deserts.

Strong claims have been made in many quarters for an absolute maternal right of abortion. A. J. Ayer, who in other contexts denied the very meaning of such concepts as right and wrong, or human rights, urged that every pregnant woman has an inalienable right to an abortion. James Gustafson, eloquently pleading the case of a hypothetical victim of sexual abuse and social neglect, pled that the social and psychic impact of an unwanted pregnancy may loom with such enormity that we must extend the permission of abortion beyond the realm of a direct threat to the mother's life.[65] Others have argued that a fetus (being dependent) is and remains an appendage, to be removed at the discretion of the mother, with no more compunction than would be shown for a diseased body part or (some have said) one's own excrement—and no more legitimate sphere of social concern or legal intervention. In some quarters more passion is expended in behalf of animal entitlements or familiar buildings than is conceded to the deserts of the unborn. The imbalance is no mere anomaly; it is symptomatic of an ethos that claims our allegiance.

The rhetoric of the abortion controversy has not abated since *Roe v. Wade* (1973). Indeed, it has grown fiercer since *Webster v. Reproductive Health Services* (1989). The claim that abortion is tantamount to murder has fostered strident demonstrations and even shootings and bombings. Among the advocates of free access to abortion, the notion of an unplanned pregnancy is frequently conflated with the image of an unwanted child; the tragic but sometimes overpowering necessity of what is paradoxically called therapeutic abortion not infrequently has been muddled with the prevention of disease or social disability.[66] Indeed, in some population control circles, population has been treated as a form of pollution. The powerful claims that urge restraint in the area of abortion are met with rhetorical and dialectical arguments about one's body as one's property or about the hazards of unlawful abortions. Such arguments have been applied in political practice to justify literally millions of abortions of healthy but unplanned embryos, whose deserts, in these pragmatic arguments and in the laws and rulings they have fostered, are set at nil. In the United States, since *Roe* v. *Wade*, the annual number of abortions has averaged over a million; in major cities the abortion rate has characteristically exceeded the live birth rate.[67] Recollection of the ontic standing of the fetus and its placement—if not as a person, then as a miracle—is a clear desideratum.

On Liberty Reconsidered

Timelessness is the signature of revelation in Judaism. Thus an ancient gloss on the *Amidah*'s striking phrase *Attah gibbor le-ʿolam*, "Thou art mighty eternally," explains that God's voice does not dwindle over time. One way for the Mosaic canon to make good its revelatory claims and for the rabbinic tradition to validate its grasp on an inspired continuity with Mosaic revelation is by demonstrating its timeless relevance.

The values of the Judaic tradition and the principles articulated in its canon stand proudly among the ancestors of modern liberal humanism. They offer striking early support to the idea of the consent of the governed (Exod. 24:7; Deut. 27:9–26), for example. But they also offer a purchase point that can aid us in teasing out some of the problems liberalism faces today. This chapter offers a critique of Mill's formulation of the liberal idea. Critiques running in the opposite direction, from Mill's principles to the various traditions of religious and naturalistic virtue ethics, have been familiar for a century or more. But my object here is not to seek prooftexts in the Jewish canon to be urged in turn against Mill. Rather, the critique is in part internal. I see the liberal tradition as a legitimate outgrowth of Jewish, Christian, and classical values, and I treasure Bergson's evolutionary interpretation of liberalism in the ideal of the Open Society. I do think that a more coherent liberalism than Mill's in *On Liberty* can be elicited from the fuller, classic repertoire, which does not draw away quite so far as Mill does from the traditions of natural and revealed law that gave birth to liberalism. But there is little point in simply confronting one text with another—biblical communalism, rabbinic humanism, or medieval pietism against Mill's liberal utilitarianism. The outcome would simply confirm the already ingrown prejudice (enunciated long ago by Cynic philosophers like Lucian) to the effect that philosophies are marketplace commodities,[1] paradigms, or worldviews that one can—at will, paradoxically enough—buy into or leave alone.

I find argument more compelling, and compelling in ways that marketing is not. The tenor of my argument is not that liberalism is mistaken but that liberals have erred in holding Mill's now canonical recension of the liberal idea at the core of the humane and tolerant tradition they espouse. I find Mill's formulae in *On Liberty* ill grounded and, partly for that reason, skewed and pinched. Further, Mill's formulations have been abused — extended by interests he had no intention of serving onto turf he never envisioned defending. I find support for a broader idea of liberty than Mill's Utilitarianism affords, in the humanism that grows from the Mosaic tradition. Jewish philosophical thinking today can, I think, by developing those humanistic values, continue to make distinctive contributions to the general political, moral, and social discourse in which the Mosaic canon has long been a formative influence.

1. Mill's Liberty

In laying out the basic principles of liberty, Mill tells us, he has no intention of appealing to any notion of absolute rights: "It is proper to state, that I forego any advantage which could be derived to my argument from the idea of abstract right, as a thing independent of utility" (*On Liberty*, ed. Acton, p. 74). The disavowal is a deep obeisance to Bentham's scorn for the very idea of rights, and to the variety of naturalism underlying that scorn. Whether Mill remains true to his decision to disavow all appeal to rights is a matter for discussion. For clearly, in the end Mill does espouse an absolute right of free opinion and free expression of opinion. He mounts on the very stilts that Bentham meant to have hidden away for good.[2] But beyond that difficulty, Mill's decision to derive an absolute right solely from its utility means that all liberties are made contingent; at the same time, the scope of the liberty the argument will support is drastically narrowed.

Mill's account opens with the broad affirmation of a universal-sounding liberty, grounded in the "one very simple principle" that Mill finds adequate "to govern absolutely the dealings of society with the individual, whether the means used be physical force in the form of legal penalties or the moral coercion of public opinion," namely: "that the sole end for which mankind are warranted, individually or collectively, in interfering with the liberty of action of any of their number, is self-protection. That the only purpose for which power can be rightfully exercised over any member of a civilized community, against his will, is to prevent harm to others" (p. 72). Mill's target, of course, is the oppressive substitution of judgment that we call paternalism.[3] But the liberties called for by Mill's standard here are just three:

> 1. The freedom to harm oneself[4] — or fail to improve oneself: One "cannot rightfully be compelled [by force, *or even public opinion*] to do or forbear because it will be better for him to do so, because it will make him happier, because, in the opinion of others, to do so would be wise, or even right" (73). Mill himself deduced, as applications of his rule, the inappropriateness of restricting the sale of alcohol, or poisons, or any commodity whatever. He specified the importation of opium into China as one of the liberties his doctrine would protect. (*On Liberty*, p. 151)

Strictly applied, Mill's standard means that if we could determine, say, that a given narcotic, quack cure, sadistic practice, meretricious or exploitative relationship were harmful only to adults who freely choose it, the state would have no authority to oppose it—even on utilitarian grounds! The argument would be that there is a greater utility in preventing paternalism than in restricting the offending harm. Even the familiar passing of responsibility to social and educational agencies, churches, schools, neighborhoods, families, or pressure groups would be normatively unwarrantable. No free society could give even passive support or tacit legitimation to such efforts. Rather, the laws would have to restrict such efforts as repressive of undeniable human liberties.[5] The sale of opium, then, could actually be enforced—as it was to be in the full flowering of British imperialism.

2. The freedom willingly to submit to the will of others.

It is hard to specify exactly what Mill should mean by this. Yet he does qualify his limitation of the abuse of power with the phrase, "against his will." He might mean to allow, say, acceptance of the authority of a government, or the conditions of gainful employment on terms mutually agreed. But even if this is all Mill means, he sharply departs from the Lockean assumption that such "submissions" are no more than expressions of one's own will and so cannot be construed as a surrender of one's interests to the arbitrary will of another. And if he means what he seems to say, he knocks the imagination sprawling among thoughts about frightful regimes that tolerate or legitimate (voluntary) slavery, mind control by cults, and penal institutions that demand control or reconstitution of the convict's will. On the most charitable construction, Mill here has simply failed to distinguish free employment from slavery, or free citizenship from subjection to a totalitarian regime, since he construes each of these as a surrender of the subject's will rather than as its voluntary adoption of another's goals (in the case of employment) or its acceptance of shared goals (in the case of government and community).

3. The freedom to hold, express, and disseminate what views one pleases, without regard to the opinion of others, and, least of all, the pleasure of the state or common opinion, on all sorts of issues, especially those regarding the nature of the world in general and matters moral, religious, or political in particular.

Like Hobbes, Mill trusts in human nature with an abiding faith in the rational pursuit of self-interest. He knows that there is no better—or at least no charier—judge of that interest than ego. So he is not concerned that the liberty to harm oneself or surrender one's very liberty will be abused or misapplied. The paradoxical liberties of harm to self and self-surrender are, it seems, foregone conclusions, or trivial consequences, of the rational egoism that anchors Mill's larger scheme. They are matters of private judgment, rightly left to individual discretion, in no special need of caveat or qualification. The benefits to be gained by debarring substitutions of judgment, Mill assumes, will far outweigh the costs incurred by the occasional irrational private decision.

Besides, there are institutions that can step in to protect the interests of the mentally infirm, just as there are parents to protect the interests of children. As for societies that are not, or not yet, "civilized," they too can be aided, by colonial powers like Mill's own East India Company, which can provide the necessary steering—the value system and the policy decisions about its implementation—that will use paternalism where it belongs, for those who lack the faculties, individually or civilizationally, to exercise discretion in their own behalf. Thus Mill writes, still speaking of his simple principle:

> It is, perhaps, hardly necessary to say that this doctrine is meant to apply only to human beings in the maturity of their faculties. We are not now speaking of children, or of young persons below the age which the law may fix as that of manhood or of womanhood. Those who are still in a state to require being taken care of by others, must be protected against their own actions as well as against external injury. For the same reason, we may leave out of consideration those backward states of society in which the race itself may be considered as in its nonage. (p. 73).

When Mill does consider such "backward states of society," he warrants a quasi-benevolent despotism in their behalf (*Representative Government*, chapter 18)—a despotism whose benevolence must be qualified by realism, and which Mill thus models on the regimes of Akbar or Charlemagne: "Despotism is a legitimate mode of government in dealing with barbarians, provided the end be their improvement, and the means justified by actually effecting that end" (*On Liberty*, p. 73). Aristotle said as much regarding ends in his justification of slavery.

Mill's consequentialism here is complete: He insists that actual betterment flow from a paternalistic regime, but he draws no constitutional restraint on the intrinsic character of the means deployed to that end. He cannot, without appeal to absolute rights. The anomaly is heightened when Mill assigns what look like absolute rights to those whose societies he does deem civilized. For that gives us societies, living side by side, and in relations of trade or even colonial—or mercantile—dependency,[6] where the denizens of one are denied rights available to the citizens of the other. The question naturally arises whether the absolute guarantees available so freely here are not purchased at the expense of their denial there.

I mention all this not to score points ad hominem from Mill's employment at the East India Company,[7] but because the anomaly persists. Under the guise of an easy relativism, some would-be liberals still hold civil rights, human rights, to be a European, bourgeois notion not readily accommodated to the values and cultures of African or Asian societies. The racism implicit in such varieties of relativism will be evident.[8] When questions of profit from cheap goods are considered, the matter of dependency, of the parasitism potentially concealed within the rights we hold so proud and dear, returns with a vengeance. Mill at least believed that India was being governed in its own interest. But the postcolonial free marketeer has left the Third World in free fall. Today's political relativists are liberal as can be about the regimes that others—including a billion Chinese—may toil under, as long as cheap goods are available in quantity at Wal-Mart and Kmart.

Confident that self-harm and the surrender of liberty itself to the will of another will be rare in what he is pleased to identify as civilized societies—notably Britain and the United States (*On Liberty*, pp. 127–29, 167)—Mill focuses on the object of his most immediate concern: freedom of thought and expression. In the end—although we parse the liberty of his title generically, as Mill's rhetorical posture expects and demands—the liberty he singles out as his cynosure is in fact just one: freedom of mind. Even the individualism that he makes the great theme of his third and fourth chapters is instrumentalized in the service of intellectual liberty.

Further, Mill's preoccupation with intellectual freedom and its corollary, the freedom to communicate, strongly color his thoughts about paternalism. For when he speaks ingenuously about the opinions of others as to my true interests and warms to the topic of my right not to pursue those interests, should I so choose, it is not suicide or mind control, tattooing, euthanasia, or even self-neglect that comes to the fore, but the presumptive interest of the soul in its salvation, which do-gooders among Mill's contemporaries (or our own) might seek to protect by restricting skeptical, heretical, or anti-religious speech. Mill's formulation may be general, but his concern is very topical and particular. The core of that concern, as the unfolding of his argument makes crystal clear (*On Liberty*, p. 91), is with the expression of moral, religious, and political ideas. Self-harm is envisioned, as if in scare-quotes, as failure to go to church or pay lip service to pious verities. That is why it can be safely left to the discretion of individuals.

The demands of great corporations for our labor and that of our children, at ruinous or exploitative wages or in unsafe or unwholesome surroundings, are not uppermost in Mill's mind when he chooses the words to be emblazoned on his broad, libertarian banner. Nor is the liberty to assume environmental and other risks in exchange for economic benefits. Free trade is protected, on the vague grounds that it is a "social act." More pointedly, it is defended on the grounds that when economic transactions are left "perfectly free," we have learned, "both the cheapness and the good quality of the commodities are most effectually provided for" (*On Liberty*, pp. 150–51)[9] So the potential harm of alcohol, narcotics, or tobacco, if these can be sold to us, simply does not weigh in the balance. Thought and speech stand paramount among the goods to be protected. And even the protections of our right to harm ourselves (or arm ourselves?) or to surrender our will to that of another are couched as protections of thought and speech. They come down to us still framed and hemmed in by Mill's rationale, as if our sole concern for the human person were with the right to refuse to pray and the right to welcome or turn away the missionary at the door.

2. Mill's Argument

Mill's defense of the utility of freedom of thought and expression is grounded in his famous trichotomy: Speech, he argues, must be either true or false, or some mixture of the two. But (1) if it is true, it merits support. Nor can we claim in advance to know which views are true. So even the most unpopular or seemingly outlandish theory should surely be allowed its chance to win men's minds. Only dogmatic pretensions of infallibility could provide the necessary assurance to those who would suppress a claim. (2) Even ideas or claims that are in fact false still have the value of keeping familiar truths from becoming dead and dormant, losing the living edge that only the honing of criticism can impart. And (3) if, as is most often the case, new and old ideas involve some mixture of truth with ignorance and confusion, the marketplace of ideas should be left free to sort out what is of lasting value from what deserves to be forgotten or discarded.

1. Mill's argument, in the case of presumptive truths, parallels the one we have already come across, which some environmental advocates use to urge that we must not destroy, say, the rain forest, since no one knows what genetic treasures it might hold—not least, perhaps, the cure for AIDS or cancer. To apply such argumentation here, one needs to know that the ideas that are unwelcome are indeed at risk of suppression that is permanent in the way that extinction is permanent. One needs to know also that ideas, like creatures in the rain forest, cannot be harmful (unless, of course, disturbed).

Mill's consequentialism here does not serve him well. It does not, for example, forestall the oppression or persecution of persons who hold unorthodox or unaccepted ideas, so long as those who do the persecuting are unlikely to succeed in utterly uprooting the ideas (or obliterating the expressions) they disapprove. An employer could dismiss an employee for holding certain views, as long as it seemed likely that the views themselves would survive unimpaired. Not appealing to any notion of rights, Mill's argument does not distinguish between censoring a newspaper and stifling a thought; it does not distinguish between burning a book and burning the author. Further, the charge of dogmatism is misplaced. A perfect fallibilist can act to suppress an idea, as perhaps Pilate tried to do, while making no claims to know what the truth is, let alone claims to infallibility.

2. If an idea is false, Mill argues, it should still be allowed its day in court—not for any absolutist reasons involving fairness to human beings, but because the challenge of argument will clarify and strengthen the correct view. But it is hard to see how any ideas can be useful or beneficial unless some can be harmful. The assumption that thought must always be held harmless trivializes the work and power of ideas, even while the presumption that bad ideas are the catalysts of good ones romanticizes that work and power.

Jewish experience vividly bears the memory of a kind of speech that can hurt and can unleash the dogs of war and the jackals of genocide. The experience, tragically, is not unique. It puts in question Mill's very premise that civilization has made some nations safe for the liberties he defined. Industrial democracies are as vulnerable to the poisons of misappropriated speech as the countries of the Third World. The experience of Bosnia is no different in kind from that of Rwanda and Burundi, or Cambodia or Congo. Education was no bar to membership in the SS. On the contrary, the Nazi officer corps drew heavily from the intellectual elite of Germany. Ideas can be a vehicle of destruction as well as of creation. The pattern runs back to the Corcyran massacre and beyond, to the Egyptian slavery and attempted genocide of ancient Israel (Exod. 1:16). Once a population has been marked notionally as pestilent or subhuman, wholesale destruction awaits only the opportunity and the means. The motive is ever present in the political power of the ideas of vengeance, hegemony, and the scapegoat.

The inference I would draw from the fact that there is dangerous and destructive speech is not to a rationale for suppressing unpopular or unwelcome views.

Rather, I find here a warrant and a need for the encouragement of critical and constructive thinking. But such encouragement has costs. It involves positive rights rather than the negative ones Mill's essay deems sufficient. The partial outcome, for all who have faith in the power of understanding, is a warrant for the creation and support of libraries, schools, museums, orchestras, educational media, and opportunities — the diffusion of books, and (in our time) computer access and informational and educational broadcasting. But beyond that arise a warrant and a mandate for all human beings, individually and conjointly, to attend to the tenor of the ethos and the ideas that inspire it. For no mere medium guarantees that love and generosity, or even tolerance, will be its message.

My own inference bears with it a problematic, the very problematic of orthodoxy that was exercising Mill at the dawn of the information age. Linked to that difficulty is the related problem of vulgarity that also surfaced in Mill's time and was an object of concern in his earlier thought — the loss of depth, complexity, and critical edge in the materials intended to convey and diffuse the ideas that make critical thinking possible. The broader the diffusion of an idea, the greater the risk of a loss of subtlety and the greater the liability of blurring argument into authority and of blunting, or even reversing, the idea's nisus.

This difficulty was recognized by Plato. He addressed it with the expedient of enlisting that class of human beings whom he called the poets in the cause of truth and justice. Plato's hope was that the beliefs and attitudes that creative works have the power to instill would coalesce in an ethos that aims at truth and fairness rather than serving one or another passional or appetitive master. His fear was that the appeals of human passions and appetites, wrapped in the rhetoric of freedom, would be used to enslave the populace politically or exploit their desires commercially, to their own detriment.

Religion is the name we now give to Plato's answer to the problem he confronted. As a human institution, religion itself is susceptible to corruption. It suffers not only from the dynamic of vulgarity that Plato hoped it would surmount but also from the original passional and appetitive illnesses that he hoped it would treat. Epicurus, whose egoist hedonism we have already observed at the root of liberalism and laissez faire, and whose individualist credentials are far stronger than Mill's (whose Utilitarian equation of the good with the greatest happiness of the greatest number readily subordinates individual interests to the presumptive common good), preferred to deny the problem Plato addressed, rather than confront it. So in Epicureanism no natural passion or appetite was admitted to be dangerous, if only we keep our heads and moderate our desires. The notion of a problem about the vulgarizing of knowledge was dismissed as elitist and confining. No moral truth relevant to all could possibly lie beyond the reach of all. Religion, the poetry that Plato had hoped would weave a ladder of love from the light of the stars to the unseen majesty beyond, seemed now to be no more than a tangle of anxieties, entrapping the unwary in their own unreasoning fear of death.

The conflict that ensued between followers of Plato and followers of his heretical successor Epicurus is too large to be more than noted here. It sharply defines two rival ideas of knowledge and of liberty. I mention it only to make clear that dismissal (as elitist) of the problem of vulgarity, in and beyond religion, is itself just one of the stratagems in the deep and ongoing warfare between rival ideas of human freedom—and to remark that the idea that no truth relevant to the masses can possibly be inaccessible to them poses a dilemma for those who adhere to it: Either they must acknowledge and adopt a kind of know-nothingism that ill befits their democratic pretensions (as familiar as it may be in populist rhetoric) and relegate the masses in whose interest they profess to speak to the sheer role of consumers, a flock or herd to be fed and fleeced or milked but not enlarged or intellectually enriched. Or they must commit themselves to the great project of universal education, to the fullest potential of each individual. In that case, they must part company in some measure with the intellectual laissez faire of liberals from Epicurus to Mill and join hands, in some fashion, with the reformism of Plato, shouldering some of the burden entailed by hopes for universal enlightenment like those voiced in the Mosaic Torah and the prophetic tradition that takes up its discourse and ideals.

3. In the commonest case, Mill points out, still dwelling on his typified polarity of heresy and orthodoxy, "the conflicting doctrines, instead of being one true and the other false, share the truth between them; and the non-conforming doctrine is needed to supply the remainder of the truth, of which the received doctrine embodies only a part." What happens most often, in matters of controversy, Mill urges, is that the rival views (one new, unaccepted, perhaps untested; the other, established, perhaps unquestioned—but both already channelized into schools of thought) each contain a mixture of truth and falsity, and suppression leads to loss: "even in revolutions of opinion, one part of the truth usually sets while another rises. Even progress, which ought to superadd, for the most part only substitutes one partial and incomplete truth for another" (*On Liberty*, pp. 105–6). For that very reason, the vigorous dialectic of open debate is surely the best arena for the threshing and winnowing that will separate the intellectual wheat from the chaff.

I have always been suspicious of Mill's easy slide from the black and white of truth or falsity to the gray tones of his third alternative. Not that I doubt the prominence of half-truths in ours or any culture, nor that I disparage the acuteness of Mill's tragic sense that something is always lost even as new insights are gained. But the relativism Mill flirts with in this third and favored member of his trichotomy (and even in the first, when he charges the intolerant with dogmatism and assumes they must be infallible to claim prudence in suppressing a view they deem dangerous or unhelpful) does not, in my opinion, sit well with the objectivism of the first two members, by which the utility of the entire process (and thus of liberty itself) is to be weighed on Mill's account.

If even progress seems to lose ground as it advances, discarding opinions that (for all anyone knows) are potentially as valuable or useful as those that replace them, then the entire dialectic of progress that Mill invokes in behalf of intellectual liberty becomes problematic. If tribal societies are as right as urban ones—and indeed much *is* lost when we leave the savannah or the Mato Grosso for the village or the metropolis—and if no one can say conclusively that there has been a net gain, or that we have not lost more by leaving the rain forest than we might have gained by staying behind, then what exactly is the payoff we are promised for the protection of dissent? The truth here is problematized by Mill in a way that makes it insufficient warrant for the bearing of any social costs, let alone the potentially heavy costs of absolute non-interference with the devising and dissemination of new (or old) ideas.

3. An Alternative Basis for Liberty

If we are to free Salman Rushdie from the threat of death, I do not think we need to find a kernel of truth in his *Satanic Verses*. Nor do I think we need to resort to the flimsy rationales of Rule Utilitarianism urging that the world would be a better place if authors were allowed to say and print what they like. That may be so. But I think it is as big a mistake to rest intellectual freedom on heuristic grounds as it is to rest freedom of labor on appeals to efficiency, or civil rights on good or "productive" citizenship. In all these cases, the assurance given is contingent and conditional, but the right we need to anchor is categorical. It must be so in some way, to make it proof against the peremptory claims of church and state — and of private exigency and bias, even when they use higher sounding names like "global competition" or tradition.

Why not offer absolute protections of our intellectual freedoms, including the freedom to be in error, on the grounds that these involve our very humanity? Our right to think and to express our thoughts, I argue, is not conditioned on the contribution its exercise might make to general human knowledge and understanding. If so, there would be more value in the effective utterance of a half-truth than in the demanding and perhaps faltering articulation of a fuller one. That way lies the paradox of the Grand Inquisitor. For a half-truth consciously promulgated is more than half a lie.

Grounding our intellectual liberties in the deserts of personhood avoids making a basic human right contingent. Moreover it affords broader scope than Mill does to our liberty of mind, for it accords us a right to think, even if we do not broadcast, teach, or promote our ideas. It allows them to be private, if we wish, since it does not predicate freedom of thought on the usefulness of one's thoughts to others. It allows liberty to fictions and artistic ideas, including fantasies that make no truth claims at all. Such ideas and fantasies might be expressed for their sheer aesthetic interest, or in play, for profit or for fun, or as objects of intrinsic interest. They need not be instrumentalized in the service of truth, or progress, or any other goal extrinsic to their own.

With these thoughts in mind, I ground our intellectual freedoms in our humanity and in the ideal of human flourishing. I do not believe that persons can flourish without thought. Thinking is as vital to humanity as breathing, and more distinctive to our natures, as Aristotle would add. Clearly, expression and communicative interactions are of the essence in cultivating thought, allowing it to move beyond daydreaming, zoning, or mental doodling, to the articulation of larger ideas. But an idea need not be put to work to be of value. Some ideas do prove of instrumental worth, but some should be valued intrinsically. Surely, if the measure of worth is the reach of a being, the measure of a human is his dreams. And not every dream need be acquisitive.

This core thesis of mine, that intellectual liberty should grow not from utility but from the intrinsic worth of our humanity, is rooted in Jewish ideas of human deserts and dignity in the same way that Mill's approach is rooted in British ideas of self-interest, rational choice, and the integrity of the human will. Intellectual freedom here is clearly a special case, albeit an important one, of our general liberties—all of which rest in the idea of human flourishing, which in turn rests on the ontological approach to value and personhood that I have championed philosophically and elicited textually from the Jewish sources, in the earlier chapters of this book and in *On Justice* and *God of Abraham.*

The timelessness that imparts a claim to inspiration to the Jewish approach to deserts, including intellectual liberties, derives not from the antiquity of the canon or the historic continuity of its elaboration, but from the precious idea of personhood itself. It is the clarity and constancy of that idea in the tradition that allows intellectual freedom to be taken for granted, built into the norms of the Torah and of rabbinic discourse, and not placed at the center of the biblical problematic of freedom, as it is at the center of Mill's idea of liberty.

One of the strengths of the biblical standpoint for us here comes simply from the fact that its historical and cultural roots are distinct from those of Mill and Locke, whose ideas were framed against the backdrop of ideological, ultimately credal disputes. The Torah imparts the guidance that gives the meaning to its name not by inculcating dogmas or making demands upon our will to believe, but by stamping the impress of its symbols on our lives. The Sabbath, overlaid upon the work and struggles of our days, becomes the living symbol of the liberating Creator's presence in our lives. The words of the Law and the epithet of its Author inscribed on our doorposts, and His expectations held up before our eyes, become ever-present reminders of the standard set before us, binding our hands to strengthen and restrain them and advertising to our neighbors the standard of perfection to Whose holiness we aspire. The seal of the covenant, stamped in our flesh, as the liturgy expresses it, signifies an intension that cannot be imposed but can only be imparted, aspired after, and appropriated. The mind is free to make of all this what it can.

We are commanded to love God—to love His goodness, His holiness, and the wisdom of His creation. We are not commanded to believe. Belief and trust, faith and confidence, are products of the understanding that grows from the Torah's way of life. They are not its foundations. Just as we are commanded not to test God, not to try His patience or put Him to experiment, so God does not test us like a suspicious lover, demanding constant feats of faith, as proof of our fidelity.

Are not the ordeals of our history trials imposed by a jealous God? In a sense they are; but, in a sense that Saadiah well understood, they are not. For they have no determinate outcome, like that of an experiment or a trial by ordeal. God's jealousy, as the Rambam shows, is His demand for exclusivity (*Guide* I, 54; cf. I, 23; II, 47); and our fidelity is loyalty to His ways—a moral, not a credal commitment. Despite numerous fallings away, it is a commitment that the people of Israel have borne, through centuries of suffering, with miraculous and inspired good faith. Its reward is compact with acceptance of the Torah's way of life. Its price in sufferings is balanced, even as it is paid, in the coin of authenticity, continuity, and righteousness. Thus again the Rambam is right in saying that the idea of a "trial" as an ordeal of arbitrarily imposed "sufferings of love" is a notion antithetical to the biblical thematic (*Guide* III, 24). For to make the reward of obedience to God's Law extrinsic to the life of that Law violates and vitiates all that the Law itself has to say in painting its rewards as constitutive in that life. A saintly life is its own reward, just as a vicious life is its own retribution. The life or death of a martyr, after all, testifies not by bearing its reward as a consequence and presenting that reward before the eyes of some tribunal of doubters, but by affirming the intrinsic value of the ends the martyr chooses, even over undisturbed survival.[10]

What this means is that our life is not a trust game, and our norms, unlike those of Utilitarianism, are not experimental. Rather, our fidelity is expressed in our way of life, grounded in the idea of goodness—in our confidence and trust that only absolute goodness is worthy of recognition as divine. The faith of Israel, to give the word 'faith' the sense that it bears in the history and lives of the people of Israel, is a quiet, non-dogmatic security in the recognition of the goodness of being in general and of human being in particular. Because our faith is manifested in a way of life rather than a catechism, questions of heresy, orthodoxy, imposed intellectual authority, dogmatic coercion, and even social or societal pressure to intellectual conformity are alien to the Mosaic universe. The openness of our Law is in the continuous reapplication of its core values and ideas, not in the contingency or dubitability of its principles.

Intolerance, intellectual chauvinism, and sheer dogmatism will be present, of course, in Jewish life, as in any other, just as theft or battery will, and for the same reason—because Jews are human and have egos, and ids too, like any other people. But no abiding and enforced norm of dogma will be found. The Torah contains social, moral, and spiritual commandments, but it does not shackle the mind. The celebrated case of Maimonides's 13 Articles is the seeming exception that proves the rule. These elements of belief are offered by Maimonides to enable him to explain how it is possible, if the human intellectual affinity with the Divine is the basis of immortality, for anyone other than a philosopher to attain what the Sages called "a portion in the world to come." Drawing upon Plato's distinction between knowledge and belief, Maimonides argues that for non-philosophers, beliefs such as those that the symbols and rituals of the Law seek to impart (although on a lower epistemic plane than perfect knowledge) allow the minds of persons who are not conceptually adept to attain their own intellectual attachment to the Divine and to realize their inner affinity to God. The so-called articles of the Maimonidean creed, then, are not obligations of faith that are to be rewarded—in proportion to their counterintuitive demands—with a ticket to Elysium. They are paradigmatic counterparts to the conceptual understanding of the philosopher, allowing intellectual access to the Everpresent, that is, to immortality, for all whose trust and practice bring them, by way of imagination and aspiration, within intellectual range of the Transcendent.

The rabbis liberate theology and release it to the free play of conceptual imagination by placing it within the realm of Aggadah and by locating Aggadah itself outside the realm of legal obligation. They can afford to exempt human reflection and speculation from the stringencies of praxis because the imagination they call upon as the vehicle of Aggadah is disciplined by the life of the Law and so can be counted on, critically, to be wholesome and not perverse—thus the abstemiousness of the midrashic *ke-ve-yakhol*, which can freely resort to the treasuries of the fabular without worry that God will be reduced to some mere super-demon. Rabbinic imagery constantly places the Divine in the role of a human king but never allows the condescension of that imagery to set a precedent or ground an inference that would degrade God to the plane of merely human majesty.

The realm of theory and speculation remains open to the creative play of imagination. I have glossed Philo's play on the playful name of Isaac in the same vein: Abraham was ready to sacrifice his laughter, but God returned it to him.[11] The laughter here, as Philo teaches, is moral and intellectual freedom. Thus Philo argues that every virtuous man is free, that liberty is the greatest of all human blessings and the fountain of all happiness, that if there is some pagan glory in dying for a sprig of parsley or an olive wreath in the arena, it is far greater glory to die for freedom, and that free speech is the birthright of the free man: "To speak freely what is commanded by a clear conscience befits the noble soul."[12] These remarks are not idle rhetoric on Philo's part. Recounting an incident at the theater where praises for the very name of freedom, embedded in a play of Euripides, brought the audience to their feet in a standing ovation,[13] Philo shows clearly how polyglot Alexandria, under Roman rule, yearned for a freedom it did not enjoy. The Greek poetry of an ancient bard, like the "proclaim liberty throughout the land" of the still older Hebrew text, kept the dream alive. Even the denial of liberty kept its taste fresh in the mouths of those who could not relish it fully.

Throughout the normative history of Jewish thought, intellectual liberty is presumed,[14] not asked for, except where foreign rule has imposed some rival scheme. Thus Josephus needs to explain that "Everyone should worship God in accordance with the dictates of his own conscience, and not under constraint" (*Life*, 23). And we find Simeon ben Tsemaḥ Duran (the Rashbatz, 1361–1444) in his *Magen Avot* urging, "God forbid that such a thing should occur in Israel as to condemn honest inquiries on account of their divergent views." Spinoza continued the same tradition. He wrote the *Tractatus Theologico-Politicus* in an effort to extend to his European contemporaries the standards of intellectual freedom that his own community had not felt itself free to extend to him. On the title page he wrote: "Not only is freedom of thought and speech compatible with piety and the peace of the state, but it cannot be withheld without at the same time destroying both the peace of the state and piety itself." And Moses Mendelssohn, defending his own religious tradition against the charge that its norms sought to bind the mind in the manner all too familiar to his adversaries from the common Christian practice of the day, was voicing the long-established rabbinic standard when he wrote, in the last two pages of *Jerusalem*: "Convert not into law any immutable truth, without which civil happiness may very well subsist. . . . Leave thinking and speaking to us, just as it was given us, as an unalienable heirloom . . . as an unalterable right, by our universal Father."[15] Underlying the centrality of intellectual freedom from a Judaic standpoint, I emphasize, is the recognition that to deny freedom to the mind, and concomitant freedom of expression, is to negate the very humanity that the Torah seeks to foster and preserve. Intellectual freedom is not simply a concession made by Jewish norms. It is part of their purpose. No system that makes it instrumental guards it as well.

4. Mill and the Marketplace

Mill himself plays with doubts addressed to the assumption that the free flow of ideas will inevitably trend upward and fulfill the human hope of intellectual progress. That hope, like the more general hope for progress and the betterment of the world, may indeed have some foundation, despite the doubts that afflict us as we reach the end of an especially bloody century. The assumption that there is progress in the realm of thought has certainly held true in some domains and for certain periods. But this contingent outcome can be judged a universal truth only when all history is finished, and then only when an adequate yardstick is found for comparing advances, losses and retrenchments in diverse realms and for diverse individuals and communities. So, short of the millennium (and not merely the coming one, or the next), the notion of universal progress seems far too feeble a stick to prop up an absolute right, one that we ask policemen (and even publishers' clerks) to risk their lives to protect, juries to uphold, legislators to define and defend, and jurists to serve.

If the benefits in which Mill proposes to ground our rights are contingent, clearly they leave those rights subject to exception, defended or enforced under the watchful eye of expediency. Implementation in a given case may look helpful or harmful, easy or difficult. Some rights may seem objectionable, say, to a great power like China or offensive to a paltry one like Myanmar, and policy will waver accordingly. Cicero, not at his best, advises his son that there are few services more highly valued than the eloquence of a skilled defense, but "take care when you want to help one group not to offend another" (*De Officiis* II, 68). We've already seen enough of the fruits of such an approach in domestic and international affairs to know the tenderness of the joint between the claims of utility and those of rights.

John Stuart Mill is hardly responsible for that melange of opportunism and rhetoric that is pleased to call itself pragmatism in politics. A liberal can be — should be — a strict constructionist when it comes to human rights and would, I have suggested, look silly at best proposing absolute rights for "us" and not for "them." But liberals often seem strangely confident — especially those who are empiricists — when they claim that the preservation of intellectual freedoms will always (in the long run, or when followed as a rule) produce more good than harm.

We have to ask ourselves, when we see committed liberals holding firm on questions of rights, standing their ground on principle: Is there not more behind their adamancy than mere expectations of the greatest benefit? The certitude that committed liberals bring to bear on the expectation that the common good (in this case, public access to the truth) will be served by doing the right thing carries an assurance that is anything but empirical or fallibilist. The urgency of the claim that freedom of thought and expression must never be violated, regardless of the costs, carries a moral, not an empiric nisus. The same is true in any defense of rights — civil rights, for example, like the rights of the accused. I see followers of Mill here playing a card that Utilitarians have not dealt themselves and that Mill has explicitly declined.

Not every liberal, and still less every politician or decision maker, is so principled as those followers of Mill who would rather risk the inconsistency of appealing to absolute ideas of right than surrender rights claims to the vagaries of history and political fortunes. I worry that resting absolute claims on mere utilities will too readily leave the absolute outweighed. But I also wonder about Mill's reliance on the assumption (which his own experience seems to call on him to qualify) that truth will always triumph in the end — if only given long enough! — in an open fight. If it will, of course, one can always say, as used to be said to Marxists, that an inevitable outcome surely needs no practical support, and still less the bearing of risks or sufferings in its behalf.

But I also feel uncomfortable here for the same sort of reasons that make me uncomfortable with Mill's assumption that individuals are the sole and sufficient guardians of their own best interests. Who, after all, guides *this* invisible hand? And how, if not by means that Mill's principles forbid, is his secular apocalypse to be achieved, the gradual emergence of the truth? How do we reach the social closure that Mill holds out to us as the payoff of our tolerance, without falling into new orthodoxies or relying on the force of public opinion? For surely tolerance alone does not produce conformity and acquiescence. What is to become of skeptical, heretical, or non-conforming opinion when human understanding becomes as universal as Mill hopes and expects and promises it will be? Do idiosyncratic opinions persist? Or in the light of understanding does the triumph of truth simply bathe away the rustic and rusticated views of the unwashed?

Polytheism, we must recall, did not die without a fight. It was not simply refuted. It was marginalized, relegated to country places, as the name "pagan" reminds us. The dress of the Elizabethan courtier becomes the fusty costume of the country bumpkin, so ridiculed as a clown that the very iconography of foolishness still wears his ruff. Hippies, now also often relegated to country places, have begun to become caricatures of themselves. The words that might have voiced the Elizabethan clown's antiquated views are silenced in his modern counterpart, but not by argument. Erasmus and Montaigne beat scholasticism not by reasoning but by laughter. Duns Scotus survives, apart from learned quarter-leather tomes, in the dunce cap. And even that bit of innuendo has become a matter of obscurity, just as popular consciousness is innocent of the linkage between Leibniz and the Pangloss who now prances on the Broadway stage. The Threadneedle Street group secured their reforms and put others in motion far beyond what they had sought, not by argument but by voting and more pragmatic means. Not that argument is irrelevant or even ineffectual, but in social or ideational struggles argument proves all too ready to defer to alternative techniques of persuasion, of the sort that Mill seems eager to disapprove, if not entirely to disavow. The problem is not that discourse or intelligent conversation is impossible, still less that there is no such thing as a dialectically informed change of heart. What troubles me is the idea of unanimity or consensus to be achieved by some way of persuasion. The promise of such an outcome seems to me to play on a form of false consciousness. Those who have made intellectual conformity their goal rarely stop at rational argument as their means of winning souls.

Mill, then, seems naive or disingenuous when he leans on nineteenth-century visions of progress to make the pragmatic, Baconian rewards of tolerance seem winnable. Consider the matter of rhetoric. For that is where at least a great deal of public discourse is conducted. Eugene Garver makes good sense in doubting that in a rhetorical contest truths will be the product or outcome of the dispute — let alone new truths. Rhetoric, by its nature, as Aristotle saw and showed us, pivots on accepted opinions. It does not make opinions out of the whole cloth. It uses them. If its discourse results in changes of heart or mind, those usually spring from the already constituted common ground that a speaker or persuader seeks to discover and solicit or exploit. The point is not that rhetoric cannot convince anyone of anything, or even that such persuading cannot be legitimate, for surely it can. But the discovery of truths is not what rhetoric is about.

Eliciting a line of thought from Aristotle's analysis of rhetoric and the springs of public responsiveness to it, Garver shows why this is so:

> While scientific principles hook up to reality throughout a demonstration, the topics in rhetoric function in situations where such a possibility is rare. . . . In each of the three kinds of rhetoric, Aristotle will begin with the political or ethical parent of rhetoric, and move toward its logical progenitor. Each kind starts with the need for the orator to know what he is talking about, to be responsible to, and reflective of, the nature of the *polis* and its laws. . . . That order is not reversible: Aristotle gives us no reason to think that starting from the free competition of ideas, one can eventually hit up against truth and reality . . . rhetorical competition works in a good polis; it does not produce a good polis. Given a grounding in a knowledge of the state's aspirations, needs, resources, and laws, an advocate can argue for policies and judgments too specific to be laid down in advance by the laws, but there is no corresponding license to begin with advocacy and end with truth.[16]

The marketplace of ideas is an oxymoron. Ideas are understood or seen through, not bought and sold. And what is bought and sold is not ideas.

Mill was long aware of this fact, as Gertrude Himmelfarb points out.[17] In an 1833 letter to Carlyle, Mill wrote: "I have not any great notion of the advantage of the 'free discussion' men call the 'collision of opinions,' it being my creed that Truth is *sown* and germinates in the mind itself, and is not to be struck *out* suddenly like fire from a flint by knocking another hard body against it."[18] Mill's *Autobiography* papers over the contradiction between his early doubts and later faith in the promised fruits of the free flow of ideas. There and in his essay on Coleridge, he locates the real benefit of intellectual freedom in the emergence of a small number of advanced social thinkers who will win over the rest of humanity to their views.[19]

Like Plato, then, Mill tries to contain and harness elitism by enlisting intellectuals in a metaphysically charged educational project. But he reverses the polarities, uncoupling from the idealism of Plato and putting in its place the positivism of Comte — if not a blander and seemingly more tolerant relativism and agnosticism. Covering his tracks, as Himmelfarb showed, by suppressing some of his earlier writings and simplifying his argument, in what Victorians called an "economy," the Mill of *On Liberty* rests his hopes on the marketplace of ideas. Free competition in the realm of thought will work the same magic that was expected of it in the world of commerce. But the argument lacks conviction. Mill knew better by his own insight; and we know better with the help of hindsight. For if good arguments drive out bad, how it is possible that homeopathic medicines are still sold that contain scarcely a molecule of active ingredient and that are blended and compounded in accordance with theories that even a self-respecting alchemist would have long ago held up to doubt or disdain?

If we have learned anything of public debate since Mill published *On Liberty* in 1859, it is something of the power of such debate — and the cloud of advocacy that surrounds it — to obfuscate and oversimplify. It does not simply tease out the subtle shadings of partial truths. As Todd Gitlin puts it, "In the country of the sound bite, the one liner is king."[20] To assay Mill's position adequately, moreover, we must consider a realm of expression that was quite marginal to his thought, although it lay at the juncture between free expression and free trade: advertising. Rhetoric makes its public appeal through a quest for shared ideas of the common good, but advertising does not confine its appeals to ideas. The textbook appeals are Food, Sex, Babies, Animals, Color/Design, Snobbery, Fear, and Humor. Lately we observe Envy, Guilt, Anxiety, even Horror. The nexus of any such appeal to a purchase (or voting) decision is largely *per accidens*. What is bought or chosen often has slight if any natural or rational connection to the promptings that led to its being bought or chosen. Indeed, in recent years the trend in advertising has been away from an appeal in the now classic sense to the building of a mood or image, pre-selling a product, service, candidate, or idea. Where rhetoric uses creativity to seek a common ground or common interest, advertising uses creativity to invent or forge an adventitious nexus between act and attitude. What does advertising experience tell us about Mill's confidence in the triumph of truth in the marketplace of ideas?

The American public has had the truth about cigarettes for decades now. In recent years that truth has been printed on each pack. There aren't many truths clear enough and simple enough to be printed legibly in a space that size. Yet the information has not cured Americans of their smoking habit. A few years ago we read that new deaths attributable to increased smoking among women had wiped out all the gains against cancer mortality made as a result of research in the War against Cancer. The appeal used to sell cigarettes to women has often been style. But several brands, perhaps most notably Virginia Slims, have compounded that affront with an appeal to women's independence and self-reliance, forging a brand identity about as focused as the notion that Joe Camel is cool — and about as relevant to decisions that might cause cancer and other potentially fatal diseases. Do people have a right to smoke themselves, their co-workers, and family members to death — and does liberty of self-expression serve that right?

The difficulty is that once mass marketers, in their role as civilizational movers, have found the pleasure centers and other motivational nodes in the brain of the body politic, reason has begun to appear irrelevant in their sights. Political, or erotic, or hedonic decisions (choices, at any rate) can be made quite readily without reliance on that now widely questioned counselor. Mill could hardly anticipate that ancient patterns of superstition would one day be marketed under the rubric of the "New Age." Yet philosophers, at least since Hume, have been saying that opinions are not what move or motivate human beings at all. That claim, in fact, underwrites Mill's intuitive confidence that opinions must be held harmless, although Hume's cynicism about the efficacy of truth tends also to undermine the trust Mill asks us to place in the practical value of truth's disclosure. Why, we might ask, do the annals and apologetics of intellectual liberty not register in their archive of cherished truths Hume's claim that opinions do not move men? But beyond that issue, why is expression still so quaintly equated with ideas?

Advertisers have long assumed that facts are not what move product. The motto is, "Don't sell the steak, sell the sizzle!" But would-be followers of Mill are slow to orient their theories toward recognition of the fact that choices or decisions, including many bad ones, are made not just by the marginal few but by the populace of great (and *soi disant* civilized) nations, not on the basis of reasoned argument but in response to all sorts of illocutionary acts and the appetites and instincts that those acts arouse, flatter, direct, manipulate, and help to define.

The image of Edward R. Murrow, looking and sounding thoughtful, cigarette in hand, sold far more cigarettes than any argument in praise of smoking or evidence in its defense. As the electronic media have begun to mature, indeed, image and mood rather than any factual claim at all are relied upon increasingly for sales. The approach is typified, as Ronald Collins and David Skover note, by "An Advertising photo of a riderless horse grazing in a snow-covered graveyard, with the caption 'Marlboro Country.' "[21] No verbal claim at all is made, but the Marlboro Country campaign, over the years, turned a lackluster brand into an industry leader: "Marketers exploited the possibilities of photography by intensifying the symbolic association between goods and the consumer's self-image." Informational advertising — although the notion is still used in the apologetics for extending First Amendment protection to what is ingenuously called commercial speech — is "an idea that's gone the way of the Remington typewriter."[22]

The Eveready people use a pink plush mechanical bunny to tag the idea of endurance to their product. Other battery companies use other animated figures to make a similar claim. But people like the bunny and identify with its repeated triumphs over adversity. The campaign works, not because customers have been shown that Eveready batteries actually outlast the competition, nor because they are convinced that batteries are more economically or environmentally friendly than electricity from the mains, but because the advertising links good feelings to product image. My point is not that this strategy is wicked, but just what we all know, that what we communicate is only in part a matter of propositional content, let alone news and views about the world. Yet Mill, strikingly, does not put his associative psychology to work on the matter of market decisions.[23] He seems to presume an earnest, Victorian consumer whose standards are those of reason. It would be unfair, of course, to expect Mill to anticipate the saturated marketplace and supersaturated marketeering of the present age. But, by the same token, we must ask ourselves how appropriate Mill's ideas of persuasion can be in an age when mass marketing has far outstripped the idiom Mill knew best.

Advertising uses identification and association along with appetite, fear, shame, libido, parental emotion, envy, familial tensions, guilt, anxieties, and longings of all sorts to move or sell. The tugs it exerts are rarely propositional. Still less are they claims about what is true or what truth is. Association is the key tool: auto (or electric paint sprayer) with authority, fun with immortality, lipstick with charisma, charisma with orgasm, perfume with mystery, and mystery with power. Much of the manipulation is relatively innocent, but not all of it is. Budweiser's frogs, the Absolut bottle, the Michael Jordan pitch for McDonald's have all scored high with a youth audience—as did Joe Camel. Youth alcohol consumption, early habituation to smoking, and a high fat diet are more than casual consequences of such mass campaigns. The makers of moral, religious, and political opinion and commitment long ago discovered that they can play the same game and work the same magic. In some respects, as Plato has it, they invented it. We also know— whether we consider the peculations of the latest televangelist, the mind control of Dianetics, Muktananda, and the Reverend Moon, or the sinister plots of Shoko Asahara to gas innocent subway commuters or spread the ebola virus in urban settings—that there is no guarantee of purity in the motives of such manipulators. Still less can we be certain of the powers of sheer clarity to counteract their messages when they become unwholesome.

How many persons were turned on to drugs in the 1960s by the maunderings of Aldous Huxley in *The Doors of Perception*? Can his proposals that psychedelic chemicals might open new avenues of consciousness and creativity (a suggestion that Mill's formulation would protect on the grounds that when it had been widely enough discussed and tested, the truth would out), or even the press releases of Timothy Leary (whose experiments on unsuspecting human subjects could and did appeal not simply to the experimentalism of Dewey but to the empiricism of Mill), compare in impact with the promotional activity and attitudinizing of the Beatles? Or are we prepared to say that the crude but sly allusion to LSD in a lyric about "Lucy in the Sky with Diamonds" was in fact a propositional claim—a claim about the truth?

How many followers of the Reverend Moon were convinced of his divinity by argument? Is it not bizarre to protect under the mantle of free intellectual exploration cults whose chief techniques and methods of operation—specifically, a cynical exploitation of the basic mechanisms of human sociality and socialization—negate the very capability of forming independent opinions? Or have we here a case of the inalienable freedom of the individual to alienate the will?[24]

I am not speaking here of the frightful denouements that set the taste of horror in the very names of Jonestown, David Koresh, the Temple of the Sun, Aum Shinrikyo, or Heaven's Gate. I am speaking of the means such figures and groups use to gain the trust and loyalty that can bring their members to kill or die in their behalf, to lead men to give up their wives to the appetites of cult leaders, their bodies to self-castration, their children to beatings and abuse or to drafts of cyanide-laced Kool-Aid. The means to such an end do not rest on the free exchange of ideas. But they are protected legally, constitutionally, by principles that were devised to defend the free exchange of ideas.

When the doctrine of free thought and expression was formulated, against the backdrop of the religious wars of the sixteenth and seventeenth centuries and their settlement at Utrecht, or in the Peace of Westphalia, or in the Glorious Revolution, the liberties championed by all friends of human enlightenment did concern opinion — the right to form opinions for ourselves, to teach them to our children, to argue them with one another, and to print them on paper. The claim of the persecutors had been, in the days of the Inquisition or when William Tyndale (the author of so much of the noble language that we now know in the King James Bible) was garrotted and burnt, that heretics or unbelievers were being saved not merely from themselves but from Hellfire. Mill could justly hide a smile at the archaism of such a thought — although, truth be told, the Spanish Inquisition did not cease its operations until 1834.

Mill's writing is full of hope that human progress would soon expose to all the fatuity of believing that a person needs to be saved from his or her own false belief — meaning, sotto voce, damnable unbelief. But unbelievers were still shunned or ostracized, or denied their civil rights, even at the time of Mill's writing. Here, in three such cases that he cites, is the still visible irritant of Mill's essay. The conscientious refusal of principled men to swear a Bible oath is the paradigm case of an act that Mill defends (*On Liberty*, pp. 90–91). But Mill's formulation, being politic and philosophical, is not pointed but general, and thus abstract. The resultant model is faulty.

If would-be followers of Mill are true to his desire to list all the possibilities, then surely we should expand his typology beyond the views and visions that are true, or false, or both, and add those that are neither. For not every expression is a self-expression, and not every vision is a theory or even an opinion. Does it not rankle, just a bit, to hear from the lawyer hired to keep a strip joint open that the poor dancers employed there would be denied their right to self-expression if the place were closed, or denied a liquor license? Is self-expression what the dancers are there for, and is Mill's quest for truth sufficient warrant for a court's decision in cases on such a matter?

Cass Sunstein has sought to rationalize our practice of bringing peep shows and pornography (and the $3 billion industry they represent) under the broad skirts of the First Amendment. "Sexually explicit works," he urges, "can be highly relevant to the development of individual capacities. For many, it is an important vehicle for self-discovery and self-definition."[25] The "it" here is pornography, and the self that is discovered or defined is one that pornography can discover to us or help us to define. Sunstein hedges his bets when he says "can be." He backs away from a categorical endorsement of pornography when he confronts, say, the life and work of Larry Flynt, the publisher of *Hustler*, a magazine whose snickering celebrations of molestation and mutilation do not readily comport with the sunny images of pornography as a form of education. Sunstein balks at press reports that treat Flynt as "kind of a hero of the First Amendment."[26] But when Milos Forman put his formidable directorial talents to work in a film for Oliver Stone, *The People vs Larry Flynt*, based on a screenplay by Larry Karaszewski, which goes far out of its way to whitewash the nexus between Flynt's viciously abusive and exploitative lifestyle and the expressive values of his magazine and to make Flynt the poster child of First Amendment freedoms, the American Civil Liberties Union felt called upon to rebut the complaints of Gloria Steinem and others by buying an advertisement in *Variety* that acclaimed Forman as a "First Amendment advocate and an artist of unsurpassed creativity, ability, and courage."[27]

Sunstein's arguments for the social value of pornography, like my own arguments against it, appeal to the ideal of self-development, in which I have found intellectual freedom constitutive, and to which he finds it, once again, instrumental. I find his rationale somewhat disingenuous. He objects to anyone's setting a standard for the self whose development the state is called upon to protect or promote.[28] But what is served, then, is not personal growth but the sovereignty of impulse — the same impulse that the marketplace seeks the liberty to cultivate and, if such is profitable, corrupt. The notion is that a free society (still bearing in mind Mill's strictures against social pressures) should have and should foster no substantive notion of self-development. Self-development, when pled as a rhetorical appeal, still carries with it a secular glimmer of the aura that once surrounded the idea of working out one's own salvation. In its humanistic form it is made to sound like Confucian self-cultivation. But when it comes to the directions individuals pursue, such expectations, having been aroused, are dismissed. Society, we now learn, must be wholly neutral to the modes of expression and symbolization that might cultivate the imagination of a John Gacy or a Mother Theresa.

A state or society as morally bankrupt as that, one might respond pragmatically, will not long endure. But perhaps it is more relevant to say that such a state or society does not deserve to endure and is not worthy of the name or the trust that we humans pose in human institutions — not for the sake of their many inconveniences, but for the sake of promulgating a shareable vision of human potentialities and creating the conditions that will nurture a wide variety of lives that realize diverse personal versions of such a vision.

If it troubles us to see pornography placed in the nurturant role that Socrates once assigned to dialectic and the love of wisdom, Sunstein reminds us that "the system of deliberative democracy is not supposed simply to implement existing desires." With the aid of this appeal to the dialectic of desires, the entire package is wrapped in a flag that Sunstein does not blush to call "Madisonian."[29] Citing Sunstein's arguments, Collins and Skover argue tellingly that a kind of Gresham's law is at work whereby the idioms and images of mass-marketed pornography are in fact eroding the very possibility of public discourse, by undermining its language and undercutting its mood:

> As long as the First Amendment is rooted in Madisonian soil, the ideal of a democratic state inevitably entails reasoned political discourse. . . . the traditional First Amendment would be unrecognizable without some meaningful dedication to the political function of public reason. A well-informed and active citizenry might best maintain a stable and just society through an open exchange of ideas rationally related to the public good. This, at bottom, is the premise typically invoked by jurists and scholars to legitimate American constitutional government. . . .

However pornography is understood, there are troubling consequences for the Madisonian ideal when the pornographic experience is coupled with public expression. In this regime, is it any longer possible to differentiate Madisonian self-realization from pornutopian self-gratification? Is it any longer possible for rational logic to trump erotic logic? . . . will this regime tend to collapse the First Amendment theory of reasoned discourse into a principle of pleasure?[30]

That, of course, is where Mill came in, urging a regime that places higher pleasures above lower ones and that pursues and provides for the education of desires rather than their mere servicing—lest sheer hedonism lead us to a porcine life that would never be choiceworthy (*Utilitarianism*, 8–9; *Bentham*, 95–96). But what safeguards has the pleasure principle against that denouement? And if a constitutional guarantism or Rule Utilitarianism grounded in the paramountcy of free expression is substituted for the pleasure principle, how can a rule or guarantee be formulated that will make free expression absolute without transforming public discourse into a cacophony of appeals to what Collins and Skover call pornutopian gratifications?

Public discourse, to be sure, is not the only free speech value. We have named others already. But if the argument stays on Mill's grounds, that is, if pornography and other modes of exploitation or manipulation are defended in the name of truth, the question that must be put pointedly to followers of Mill's doctrine is this: Is this form of truth worth what society will pay for it? If truth is the object in question, are truths of the kind that strip joints traffic in to be the highest values recognized by the law? Does the dignity of women, or the sexes, or the human body, as a repository of intrinsic and semeiotic value, have no standing? Are the image and the dignity of women or of the human body—whether of the dancers in this strip joint or of other women whom their art may typify in the minds of sundry viewers, and thereby implicate in its semeiotic web—are these values too intangible to hold a place alongside commercial interests or the appeal those interests make in the name of artistic liberty, or the sheer idea of truth itself?

5. Mill Abused

What is unwholesome, it might be said, is a matter of opinion. Here again we slide from a Utilitarian objectivism that puts a cash value on truth to the relativism that can find no truth about values. I vividly recall the days when we were told that LSD was a drug with no side effects; and later, when cocaine was promoted, not just on the street but in mainstream national magazines, as a harmless and non-addictive thrill. How many minds must be blown, how many Jonestowns must we witness, how many addicts must die, and how many infants must be born addicted to crack and infected with AIDS before we are ready to acknowledge that harm has been done—and some of it by what we classify as speech? We rightly shun government intervention against every sly innuendo. Still we must ask, regarding the mass marketing of drugs in the 1960s and 1970s, where were the protests and boycotts? Where was the Fourth Estate?

I see no difference here between, say, the labeling of impure rapeseed oil as good food (although it can cause blindness and death) and the promulgation of stereotypes that degrade, dehumanize, and nurse violence, or rock videos and haut couture magazines that tout narcotics — least of all do I see a difference measurable in Utilitarian terms. Mill's argument, I am saying, does not shield the mislabeling or the misleading. It does not protect hate speech or narcotics promotion or the marketing of homicide or suicide, any more than it protects fraudulent sales of tainted foods or unsafe pharmaceuticals.

True, the magazine publishers who ran features on the virtues of cocaine and LSD, long after the counterculture psychodelicatessen had closed, were not the actual drug dealers. And the purveyors of virulent racial and sexual stereotypes — or potent mixtures of the two, say in rap music, videos, and performances — were not usually the actual skinheads, klansmen, militiamen, or gang thugs who perpetrated violent acts of racial, ethnic, or sectarian hatred. But apologues couched in such terms ignore the ways in which magazine articles are placed and popular music sold.

Mill's argument does not differ from my own in condemning what is dangerous. It does not support the weight of degradation, exploitation, or manipulation that masquerades as expression of ideas and shelters under the banner of the pursuit of truth. It is not my humanism, however, but Mill's version of liberalism that is pled in behalf of the violence of pornography and the commercial promotion of violence as an end in itself. The disingenuous equation of pornography not with degradation but with personal or political revolution is sugared with promises of freedom — self-expression for the purveyors and the exploited actors, models, and dancers; self-discovery for the leering audience. Such fictions and pretensions make Mill the apologist for degradations that he did not remotely envision. We can see how disingenuous such pleadings are if we hew closely to the values to which they appeal. If our earnest desire is indeed for the development and expression of human potential, we should not shy away from envisioning that potential in all its creative varieties. Appeals in behalf of intellectual freedom, in that case, would look not to the presumptive fruits of freedom but to its intrinsic value as a constituent of human fulfillment and the good life.

When we value intellectual freedom for its capacity to foster creativity — if we understand creativity not in empty, formal terms but in a substantive and life-affirming vision of humanity — then the ideal of intellectual freedom will not sustain just any form of expression that might work as a poison to personhood and a source of dehumanizing violence or abasement of the human spirit. Nor will it protect modes of action that deaden the very freedom that is pled in their behalf. Still less will it warrant state sustenance of modes of expression and social relation that are destructive of the very capacity to form ideas or sustain relationships.

Those who urge ingenuously that ultimately the truth will out — that people will learn to avoid what they know is harmful and to ignore the poisons bred in words and images — are neglecting at least two facts: First, by the time such lessons have sunk in, the damage, sometimes irreparable, may be done, and the actual purveyors, whether of thalidomide, asbestos, impure rapeseed oil, cigarettes, cocaine, or racial or religious or gender hatred, will be vanished into the shadows, their profits secured or their agendas served. The world may learn, perhaps. But when the world learns in this way, it learns as victims learn about confidence games, after their bank accounts are emptied. Such learning is always temporary. As grifters and stand-up comedians say, there's always the younger generation, who haven't yet heard the joke or smelled the strange fruit of ethnic cleansing. Meanwhile, those who have done the damage, sold the goods, gotten the store burnt down, altered the rates of marriage, divorce, suicide, or matricide, are safe behind a screen of anonymity or corporate inviolability, well along with their next assault, their latitude of action well protected by academic hired guns, journalists, and highly principled lawyers and politicians, whose job it is to ensure that rising generations of the populace do not learn from the experience and the errors of their elders.

The second fact often forgotten by those who take comfort in the hope that truth, like murder, will out is that there are impulses toward death. So, even when the condom people, say, have sold the television audience on the proposition that indiscriminate sexual activity can be fatal, there are those who will be drawn to that very fatality.[31] They are drawn not simply by an exuberant libido but by morbid fascination, transformed by various social and psychological dynamics, into an obsession that may be linked adventitiously (as those who manipulate such emotions well know) to the impulses of libido itself.

But quaintly, I say again, we who cherish liberty, and intellectual liberty in particular, still labor with a 150-year-old theory based on a popular, topical essay[32] embodying the assumptions (1) that speech is the heart of liberty, (2) that speech is a matter of opinions, (3) that opinions and thus speech cannot be harmful in any critical measure, and (4) that neither the government nor the public has any rightful interest in the harm individuals may choose to do themselves, or the good they might have done instead.

The impact of these four assumptions of Mill's account of liberty is exacerbated by the overextension of the conclusions to which he intended them to lead. So that even for a private person, a college community, or a moral critic, journalist, or minister of religion to object to tasteless racial or gender humor or threatening speech on the grounds of its destructiveness, or to call pornography by its rightful name, is widely deemed censorious and rejected on grounds adduced from Mill. Ultimately, in effect, the claim is that human knowledge and understanding depend for their advance on the freedom of every stand-up comedian to portray the Poles or the Portuguese as stupid, the license of every pub owner with a cabaret permit to degrade women for the edification of paying customers, the liberty of every Klansman to paint the ethnic or credal other as a racial blight or moral threat, and the freedom of Al Sharpton, Louis Farrakhan, and every other street-corner Hitler who can arrange a subsidy from the Saddam Husseins and Muammar Khadafys of the world (or a marriage of convenience with a mainstream politician) to represent Jews collectively as bloodsuckers or all whites as oppressors.

6. Beyond Mill

I want to take issue with each of the four assumptions I have listed, and with the overextension to which they are linked. I am seeking to lay out a conception of liberty that is broader but also more perspicuous than Mill's. I think it high time we had one. We have learned too much to be able to rest our idea of liberty, its scope and boundaries, on Mill's arguments alone. His categories are hemmed in by the limits of his concerns and hidebound by his assumptions and those of his age about human motives. Indeed, they are hamstrung even by Mill's capacity to rely on the civilizing pressures of the very conventions whose engines in public opinion he was seeking to restrain. Yet we still cling to Mill's argument as though it gave us the only theory capable of protecting the liberties we rightly cherish. Mill's essay itself has become a shibboleth, a mandala, and a shrine. Many liberals are more willing to see the flag burnt than Mill's arguments challenged.

I think there is more, much more, to liberty than freedom of speech and thought, that there is more to speech than the expression of opinions, and thus that Mill's Utilitarian reliance on the emergence of truth as the warrant of freedom is neither necessary nor sufficient. I think that there are kinds of speech that can be harmful and indeed poisonous — not by enunciating "heretical" opinions (rosily envisioned by Mill as potentially too advanced for those who first hear them) but by diminishing or degrading the humanity of individuals or abasing the social standing of an entire race, people, culture, or gender. All of which is to say nothing of the dissemination, say, on the Internet, of instructions for making pipe bombs, polluting the water supply, constructing computer viruses, or sabotaging the power grid — information that can be obtained, in some cases, from diligent research in the library but that yields a world more damage when freely and graphically accessed and topically organized on the home computer.

I want to argue that society has a responsibility — through public expressions of indignation and through concerted actions that give force to public disapproval, sometimes including organized communal responses and programmatic undertakings by government acting as the agency of society — to uphold interests that are degraded and to sustain the worth and dignity of the human person. I would argue further that the public airwaves and the ethernet are no more free for the appropriation of every molester and purveyor of images and instructions that foster violence and molestation than are the public roads and sidewalks.

Willmoore Kendall makes some valuable points about the bankruptcy of the notion that the state should be wholly neutral in the realm of ideas.[33] He raises legitimate worries about the impact of making freedom of thought and speech the paramount social good. Indeed, had Mill held consistent to the Utilitarian principle he announced at the outset, all goods would be interchangeable in Utilitarian coin and none would be placed on a plinth high enough to demand the steady sacrifice of any other. But how can we accept Kendall's efforts to hedge the freedoms Mill does protect, in the interest of what Kendall calls "a public truth"? This smacks too much of dogma. And I worry about the disutility of ham-handed attempts to curb offensive expression, since we know very well that there are places, and not just overseas, where what is offensive is the sight of a woman's arm or ankle, or her face, or the sound of a questioning or cynical voice, or the presence of a black child or a Jew.

I propose to address the dilemmas that Mill faced and those that he still poses not by narrowing but by broadening Mill's idea of liberty. I do believe that society has an interest, a public interest, in promoting individual discoveries of the truth and not merely in clearing the ground for them. Yet I think that many liberties intertwine inseparably with freedom of expression and can never therefore be rightfully sacrificed to it—still less to any eidolon puffed up about its name. The problem with the ideal of intellectual freedom is not in making our liberty of thought and speech uncompromisable, but in construing the reference class of actions protected by these liberties so broadly and indiscriminately as to force conflicts among the deserts that we legitimately treat as rights. Complementarity is the key to accommodation, that is, to the avoidance of conflicts among rights. This means that for practical as well as conceptual reasons, we must inform our idea of free speech by the idea of personhood, on which it is founded. We should regard destructive and anti-human expressions not as exercises of liberty but as abuses of it. For, as Locke made clear, what is self-destructive is not a power or liberty at all. If Mill and his followers erred in privileging expressive liberties, the wise and prudent response is not to cast about for some other shibboleth or icon to set up in their place, but to study the modes of expression that are compatible with the preservation of all our liberties and vigorously to pursue the protection of these.

Mill faces his followers with hard choices—conflicts of right and obligation (and of rights with obligations)—that hark back, beyond the moral empiricism of Epicurus, to the value relativism of the Sophists. He vigorously enunciates his respect for liberties other than those of speech when he warms to the cultivation of individuality in the third and fourth chapters of *On Liberty*. But he subordinates these liberties to those of expression, by making the advance of thought the goal of human development and by failing to find any circumstance that would curtail liberties of expression in the interest of human fulfillment. He clearly did not foresee the threat to human individuality, personhood, and personality that would arise from overextension of liberties that parody the ones he zealously protected. And, by comparison with thinkers of both earlier and later periods, he worked with a much diminished idea of the need and obligation to foster human growth and individuality. This position was no mere accident or casual outcome of his views on political economy and the market—his worries about public education or his sometimes faltering support of free trade. Mill's prejudice against (and willingness to take for granted) the concerted cultural and religious systems that have traditionally addressed the fostering of human individuality made him gun shy of any effort by church or state to guide humanity in the quest for its potentials.

Mill was attracted to the humanism and even the teleology of human nature that he found in Humboldt's idea of human development. But he eschewed any form of essentialism. So he could describe the goals of human development only in terms of maximal diversity, even eccentricity, in modes of life and "experiments of living." Reacting against dour Calvinist notions of man's sinful nature, he was prepared to valorize all manner of desires and impulses but could not impart a similar legitimacy to human nature itself, as rendered canonical, say, in the Aristotelian eudaimonistic tradition. The ability to integrate competing impulses through the notion or ideal of an organically integrated self (whether that self is construed as a given of nature or as an achievement of cultural investment and individual effort) therefore eluded him. Nor did his knowledge of educational methods and practices make him sanguine about the impact of the broad efforts of humanity and humanism, over time, in fostering and refining human nature, or its social face, through the mediation of culture and tradition.

Mill knew that individuals, especially when cut loose from communal and credal ties in a society that gives formal acknowledgement only to civil relations, would have difficulty in fruitfully defining identities for themselves. But his response, once again, was elitist: All was for the sake of a few emergent geniuses, whose worth would be redeemed by their teaching. Yet it remains in doubt whether experiments in living like those found in any inner-city tenderloin have any helpful relation to the production of genius; and it remains unclear as well how Mill's idiosyncratic geniuses can be expected to teach, or what benefit (if others popularize their ideas and lifestyles) can be expected to arise from the practice of their precepts. Experiments in living that are even a fraction as wide-ranging as those that Mill notionally urges will, of course, have their victims. The benefits of even one social experiment—say, no-fault divorce—are heavily counterbalanced by its costs. The idea that lifestyle experimentalism and eccentricity of lifestyles, pursued as intrinsic goods and equated with individuality and human development, must inevitably produce more good than harm seems not only counterintuitive but remarkably a priori by Utilitarian or empiricist standards.

Yet the outcome of Mill's abdication of the philosopher's role in speaking normatively about human nature and the human good is neither the anarchy that Willmoore Kendall feared nor the Edenic efflorescence of individuality for which Mill hoped. Rather, it has been the invasion of individual imagination by commercial, sectarian, and other interests that do not respect Mill's standards any more than they respect the individuals whose minds they seek to colonize. Clearly Mill is not responsible for acts that violate the standards he enunciated. But the fact remains that Mill did not reckon with the vulnerability of individuals, including adults, to manipulation and exploitation. The openness that Mill's standards intend to preserve becomes an invitation to parasites; and those standards themselves, enacted into law or enshrined as constitutional paradigms, become a sword and shield to the manipulators of public consciousness, exploiters of human weakness, and would-be enslavers of the human mind and spirit.

Guidance is no less problematic for being made a social or a public responsibility. A group or culture can err at least as catastrophically as an individual. But neither is the sanctity or sovereignty of the individual adequately protected once all responsible social agencies—whether communal or societal—have left the individual to his own devices. If history teaches us anything, it is that individuals need and deserve all the help they can get; and if the study of politics and society teaches us anything, it is that it is for the sake of such help that social agencies, from the family to the state, are legitimately formed, fostered, and, I say again, tolerated.

My argument in defense of human liberty rests on an expanded conception of the human person, assigning a penumbra of deserts to the human name and image, enlarging the sphere of protections beyond what Mill had in mind when he spoke of harm. But my argument goes beyond Mill in another way as well, since it

assigns positive deserts to human personhood, including a desert of honest information, fair labeling, and indeed liberal education of a kind that will enable its
recipients to rise somewhat above the human vulnerability to invidious and manipulative appeals and to scorn them with the same sort of scorn, although far
better justified, that Bentham applied to the idea of rights.

i. Liberties that go beyond self-expression.

A central plea of this chapter is that we need broader-gauge conceptions of our
human rights than those afforded in *On Liberty*. I derive these broader rights not
simply by stretching Mill's argument or making positive rights the precondition or
concomitant of negative rights, but by appeal to the idea of self-perfection. Rights,
and deserts of all kinds, including the right of free inquiry, free thought, and free
expression, derive from personhood. It is personhood that is thwarted vitally when
thought is curtailed or expression denied. But the function of law is the protection
and furtherance of personhood, not the protection of persons for the sake of what
they might have to say, nor the protection of personal sovereignty for the sake of
a diversity or experimentalism that will, in turn, on occasion yield interesting or
fruitful statements.

The function of the law, and more broadly of the social ethos, is not to keep
the world safe for science, or for discourse, or even for conversation. The life of
the mind is not in that sense the paramount good or goal, although such a life
does have intrinsic and not merely instrumental value. The substance of liberty is
not confined to the freedom of the mind to roam at will. Rather the substance of
liberty is the freedom of the whole person to act and grow, to forge relationships
and friendships, to learn and discover, but also to be nourished physically, to
flourish in sensibilities, to raise children and enjoy grandchildren in intact and
integrated families, neighborhoods, and communities.

To focus the rights of humanity in one, paramount negative freedom, the
freedom of the mind and mouth, pen and keyboard, is the same as to suppose
that a city can get by with libraries and does not need hospitals, playgrounds and
parks. Indeed, it is worse, since sheer non-interference with expression, the reduction of intellectual freedom to a merely negative liberty, robs minds and mouths
and pens of much that they might think or speak or say, and leaves the channels
of communication open to whatever combination of commercially promoted content might stimulate a demand and whatever melange of politically motivated
messages might make one.

The laissez faire approach to intellectual liberty will generate clutter, and in
time a glut, as any bulletin board or newsgroup where access is free and anony-
mous will demonstrate. In the information age, as in any age of affluence, the
tragedy of the commons is not neglect but pollution. The information superhigh-
way is already clogged with roadkill, and the ether is infested with viruses that did
not spring up by spontaneous generation but were artfully devised by the anony-
mous Schadenfreude of the alienated.

The same considerations that expand the idea of rights to the sphere of health
care, or that spread out the safety net by which a humane society husbands and

invests its resources (that is, the energies of its members) for the sustenance and education of all those whom it can aid effectually, also describe for us the limits of free speech—just as they help us to delineate what is actually help and what is not. The orienting principle of all rights is in the projects of persons, and there is no right of self-destruction or of fostering or facilitating destructiveness.

ii. Speech that is not about opinions.

I have clearly sought to narrow the reference class of the presumed liberties that are commonly sheltered under Mill's defense of intellectual freedom. Commercial speech is not my major concern here, but we need to note not just its presence but its methods, which are often subtle and indirect. We need to note too the nisus embedded in the dynamic of those methods, not only in undermining discourse (which is serious enough), but also in all sorts of social impacts and pathologies that advertisers and opinion makers shelter under the aegis of free speech. Society and society's children, to mention just one example, have paid and continue to pay a social cost from the promotion of free love or sexual revolution. But for the promoters of, say, steroid contraceptives, such costs are as irrelevant (or as necessary to suppress and remove from the realm of choice making) as are the claims that a given product heightens the risks of uterine or breast cancer.[34]

Leafing through a women's magazine at the supermarket checkout counter, I am not surprised to see this month's formulaic article on extramarital affairs tucked in among the contraceptive ads. It opens with a lead about the need for planning: One might imagine that spontaneity and passion are the issue, we are told. But an affair requires preparation and expense—from leg waxes to lingerie. Lifestyles are marketing clusters, and indirection in marketing need not be subtle: The reader has not gone beyond 200 words before she has been given a shopping list.

Perhaps commercial speech needs clearer labeling. If it has consequences for public policy and public welfare, perhaps the makers of public policy and the servants of public welfare, whether state funded or privately sustained, should at least be aware of what they are facing and find a voice and venue to respond. They will need more than their usual subtlety if they are to be effective, or even to be heard.

Let me be very concrete about this. If there is a link between extramarital affairs and the vicious abuse or murder of spouses by their outraged mates, that linkage should be established in the minds that matter, and not just in the methods of the police. Yet this is not the sort of linkage that campaigns appealing to anger over the abuse and murder of spouses have singled out for attention. In fact, such campaigns tend to treat the very mention of such a nexus as part of the abuse, or as an apologetic in its behalf.[35] Nor is such a linkage a matter that the purveyors of the lifestyle goods that can be listed in a checklist feature article are likely to want prominently discussed among the presumptive pros and cons thoughtfully, titillatingly, lovingly dwelt upon in the pages between the advertisements for the hair dyes, hideaways, and shampoos that feature in the shopping list of indiscretion.

I have argued that Mill's intentions, and more critically, his argument, do not extend to the protection of violent or violative pornography, racist caricature, incitements to violence against the members of a class, race, sex, ethnic group—or humanity at large. For what opinions, whole or partial truths are conveyed by sado-masochistic materials on the Internet? What form of enlightenment is promised by the use of gore as a token penalty or reward in video games like Mortal Kombat, or by the crude humor of video chess games that graphically represent a rape when the queen is taken? Is there an ideational content that merits shelter under the cloak of Mill's defense of intellectual freedom in rock music that promotes suicide, parricide, racial violence, rape, violence against police officers—not by enunciating a doctrine but by mere suggestion, celebration, and innuendo? Clearly Mill's conclusions are being applied where his arguments do not reach and where they were never intended to apply. Mill's arguments—his appeals to intellectual advancement and the rise of truth—do not protect representations that dehumanize persons or promote genocide or that inculcate cruelty or destructiveness as values, and they should not. Nor should they be allowed to protect the dissemination of technical instructions for the implementation of mass violence, teleplunder, arson in the cities or the forests, or other sorts of depersonalized brutality.

Once we get past the initial phase of denial—that is, the denial that such incitements take place, that destructive caricatures are drawn, that there is anyone at all who would be influenced by such portrayals or who would instigate wanton acts of vandalism, theft, invasion of privacy, sabotage, indiscriminate murder, or fraud—we encounter a subtler form of denial: the claim that regulation of information flow is too sensitive a matter for public concern, that even the critique of representations of any sort is too subjective a business to be a concern of social response, let alone of legislation. Pornography is not presented as an assault on the human image, an assault whose frisson derives from the differential between dignities degraded and the levels to which they are abased. Rather, it is described in terms of the "graphic" or "explicit" portrayal of various anatomical parts and physiological acts, whose representation may or may not be "offensive" to some.

This characterization is naive or disingenuous in the extreme. It is stunning to see philosophers, in particular, who long ago abandoned the "picture" theory of language and expression still clinging to it when they speak of pornography in terms of the "graphic" or "explicit." Representation is always the portrayal of X as ϕ. The response of a viewer, especially the affective response, is attained not by some "willing suspension of disbelief," but as a by-product of the recognition of what is represented. When a human individual is represented as degraded, the immediate emotive impact is one of dehumanization. That response can be suppressed or rejected, leading to pity on the one hand or cruelty on the other, by a dialectic that Spinoza brilliantly described (*Ethics*, Definitions of the Emotions, 38). But when the affect is made a goal of gratification, we have not merely cruelty or its portrayal but the roots of sadism. Is that an ideational content, a germ of progress? Or is it an adventitious product? What Mill took for granted and therefore did not notice as a material premise of his program now needs to be stated explicitly: *Pace* the ardent adherents of bad-boy sensibilities, the Marquis de Sade was a depraved individual, not the leader of an intellectual vanguard.

Once the affect of cruelty is a matter of gratification, a hedonic goal, there is a corresponding appetite to be addressed; the act of degradation itself, or its imagery, which is itself a degradation, can be marketed, made an object of prurient but also hedonic interest and a source of artifactual value. At this point not only is the dignity of the initial object degraded, but so is that of others who are assimilated to her image by the psychology of association. Permissions are extended by the very publicity of the degradation. And, since we are social creatures and the dynamic of cruelty began with identification, the degradation of the object generates a concomitant degrading of the outlook and character of the viewer or participant.

At issue here is not the merely symptomatic question of what an unreflective bystander might find "offensive," say in the portrayal of the human form, but the core of the ethos that is a society's lifeblood. It is the colorations of a culture's ethos that are the clearest markers of decadence or morbidity, the clearest indications of the regard or contempt that we hold toward one another as sentient and sensitive beings. Is there a proper moral concern with such outcomes? Clearly there is. The tenor of human character is the core subject of morals, for the ethos is what informs our actions. Is there a proper social concern? Once again there is. Cultures and the vehicles of culture are the seedbeds of the ethos that expresses and perpetuates the traits of character by which we live with one another, amicably or desperately, peaceably or in the anxious anomie of alienation. Is there a proper legal concern? There can be. Jeffrey Dahmers are made, not born.

The objection to a legal, programmatic concern on the part of government or other social agencies with violative pornography is that such efforts inevitably involve attempts to legislate or coerce morality. Morality, it is assumed, is a private matter. But the first premise, about coercion, is false, and the second is equivocal. For law need not mean the police, and character is never wholly a private concern. Of course there is a sphere of private morality. The open-ended cultivation of the virtues is too long, too arduous, and too many-branched a path to be specified by the exigent and sanctioned imperatives of the law, or even the neighborhood — although, in my view, the machinery of the law and the standards and atmosphere of the neighborhood should be used to make that path and its byways more open and accessible.

But if the notion is that laws and social pressures can and should have nothing to say about the framing of an ethos, that notion is far more problematic — certainly not a question to be begged by appeal to an equivocation on the familiar private sense of the idea of morality. I think the claim is false, precisely because culture is the vehicle of morality and culture is a social, not a personal creation. Consider the alternative: If morality is not legislated, even indirectly, then what will be the subtext of our laws? Some arbitrary construction that has, *per hypothesi*, no relation to right and wrong? And if moral standards are not made expectations, not even by the pressures of public manners and opinion, what motivational standards will hold the field? Those of commercial, sectarian, partisan, and factional interests that care nothing for Mill's standards or any other than their own?

Accepting the keystone of liberalism, that laws must be minimal to allow maximal scope to human freedom, we still reach the view (well stated in Islamic jurisprudence) that laws legislate to sustain what is right and good and to restrain what is wrong and evil. As a liberal, I must add—especially with the images of embattled Algiers and prostrate Kabul vividly in mind—the laws must not attempt to do so in every case conceivable. This is so not because there are no objectifiable standards of right and wrong, but because the human condition is too complex and delicate and the realm of human action too vast and ramified to permit a simple rule, let alone a government agency, to enter and act without violating the freedom and individuality that laws exist to protect and sustain. Typically, laws focus, as they should, on wrongs that are palpable and indisputable, extreme in consequence, significance or extent. The goods that laws pursue must, similarly, bear a social interest that reaches the threshold of public concern. And the laws themselves must cross even that threshold equitably, gingerly, and with respect. The goods that laws serve must not only stimulate or demand legislative attention but raise issues deep enough to foster and warrant public acceptance of the costs and inconveniences of legislative intervention and governmental engagement. There are principles to be respected, trusts to be kept—the first of which is the trust reposed in government as the champion and not the bully of human individuality, creativity, and personality.

Taking pornography as a test case, the defining issue is not offensiveness, a standard that is subjective in its measure and scope and in its ictus. Individuals vary in what offends them and in the extent to which they are offended by a given act or expression, or to which they say they are. Beyond that, when I speak of the ictus of the act, I mean that the affront itself is subjective, a blow to the sensibilities, not to the body or the pocketbook. For that very reason, legal authorities are rightly chary of intervention; and they often treat such affronts, nominal or notional as they are, slightingly. Yet we do not hesitate to condemn and restrain acts of libel, where the ictus again (or much of it) is in the mind. We rightly restrict pandering and sexual soliciting, incest and child pornography. These do not differ in the locus of the damage from several types of commercialized demoralization that are not restricted—or that are indeed defended as commercial avenues to a special kind of enlightenment.

Assaults to sensibilities may deserve legal attention. But in the case of pornography, we need not and should not rest our case on the subjective dimensions of the offense, where able advocates who wish to classify pornography simply as a special case of free speech, speech that might offend, have knowingly located it. What arouses legislative concern that goes beyond the issues of sensibility and privacy is the potential in pornography for palpable, indeed wholesale harm. Here the question we must ask ourselves, as we scrutinize the principles on which we legislate, especially against the backdrop of Mill's liberal manifesto, is when does the utility principle, on which all of Mill's legal interventions rest, reenter the picture, so that data can be evaluated and impacts assessed?

Clearly a critical test for expressive acts is the likelihood of their producing violence. Leering or tasteless representations on the order of "What the Butler Saw" might be deemed morally objectionable as acts of violation, in that they debase the human image and sour the ethos of intimacy, even if they do not reach the threshold of legal response. But some representations so degrade the human image and so abase human dignity as to amount to clear and present dangers, even though their impact may be diffuse or delayed. A time bomb is no less a clear and present danger because its impact is delayed or because its victims are an indeterminate number of a somewhat ill-defined class—for example, subway riders.

Where a jury is capable of finding that a given representation or source of representations is harmful or dangerous to humanity, say, by its degradation of the human image or its dehumanization or demonization of an individual or a group, there may be grounds for a legislative response. For, as I suggested in chapter 1, dehumanization is a device for excluding others from moral regard; and demonization is a device for legitimating violence against them. Like any legal principle, the principle of recognizing that some representations are dangerous can be abused. But it won't do to say that the judgment called for is too vague or arbitrary to be fairly made. Judgments about such matters are no more problematic than judgments about malice aforethought or *mens rea* in the realm of intention, or about restraint of trade or environmental pollution in the realm of consequences. Legal tests and standards of evidence are precisely what laws and courts are called upon to devise and marshall. And the basic standard of potential for harm, demarcating what is morally noxious in a grave enough way to become an object of public concern, is less arbitrary and problematic than the presently used vague and concertedly flimsy notion of offensiveness to community standards.

iii. Harmful speech.

What, then, of harm? I do not concede that physical or fiscal harm is the only harm that matters, or that victims of a crime or tort must be named or nameable individuals. I have in fact urged that society has a legitimate and vital interest in protecting the ethos that gives definition to its project and that underlies the possibility and value of its survival, let alone its self-integration and advance. But I agree that most of what concerns the ethos, as a moral matter, is beyond the purview of the law—not because laws have no business with morals, but because most moral adjustments and concerns do not reach the threshold of significance that warrants legal intervention and because most are too delicate for the clumsy operations of the public apparatus to address case by case. For this reason, it is not improper for laws to focus on utilitarian standards, since these are the most palpable and least controvertible. It is here that liberals must face the music and submit their empirical claims to empirical tests.

Exponents of media interests are fond of saying that media violence is a safety valve allowing the harmless release or sublimation of energies, anxieties, hostilities, and aggressions that might, if frustrated or pent, cause real damage. Evidence has been mounting in recent years that with certain kinds of representations and expressions, this brand of denial or defense simply will not wash. The backup claim that television, movies, and sensate literature are the mere passive mirrors of (a decadent or violent) society—rather than the active instruments or megaphones, permission givers, or popularizers[36] of standards sensationalized from the ambient extremes — is particularly disingenuous. It assumes that the makers and users of cultural artifacts simply do not know what they are doing. But many of them, especially the most effective, know exactly what they are doing.

Dashiell Hammett *intended* to produce sensate literature to feed the unwholesome appetites of what he viewed as a decadent society, and thus to accelerate its fall.[37] Steven King could not be as effective as he is if he did not know what he is doing, or understand the emotional impact of his work on its audience. Television people research such questions with the same care that the cigarette industry used in researching the addictive properties of nicotine. When the small screen repeatedly shows the rape scene through the eyes of the rapist, the images projected in our homes are as attuned to the sensibilities of the viewing audience was O'Brien's choice of rats in the final torment and temptation that will break the spirit of Winston in Orwell's 1984.

The standard I am proposing with regard to symbolic or representational violence is similarly an empiric one. If the issue is to be one of utilities and not of arbitrary privilege for politically potent interests, let the studies be done and the damage assessed. The techniques of measurement are in place, and the great strength of Utilitarianism is that the harms and benefits on which it concentrates are measurable. So let us see, without special pleading, whether certain forms of expression that are not in fact expressions of opinion, or that express opinions only or largely as a vehicle for venting hatred or fomenting generalized resentment, have as part of their effect an impact that heightens the level of violence in our society, against persons in general, against women, against parents, against persons of one or another racial, ethnic, or religious background, against homosexuals — for no one should be beaten senseless or murdered for his sexual orientation.

Let us investigate, impartially and without the kind of backroom lobbying that allows newspapers to exempt themselves from the child labor laws or broadcasters to monopolize the airwaves at no cost, whether sado-masochistic expressions, drug or suicide or parricide promotion, or apocalyptic racism, have palpable negative effects on our society. Then let us regulate and restrict those expressive acts that are shown to do damage. The V-chip is not the answer, but simply a standard buck-passing appeal to our protectiveness of children — an advertising gimmick: child appeal linked to a bait and switch. The damage and the danger we confront are not confined to children; and the idea that the fare provided by the World Wrestling Federation could not foster sadism anywhere, or that the TV programming that any indulgent parent might permit, or ignore, or use for baby-sitting is *eo ipso* perfectly acceptable for children, is no longer acceptable on a priori grounds but must stand up to empirical test and refutation.

In a market-driven society, audience is the court of last resort for any mode of amusement or communication. Why not some effort at educating more critical and discriminating audiences, instead of working on the assumption that all reading, all opera, all art, music or poetry is worthwhile — and all created equal? Some followers of Mill object to the mobilizing of social disapproval, say, in group boycotts of the broadcasters or sponsors of materials or representations that a community finds repugnant. They see here the very pressures against which Mill spoke out. But consumer sovereignty is as much a reality as are the market forces that feed and are fed by, say, rap music and videos, or combat videogames — the market forces to which the purveyors make their ultimate appeal. *Seventeen* Magazine has avoided religious topics for years, not because the subject is uninteresting to adolescent girls, but because it is a focus of anxiety to potential boycotters who do not think *Seventeen* the proper vehicle for religious discourse. The motives of the boycotters may be as unsound as those of the publishers, but the effectiveness of the threat demonstrates an avenue of response that could be more judiciously explored if thinking rather than raw prejudice and fear were enlisted, and if thinking were not hamstrung by the notion that no one but the market makers has any business having views about what teenagers should be reading.

What is critical, if the market is to act wisely, is education, including the education of taste and judgment — not indoctrination, which does nothing to contain prurience, but the growth of sophistication and discrimination. Caution is needed, since education is so often the politician's counterpart to the football punt. Intractable social problems are laid at the schoolhouse door, as though schools, rather than parents and peers, were our chief role models. But schools help. To name just one problem area, that of our human diversity in a pluralistic, multicultural society: Schools can provide a primer, as it were, in tolerance; so can the military and other forms of national service, at a very experiential level. America has made some halting steps away from normativizing an artificial, white-bread amalgam identified proudly in the 1950s under the rubric of conformity — perhaps the last vestige of Zangwill's melting-pot idea. We have not yet wholly given up the notion that the chief function of the public schools is to serve as the crucible of conformity, or of whatever newer standards of political correctness may be offered to replace it. Thus intellectual interests are neglected, and the vulgarization and politicization of the idea of diversity, for example, has rendered it down to a celebration of stereotypic identity markers while attaching to the pluralistic ideal the same repressive anxieties that long accompanied the conformist paradigm. Deeper and more sensitively guided study of literature, of history, of biology would be far more to the point than painful role-playing exercises and noisy sloganeering. The more cognitive path is always harder than lip service, but it produces results that are more lasting and more real, because it preserves the content and not just the name of education.

In addressing the negativities in the media, however, the immediate task is simpler than the long-term one of educating the taste and analytical sophistication that frustrate prejudice. Why not start with full disclosure of the sources of income that support any published or broadcast communication? That certainly is no panacea, but I suspect that the policy, if implemented, would have powerful effects. We can get some idea of its prospective impact by the hue and cry that echoes even suggestions of any form of media regulation, which is labeled "chilling" by those whose practices it might affect. But I have trouble understanding in Madisonian terms the notion that political influence, *or* media exposure, can legitimately be bought and sold through a junket, an emolument, or a lunch. Perhaps the nexus lies closer to Madison Avenue. And if such practices really are perfectly sound, there should be no objection to public knowledge of them, just as we publish the scores of health department inspections of restaurant kitchens.

iv. *Harm to self and help to the ethos.*

Rights are a species of desert, and deserts are the claims of beings. Deserts, prima facie, are the program or project that a being defines and develops in the affirmation of an identity. It is because all deserts are ontically affirmative at base that there are no rights to harm the self—no right of suicide or self-mutilation, self-degradation or self-destruction, although heroism and martyrdom, when they affirm the dignity of personhood and uphold humane values, are another matter entirely.

I take it to be an authentically Jewish view that it is paradoxical to urge a right to harm one's own genuine interests, and I locate the metaphysics underlying the exposure of that paradox in the positive valuation that the Jewish tradition places on being—not because it is the handiwork of God but rather (proceeding from moral insight upward) as the *warrant* of our inference that being is God's handiwork and expressive act. To apply the relevant insight concretely: It would be absurd, say, to make a right of sadomasochism, even among consenting adults. I link sadism and masochism here not only because they are linked clinically, but because the moral standpoint (despite the commonplace confusion of morals with altruism) regards the interests of ego as no less worthy of consideration than those of the other.

Kant might imagine, along with others in the liberal tradition—Mill, Locke, and surely Hobbes, who was no liberal but laid out the ground on which liberalism pitches its tents—that self-interest can take care of itself, and that self-serving cannot be moral, since it would not naturally be praised. But we know enough of the perils of internalized resentment, the hazards of ambient hatred and rejection, and the struggles of personal integration to know that the constitution of an integrated personality and plan are achievements indeed and well worthy of praise. Further, we can hardly presume that self-interest will be adequately understood, let alone effectually pursued, without social support, in infancy and childhood or beyond.

Where social and economic pressures militate in behalf of euthanasia or infanticide, the task of society is to combat them. Doing so means not simply and crudely opposing such practices politically, but providing the kind of sustenance to human life, health, and well-being that will make the hard choices rare. Again, if there are social and cultural currents, including ideational currents, that disrupt the environment in which individuals can discover their own identity and devise their own life plan, it is the task of society to channel those currents more constructively, to foster the emergence of selves—not to form them, but to free them and nurture them, allowing them to discover their own paths of growth.

Many of the social pathologies on which traditional religions and moral systems frown, it is said, should not be restricted or even disapproved, since they harm no one, or no one other than their willing participants. But there is no victimless crime, and that for two reasons: first, because all the members of a society are interlinked with one another, so the motorcyclist who rides without a helmet will almost certainly share the heavy cost of his head injuries not only with family members but also with the co-insured and with the taxpayers who must mend and heal him; second, because the status of victim does not exclude the freely consenting adult. The alcoholic or compulsive gambler—or the impulsive gambler, for that matter, who gambles and loses what he cannot afford—shares his habit or his lapse, and his losses, with his family, and, in a lesser degree with co-workers and society at large. But he is himself, by many measures, the most damaged victim of his own behavior.

Prostitution and drug addiction, similarly, have multiple victims: the family of the john or user, whose trust is violated, whose hopes are hazarded or dashed, and who are exposed, among other detriments, to AIDS. These victims include even the unborn, who may contract AIDS and other diseases in the birth canal. But hardly negligible among the victims is the individual prostitute or drug abuser, who perhaps freely chose a course that jeopardizes every chance of human fulfillment. If the libertarian slogan is mooted at this point, urging that my body is my property, to do with as I like, we must ask the very Jewish question, when did the self become property? And doesn't even property demand responsibility?

The work of society and of culture, their sole task, is the fostering of identities and the favoring of circumstances in which identities can self-define and flourish. Despite the appeals of many advocates to the contrary, I have suggested, pornography is not quite the best starting point or vehicle in this task of self-definition. I say this advisedly, even bearing in mind the mixed results I know of in one or two cases where something of the sort did occur. I'm not at all sure that the casualties and occupational hazards of the industry are worth the payoff. But in a positive vein, there are many fruitful avenues to be developed and explored. Legally, institutionally, societally, the task is one of richly endowing the moral environment with the models and materials that will allow and promote human self-definition. It is certainly and centrally the task of the family to provide such nurturance. Communal agencies like churches and synagogues, Y's and Jewish centers, neighborhood groups and clubs, sports teams, exercise groups, dance clubs, and community bands and orchestras can help individuals to give definition to their personalities and foster the emergence of more developed identities. And that is a relevant matter not only for the young. By such means, communal enterprises like these combat anomie and demoralization. They not only build self-esteem but help to give it grounds.

Government lacks primary expertise here, and we tend to prefer that these tasks be undertaken privately. We rightly worry that when this kind of moral work is done by societal rather than communal agencies, it will be done badly. Not that governments do all things badly. But a certain crudeness of touch and blandness of taste naturally result from seeking a lowest common denominator. We are rightly chary of slighting individuality, and of the adverse reactions that impersonality can provoke. These are among the reasons, surely, why we do not, if we can help it, prefer to have our children raised by others but would rather keep this onerous task (or at least control of it) to ourselves, within the family and in institutions that are as close as possible to the oversight of the family.

Even when we pursue activities that seek to integrate our communities more broadly than can the family or the neighborhood, we see increasingly the need for sensitivity to interests, outlooks, and sensibilities that are "sectional," as Mill might phrase it—ethnic, regional, gender, and generational identities. Every folk song and piece of teenage slang is founded on the notion that "We alone know what sex is" or what life or death are. The exclusivity of that "we" is naive and potentially dangerous. But it should not be too rudely awakened. It rests on the negation and exclusion of what is seen as alien or exotic, old fashioned or simply old hat. This is a negation that we all must learn to grow beyond, by coming to see our social identities in positive rather than negative terms. But nurturance of that kind of growth requires sensitivity and sophistication.

Granted that jingoism is not an exclusivity that everyone, in the best case, is simply jolted out of, there is a public interest in the forging of larger than local identities. National service is a good vehicle for such efforts, because it draws energies and attentions away from locality and idiosyncrasy and toward a common goal and task. Regardless of the vehicle, there is a public responsibility to foster deeper, sounder, larger, and at the same time more individual conceptualizations of the self and its project than would typically emerge in, say, a neighborhood playground or an ethnically homogeneous recreation program. Clearly there are cross-pressures between the public responsibility for fostering personhood and the dangers of standardization, with its relatively empty secular and minimalist notions of "good citizenship." In acknowledgement of those cross-pressures, pluralistic societies seek means of sustaining highly varied approaches to the formulation of ideals and the forging of identities.

The tax deductibility of philanthropic contributions to educational, social, recreational, religious, and cultural bodies is one rather successful means. It provides both an index and a suitably pluralistic medium for the valuing of all sorts of programmatic efforts. By proportioning state support to articulated communal interest, and by offering that support obliquely, through tax forgiveness, it preserves a high degree of independence in each particular effort and permits self-defined communities to formulate their own objectives and devise their own means of pursuing them. Programs grow, change, and disappear according to the effectiveness of their message and the appeal of their goals. No private agency, however, is sufficient to attain all the social goods that lie in the public charge. And none is so infallible, we might say, with Mill in mind, as to be left to define its goals without let or restraint. Critically, for example, why should we condone the abuse of indirect public subsidies by abdicating the responsibility to ensure that they are not appropriated by hate groups, criminal gangs, or mind-controlling cults?

Public education, at least in recent years, has sagged under the weight of its responsibilities and has not, as effectively as might be wished, promoted the emergence of personal, communal, or national identities. Public libraries, public broadcasting, arts and cultural programming, although less frequently and less presumptively criticized, have produced even more mixed results vis-à-vis the ethos. For here, despite the mingled hand-wringing and self-congratulation, there is often not even lip service to the shallow and minimal educational ideal of good citizenship. Indeed, the mere suggestion that there is a public responsibility for the public ethos is likely to be met with charges of big-brotherism or Pavlovian conditioning. The idea that public (or even private) expenditures on art or music should aim to enlarge the sensibilities of the public is rhetorically conflated with socialist realism or fascist kitsch. And the idea that music (or fiction) is an important public institution, a realm in which identities form and spirits grow, a vehicle through which, as Aristotle suggested (*Politics* VIII, 5, 1340a, 11–29), our moral experience can be enlarged, is liable to be conflated with a Stalinist arts policy. Yet the ethos that is thus left to the intense and highly focused vagaries of commercial and political manipulation is counted on in every public institution and presumed upon in the most elementary of our notionally private acts.

My final proposal here is a modest one: that we should regard and treat our cultural institutions as if they matter — since they do — not merely to the welfare and survival of our society but to the worth and credibility of its claims upon existence. If Little League and Pop Warner are really where characters are forged — if these are really the places where boys become men and learn the meaning of teamwork and cooperation, not to mention masculinity — then we ought to reflect on the rules by which we play and study the lessons actually taken home from the playing field. If the arts are as important to us as we say they are and as the attendance at arts events testifies — for it outdistances the attendance at all sports events — then we ought to consider what our arts are saying about us and what we are saying through them about our visions of ourselves and one another. Ballet says as much about us as baseball, and if ballet is decadent, that is as serious a problem in our culture and mode of education as is the corruption of our sports.

The reflection I am calling for is something we need to do publicly and deliberatively, through the boards and committees of our arts and sports and other cultural institutions. That, I believe, is the key to escaping paternalism in our decision making on these matters. That is, conjoint, deliberative discussions are just the opposite of the sort of substitution of judgment that is morally problematic because it robs individuals of their free agency and usurps from them the dignity of choice. It is the manipulative and surreptitious preemption of judgment by the makers and purveyors of destructive and exploitative representations that is paternalistic in the morally objectionable sense. For the advocates of such representations rarely admit publicly either its intensions or its impacts and are loath even to discuss the matter, let alone to deliberate about the scope and ictus of its costs. The proper, and non-paternalistic, response is not a countervailing manipulation of the media (which will only succumb to the sensate imagery and idiom of what it professes or intends to counteract) and not a triumphalist attempt to impose uniformity or conformity to some preestablished standard of minimal (or maximal) acceptability, but a collective assumption of moral responsibility and responsiveness on the part of those who generate the imagery that is the moral life blood and spiritual breath of any culture. Reaching beyond the invidious display of the symbolisms of wealth and power that attach themselves to art and sport and all cultural institutions, we should deliberate together with a view to the enrichment of the human experience, pronouncing to ourselves, through our institutions in all their diversity, who it is that we think we are. It is by doing this that we can escape the trap of merely paying lip service, when fund-raising time rolls around, to the notion that our cultural expressions are the vehicle of our communal memory, social identity, and civilizational future.

The Rights and Wrongs
of Nations

Despite the metaphor of a common descent and the fiction of ethnic homogeneity, nations are more the stuff of history than of birth — just as cultures are more the stuff of birth than of independently achieved conviction. Mazzini's world of nations, each situated in a single contiguous land mass, providentially fenced against invasion and warned against the hubris of expansion by the natural barriers of mountains, deserts, seas, and rivers, was always more ideal than fact. Hegel's pure types were more the reflex of an armchair tourist's fancy than the realization of any authentic encounter with the races and cultures he so pungently described. Outsiders often typify extremes, making essential what seems exotic, negating the deep unity of human experience. Whatever that experience may be, it is never, while we live, static or uniform — not in individuals and still less in groups.

Nation by nation, minorities are always with us — the *ger*, the metic, the helot and *mawla*, the person of color, or of too little or none. Their numbers, as in American cities, may outpace the ranks of the notional majority. Their pedigree, in town or on the land, like that of the Jews in Muslim Spain, may antedate the title of the notionally indigenous. Despite the claims of irredentists, purists, and essentialists, there is no one ethnicity per land, and no one idea per ethnicity. The conviction that there is or should be is the kerosene of ethnic cleansing, leaking or welling up from historical false consciousness. It ignores the diversity even at the heart of *soi disant* homogeneity — the Tatars of Russia; the Dai of China; the Kurds of Turkey, Iraq, and Iran; the Turks of Germany; the Russians of Latvia; the Welsh, Irish, Greeks, and Pakistanis of England; the Filipinos and Filipinas of Japan; the Indians of Fiji and South Africa; the Chinese of Montreal; and the Koreans of Kuwait. It also ignores the latency of difference and potential for change within a nation, in the variety of constructions that individuals may put upon their identities from one historical moment to the next, exposing its dependence on a simplistic and reductive externalism that seeks to pigeonhole the *other* as a type.

Mazzini's map today more accurately projects the play of an old-fashioned board game than the realities of the human globe. In our world, minorities arise within minorities; the alchemy of opportunity and grievance can, in a generation, make a nation where there was none. Or the horror of genocide, no recent invention and no European monopoly—or simply the eager assimilation of conquered to conquerors, or of conquerors to the culture of the conquered—can leave one nation where once there were many and where even the surviving nation is hugely altered in the wrack of history. Hamadhani (968–1008), a celebrator of dissembling, and of the truth about change, saw in the iridescence of human populations not the least of what he archly called "the tricks of time":

> God may mingle His creatures in form or in style.
>   And some, with forms hyper-protean—
> By night they are Arabs, clear of birth and of blood;
>   By day they become Nabataean.

A Nabataean, in Hamadhani's days, was a Syriac-speaking peasant—alien vassal to the conquering elite who proudly claimed the name of Arabs—a title that in other times, dismissively, meant Bedouins.

Language and culture are real. The boundaries they create, marked by nuances of phonology and ritual, are not impassable. Yet they are dangerous. For these pickets mark not the mere topography of some geographic domain but the deadlier distance between *us* and *them*, free and slave, foe and friend, the forbidden bride or licit victim. The moieties of blood between Hutu and Tutsi; Serb, Bosnian, and Croat; Chechen or Russian; Georgian or Abkhazian—or that such markers fail fully to segregate in polyglot nations like the United States or the former Soviet empire—are not those of lineage; still less are they discrete gene pools. They are pools of blood in a ghastlier, more vivid sense: our own and theirs, to be spilled in our cause or in theirs.

My purpose in this final chapter is first to ask what a nation is, what makes possible the existence of nations. Then I want to ask two normative questions: first, how the existence of nations is justified; and second, how the legitimacy of nations can avoid falling foul of the exclusivity problem we considered in chapter 1. My thesis is that a nation is a large community, bound together by a shared sense of identity and capable of acting in concert. It is this possibility of coordinated action that can give legitimacy to nations. Nations, I will argue, are justified by their projects—more pointedly, by their special capabilities in pursuing projects of genuine worth. The inward-turning characteristic of nations, as of all communities, then, must be justified by the contributions that such turning can foster. It follows that the goods served by a nation's capabilities are not legitimately confined within the boundaries it claims, although such goods will naturally be achieved more effectually where the reciprocities that fund and energize them are most effectively in operation.

1. What Is a Nation?

Nations exist only insofar as they have a cause, just or unjust, wise or foolish, generous or deluded. They survive and thrive only by enlisting action to their cause. *Action* here, contrary to the usage of the movies and the Third Reich, is not synonymous with violence. It may be creative or destructive; intellectual, spiritual, or artistic; moral, social, or cultural; but it does not exclude suffering or death. Nations die when their cause is dead, when there is no one to live by it, or die for it. Nations have never been impassable geographically, impermeable genetically, impenetrable economically, impervious culturally, pristine or inscrutable linguistically. Yet war can call home exiles and expatriates as well as make them. When war threshes the nations,[1] it tests the least named but farthest reaching bond of human fellowship, the readiness of some to die for others. That readiness makes *these* others more than merely others. It sets them apart from the rest, who are now called "them."

Morally, we ascribe a right of self-determination not just to individuals but to nations. Nations in this sense are not mere populations with some arbitrary trait in common like eye color or obesity. Still less are they to be identified by some sheerly ascriptive trait like a telephone dialing code.[2] Nations are communities, and communities, more often than not, are natural groups. This does not mean that they are organisms, or genetic isolates, or wholly self-sufficient markets, or indomitable military machines. Rather, communities are natural groups because membership in them is not purely voluntary; and obligation toward them is a matter, in the first instance, not of contracts or abstractions like money, but of realia like interdependence and existential need. Our obligations in communities depend in the first instance not on what we have agreed on but on who we are, where we stand, what we can be expected to contribute. This matter, the primacy of roles and expectations in social identity, is a given of human existence, part of what is meant by *zoon politikon*.

All communities have a cause, not always in the subjective and forward-looking sense of a shared idea, but minimally in the objective and retrospective sense of antecedent and persistent conditions for standing together — shared need.[3] It is in this sense that communities are natural groups, not mere voluntary associations. The family is a paradigm, but hardly the only instance of such a natural group, as the rhetoric of blood and brotherhood, taken literally, might suggest. Clans and tribes are also communities, although their members may be kin only notionally. Neighborhoods too are communities, if their denizens have some common life.

A people is a rather large group of human beings who identify with one another in the critical sense that they regard and treat each other's interests in some measure as their own. Identification can mean sharing a common goal or vision. But the members of a people may differ in their personal goals and well may differ in their visions of the common goal. If individual visions are to conjoin, without suppression of individuality, the broad base they share must be rather generic and in many ways undemanding. Yet peoplehood does entail community, and here — as in friendship — interests, and thus identities, are shared. There is mutual support. In some way, the members of a people sustain one another's goals, not regardless of their content but not solely by reference to that content either.

The mere fact that you are my neighbor or my fellow countryman, if these notions are to have any operative force, enlists me in some way in your project — not as intimately and intensely as if we literally were brothers, spouses, parent and child, but in just as real a sense — in view of the interests we share. Our linkage to one another facilitates our conjoint pursuit of common interests and fosters our sustenance of one another's private interests and projects as well. With peoples, this linkage is not a matter solely of vicinage but of appropriated identity. Thus peoples share not simply real estate but pain and shame, hope and fear. Peoplehood seeks embodiment in geography not because land is its essence — for the country is not the nation — but for the sake of action, since it is in a land that peoples as such most readily can act.

A people is a collectivity whose members conceive of their interests not only as linked but as constituted in some measure by one another's good, and who act on that conception. The roots of such identification may lie in a sense of common history, common situation, or common destiny. Typically these are combined, but they need not be. What matters is the identification, especially its practical side. This is what makes communities, for we have defined a community as a group whose members depend on one another.[4] Their ability to do so in a stable, effective, and ongoing manner requires some form of mutual recognition. But not just any community is a people. A people is a collectivity large enough, bold enough, and diverse enough to breast the seas of historical circumstance and change.

It is because peoplehood involves conscious participation in a shared identity that nations can be born and live and die. They are not immemorial features of the landscape like mountains and seas — or rather, like mountains and seas, they grow and erode, swell or subside, vanish or shift. That peoples are natural groups means only that their existence depends on no explicit compact or formal undertaking. It does not mean that they are temporal archetypes, in the manner, say, that Toynbee — or Hegel — imagined.

It may seem invidious to mention size. But I think numbers are critical, if peoplehood entails group persistence over time. Boldness and diversity are critical too, for history is rarely gentle. To weather its storms demands a certain robustness. To hold terrain without quailing or vanishing at the threat of interference and to sustain itself across the generations, a people needs numbers. But it also needs the diversity that numbers make possible. Just as a gene pool needs diversity as a sump of variability and responsiveness to altered circumstances, a people needs diversity for the division of cultural labors and as a reservoir of intellectual, technological, and moral strengths. What is evolution in a gene pool is experience in a nation.

An ethnicity need not be a people. Whatever objective or ascriptive characteristics are used to differentiate one group from another,[5] and whatever genetic heritage they may share, a group will not begin to function as a people without the internal bonds of identification. A common language, culture, or religion may strengthen such bonds, but these affinities may also reflect the sense of common interests and commitments, grievances or opportunities that makes for peoplehood. They need not be its cause. Indeed a nation risks attenuation of its national life if any one of these alone is taken as its raison d'être, just as it reaches stultification if it makes survival alone its goal.

Reproduction is necessary in any population, both to replace lost members and to preserve genetic diversity. A common homeland is precious to a nation, as a nursery, an economic base, and a locus of national life. But what makes a people effectual as a people is neither shared land nor shared genes, but a shared sense of identity. This sense of identity is more the cause than the effect of any tendency of peoples toward endogamy or territoriality. Vis-à-vis such an identity, the countryside and even the gene pool are instrumental goods — resources of the commonweal and emblems of the unity that allows coordinated action.

Nations do not coalesce around just any ascriptive trait, but peoplehood does have an ascriptive dimension. It depends on what individuals think about one another and themselves as members of a group. The need for mutual recognition gives nationhood a subjective side. But it has an objective side as well. For the practical impact of group identification can be tested by circumstance, and often is. Indeed, there is no survival without action, not merely because life requires defense but because life is activity. National life entails the concerted or coordinated activity of a people. A nation is a people that has learned to act.

Omar Dahbour points to two rival accounts of nationhood: "primordialist" and "modernist." The first traces the birth of nations to factors such as kinship, geography, sentiment, or history; the other, to such factors as cultural attitudes, social aspirations, or political beliefs.[6] Since our task here is not the historical one of explaining the rise of the nation-state and does not depend on identifying a single cause in the rise of modern nations or the ideology of nationalism, it is not necessary for us to choose between these rival models. What is needed for our purposes is a conception of nationhood broad enough and generic enough to avoid procrustean quarrels with the facts on the ground but still pointed enough to differentiate nations from other phenomena and groups. We start from the recognition that nations are human groups — communities, indeed peoples — and we differentiate them from other such groups by the articulation that makes possible concerted action. The bonds of identification that differentiate peoples from other groups or groupings of individuals and that are prerequisite to coordinated action may rest on a variety of factors, real or mythic, but necessarily notional. Clearly, as the facts of history and current events reveal, homogeneity of an ethnic or linguistic or religious character is no more necessary to nationhood than is a shared ideology or credo. But all of these factors can contribute to nationhood and are valued (or feared or resented) accordingly. Our reasoning is simply that if a nation is an entity, it is distinguished as such by its ability to act.

The affective bonds of unity that unite a people find concrete expression in shared practices and gestures. Shared joys and griefs, achievements and defeats, can strengthen such bonds; and, as shared experiences are appropriated and interpreted, they may contribute to the framing of an idea. This need not be a national ideology or credo. More often it is simply a sea of overlapping values. But such values give content and focus to a shared identity. What distinguishes a nation is that the bonds of identification that set apart a people from a mere collection of individuals have reached a stage of integration that allows that people to act as a people.

Regardless of the character of its formative experiences, a nation is a nation by its project, not merely by its past, and still less by its perception in the eyes of others. A project is a conative and active undertaking. Just as a random grouping of individuals is not a people sheerly in virtue of what others may think, so a people is not a nation by mere self-perception—although the perceptions of others can contribute to the making of a people, and self-perceptions are what make a people capable of nationhood.

Nations are peoples that have brought their sense of communal identity to articulacy in formal or informal institutions aimed at serving what are seen as common interests. It is here that we find whatever aptness there may be in comparing nations to organisms: not that their members are no longer individuals but that in a nation, as in an organism, reflexivity and mutuality reach a pitch that gives pragmatic import to a single identity, and, in the case of nations, even across the broad diversity of an entire people.

It is because nationhood rests on the idea of a common interest that a common language is so treasured by the makers and preservers of a people's nationhood. It is for the same reason that they hold precious a literature that can give voice to the sense of common weal and focus the perspective that defines a shared identity. A common religion or culture, moral code or creed, can crystallize shared or shareable ideals. A common law can concretize and seek to effectuate those ideals in practice, and a common body of historical knowledge or lore can project ideals from past to future. None of these factors is necessary to the birth of a nation, and none suffices to ensure a nation's survival, but all can contribute vitally. This is one reason, apart from credal triumphalism and quite apart from all matters of mutual intelligibility or commerce, that peoples have fought and still fight to preserve their own language and literature, the archives and artifacts, facts and myths, monuments and tumuli of their history, the peculiar or archaic customs, celebrations, values, and mannerisms that become tokens and repositories of the national idea. The niceties of theology scarcely graze the surface in interpreting the tenacity of the world's distinctive religious ideas and institutions. For these are often thought by the people of a nation to enshrine the highest reach of its national ideal.[7]

A nation is not a state, but a state may be the instrument or organ of a nation, the societal institution par excellence, charged with oversight of the national project and thus with assuring complementarity in the activities of its members and the compatibility of their actions with the principles that underlie its project. For a state, as an institution, an overarching institution, can give articulation, in laws and not just words, to the values that a people share or the ideals for which a nation hopes to stand. By overarching I mean what once was meant by the now disfavored word 'sovereign.' For justice is the implicit condition underlying all national projects; no nation will long survive without justice, and no state is tolerated except for its capability of providing justice. But there is no justice, finally, where there is no court of ultimate appeal; and no court of ultimate appeal, where law is not sovereign.

The rhetoric of national bombast and the priggish self-righteousness of national or ethnic self-assertion may claim that sovereignty means something more— that because states bear the responsibility of affording ultimate justice to their citizens, states, nations, or peoples are therefore sovereign in quite a different sense, as ultimate arbiters of right and justice, immune to higher or external norms, answerable to no one, and incapable of wrongdoing. There have always been states that behaved as though the distinctness of their laws from those of other states somehow sealed them against the universal claims of human and natural justice. Some ethnic movements have seized upon the word sovereignty in a similar sense: not that they are prepared to assume the responsibilities of national self-sufficiency but because they seek exemption from certain of the laws and imposts of a larger and more pluralistic society. Such claims rest on an equivocation, seeking to split privileges from the cares of government. The related moral flaw in claiming exemption from any law beyond those of a de facto state is more serious. Yet the fallacy of sliding from ultimate responsibility to ultimate arbitership must be obvious, and the illegitimacy of claiming national sovereignty as a shield against the claims of universal justice is all too plain against the backdrop of the Holocaust.

Is it proper to speak of a nation's hopes, ideals, or values? I think it is plain that nations have agency. They can act as well as suffer. Indeed, it becomes difficult to speak of genocide and certain other crimes, including slavery and other forms of oppression, without acknowledging that nations, and peoples, act. There are some crimes and other acts as well, including acts of reconciliation, or of providing adequately for the needy, that only nations can perform or commit. Nations can be negligent. So, evidently, nations can be caring. A nation can have an ethos. So a nation can have a character.

We must be on guard, however, against supposing that when actions are ascribed to nations or other groups, the terms in which this is done can be simple one-place predicates, applying univocally to the members of the group or aptly contrasting their personal character severally with that of any member of some other group. We must also recall that an ethos, in a nation as in an individual, is of moral relevance only insofar as it is acquired or expressed through freely made choices, appropriations of a chosen course of action by those who are, in one way or another, complicit in it.

Margaret Gilbert offers a model of social action based on the idea of explicit consent by participant individuals who take part in a specific cooperative or collaborative act.[8] I would spread my net somewhat more widely, since I think we can be complicit in acts that we do not acknowledge if we are parties to the enterprise that effectuates them. Such complicity may involve overt undertakings, but it may also involve acquiescence in a variety of intermediate and complexly mediated modes of participation. I certainly do not consent to the employment of child labor in India or prison labor in China, but when I fail to check the labels on the goods I buy, to determine their origin, or when I permit my government to acquiesce in such practices as these, I am, in an admittedly indirect but still real way, complicit.

A corporation can have a corporate culture or climate, or ethos, and can deserve moral criticism or praise in virtue of the decisions its people make, despite the complexity of their nexus with one another in decision making and despite the fact that corporations as such are devised, in the first instance, to render difficult the assignment of individual accountability for conjoint actions. Nations too may have a culture in this morally freighted sense, despite the fact that our notions of accountability here are almost as primitive as our notions of corporate or communal praise and blame. The idea of corporate responsibility is obscured by the artificial anonymity of corporate undertakings and the invention of numerous devices, from insurance schemes to stock equity transactions, that are designed to mask and diffuse responsibility, mute and dissipate accountability. The notions of national responsibility and accountability are even more systematically obscured. They are positively shrouded by rhetorical persiflage and the systematic conflation of national acts with the acts and choices of national leaders. Since Deuteronomy and the Prophets of ancient Israel, few public documents, with the telling exception of the eloquently elliptical prose of Lincoln's Second Inaugural Address, have dared touch the subject. But the technical problematics of communal responsibility are not the only moral difficulties posed by the fact that we human beings constitute ourselves into nations.

Because nationhood depends on mutual recognition, nationhood always involves some level of exclusivity. It may be an ideal to treat all our fellow humans as our brothers and sisters, but human beings rarely do that literally. They rarely make the public their heirs, especially not when the tax laws do not mandate such generosity. And even when estates are left to the public in whole or part, the beneficiaries are most often the benefactor's own people, not the people of the world. An art collection or a library, say, is left to "the nation"; anyone may come to see it in the museum, but the museum is sited within the shores of the donor's land, and its integrity is ensured or neglected by trustees appointed under the favored nation's laws.

Granted no nation is watertight, nationhood defines itself through identification, and we humans seem in general to find no readier means of establishing identity or validating identification than through (or against) some category of difference: Inclusion typically seems vacuous if it cannot make reference to what is excluded, and nationhood is at least as much about exclusion as it is about inclusion. Whether we speak of customs duties or college fellowships, awards for creative achievement or obligations for conscription, health benefits or the right to vote — participation in the activities, responsibilities, profits, and losses of a society is most typically boundaried. Societies are complexes of formal and informal institutions; and, like organic bodies, if they are to have any structure at all, they must have some semblance of a size and shape, some basis of distinguishing interior from exterior — participants from non-participants — and some means of articulating their members in interconnecting roles. The large barriers that mark or limit the internal from the external in shaping the life of a society, in regard to residence, work, trade, political activity, or social participation — be they ever so permeable or flexible — are typically set up on national lines and regulated, policed or enforced, modified, reduced, or eliminated, as are the large parameters of the roles themselves, by national authorities, values, and institutions.

It is with these thoughts in mind that I want now to turn to our questions about whether (and how) nations can be justified. On the one hand, the very existence of nations involves differences in the treatment of those who belong and those who do not. The existence of nations, then, may seem antithetical to the egalitarian thrust of democracy and to the humanistic values and traditions from which democracy draws its moral claims. On the other hand, to negate a people's nationhood is clearly a kind of genocide, since one can kill a people even without killing large numbers of individuals if one can demoralize them and rob them of that dimension of their identity and self-confidence by which their peoplehood might realize and express itself in nationality. This fact suggests, contrary to the idea that nations are merely groups of individuals, that there is a value in the survival of a nation as such, over and above the value of preserving the lives of its members.

It might be thought that the enormity of genocide arises solely from its scale and that there is no difference between genocide and mass murder. But this notion, I would argue, is a mistake. Compounding, but not eclipsed by, the horror of mass slaughter is the further crime of suppressing a nation's project. Thus, Jews in the death camps, even when there was no hope of personal survival, sought to preserve some act or memorial of their culture—a scrap of liturgy, a poem. They painted, sculpted, made clandestine newspapers, even organized musical performances or preserved some reverent semblance of ritual practice—some expression of what had been their life. What we see here is that the snuffing out of a culture is a crime, compounding the crime of mass murder and thus distinct from it. Cultural genocide is distinguishable as part of what the Soviets attempted to perpetrate on their Jewish subjects in particular. And our theory of deserts makes very clear why it is a wrong to thwart a nation's creative purpose or block it from fruition. We need not hold that nations are substances or organisms or in any way ontically or axiologically prior to individuals to recognize deserts in the entitative claims that nations make by the very activities of their national lives.

Fecundity is critical to any nation's project. It links personal, familial, and communal hopes and dreams, for it conjoins the futurity of a couple with that of their people. We learn something about that nexus of personal and communal futurity through facing the fact of the use of rape in warfare—as witnessed in our own historical moment in the barbaric practices of the Serb fighters in Bosnia or the Iraqi troops in Kuwait. Here rape became an instrument of genocidal policy, not by the Nazi expedient of seeking to erase a gene pool, but by the hijacking of gametes (where the ancient practice of enslaving women was impracticable)—executing men but scarring the bodies of women with the marks of national humiliation and cultural evisceration.[9]

All schemes for the dispersion of peoples, the suppression of their language, literature or customs, delegitimation of their traditions, unmanning of their men, and defiling or debauching of their women follow the same pattern. A case in point: The Romanovs and the Hapsburgs promoted prostitution among the Jews of their lands, as a calculated tactic of degradation.[10] Narcotics have been used to similar effect in this century against more than one nation. So have adoption policies like the practice of Australia, between 1910 and the early 1970s, of forcibly removing children of mixed aboriginal and white ancestry from their familial homes. Such acts are not policies of mass murder like that practiced by the Nazis in the Holocaust, but they are genocidal nonetheless, of a piece in theory and practice with the more violent forms of genocide. As Ronald Wilson, president of the Australian Human Rights and Equal Opportunity Commission, put it: "Genocide is not the attempt to destroy an individual. Genocide is the attempt to destroy a culture."[11]

At the very least, I argue, the enormity of cultural genocide suggests that something in nationhood is of value beyond the survival of individuals—even despite the invidiousness inherent in the constituting of a nation, and even despite the many crimes (genocide among them) of which nations are capable. The fact that persons can be guilty of murder does not negate the value of personhood but presupposes it—in their victims. And the fact that nations can be guilty of genocide does not negate the value of nationhood but again presupposes it. The instinct or intuition that cautions us against the violation of a people's nationhood is alerting us to the presence of some real value, at least prima facie. And this we need to explore.

If we can make out the legitimacy of the life of nations, we have a basis for determining the extent of their sovereignty. I have already suggested that the right of national self-determination cannot warrant anything like a claim to moral self-sufficiency. There is no basis for the claims, long made in the name of nations, that their autonomy, the sovereignty professed to be rooted in divine right or the *vox populi*, can give nations any basis for the claim to be above all laws—or any. But what is a nation justified in doing or being?

The brunt of my argument will be that the existence of nations is justified and the modalities of their existence and activity, accordingly, regulated normatively, by the worth of individuals. It is because individuals, when they collaborate as members of a nation, can achieve things that they cannot otherwise achieve, both in their own behalf and in behalf of others, that nations are worthy of moral recognition. Indeed, it is because nations can serve and foster the interests of their members, and those of others as well, that some of the acts that individuals undertake in concert, through national institutions, are worthy of description as achievements.

The entitative claims that nations make through their activities as nations are not reducible to the individual claims of their members, because nations are capable of activities of a kind and on a scale that individuals could never undertake. But the warrant for those activities must in the end redound entirely to the benefit of the primary sorts of beings—not the corporate entities but the individuals whose deserts are affected, and indeed whose fates are in great measure constituted by the acts of nations.

2. Justifying Nationhood

The locus of value is in beings. I have great difficulty, as I have argued, in seeing where, if not in beings, value could reside. That is why the denial of value in beings seems to me tantamount to the denial, whether genuine or only verbal, that there is any value at all. Indeed, I must take such nihilism to be only verbal, for it seems to me that a genuine negation of all values would prove unable to find any motive even for its own enunciation. But if value resides always and only in beings, then surely there is value in nations, for nations are real.[12]

But more needs to be said if we are to value things for what they are. For the value ascribed to nations might seem to go no further than the value of some contingent concurrence or relationship. Granted that nations have members who in some sense act in concert, does a nation's existence have no greater worth than that of a mere interest group, say, a college fraternity or a lobbying coalition? To dissolve a fraternity need not do real harm to any existential deserts; to dissolve certain lobbies might in fact bring about a net gain in human welfare. There is no special reason for concern if, say, redheaded people do not stick together. Indeed, redheads tend to marry non-redheads, and no one sees that choice as disloyalty or injustice. But to dissolve a nation is, at the very least, to destroy a part of the identity of its members and to undermine aspects of their power as persons. Even the considerations that would warrant dismantling a state, by internal forces of revolution or external forces like those the Allies brought to bear on the Nazi Reich or the Tojo regime, would not justify destruction of a nation. Ratko Mladek is no George Washington.

The recognition that nations have deserts does not establish the extent and limits of those deserts. After all, nations make claims upon us as well as in our behalf. In what measure can the claims of nations legitimately invade our personal space or curb our private rights? Our recognition of the paramountcy of persons as subjects, on a moral plateau above all mere things, places us firmly in the liberal tradition and cautions us against turning communal values into fascism writ politely. Specifically, it warns us against substitutions of judgment. Although personal choice is hardly an infallible guide to individual interest, and still less the equivalent of moral rectitude, it is typically the most effective index of self-interest we have; and government should not be a second guessing but a reconciliation of interests. In our discussion of Mill we have already qualified our concern with substitutions of judgment, in the interest of protecting the ethos. We found, for example, in certain semeiotic threats a moral equivalent to shouting fire in a crowded theater. Expressive acts and representations that demonize or dehumanize their victims were identified as legitimate objects of legislative, juridical, communal, and societal concern, regardless of what variously focused market interests might be coaxed or teased to say in their behalf. But the gravest form of substituted judgment, lying at the opposite extreme from racist and pornographic expressions, is that which seeks to manipulate into subservience our natural human capability and penchant for forming a social identity. Indeed, it was by reference to the very real possibility of such manipulation that we identified the paradox in treating mind-controlling cults as just another form of spiritual expression or credal affiliation. But cults are only the microcosm of what is sought, and unstably achieved, by single-party movements in totalitarian states. Like cults, fascist parties — both those that have flown red banners and those that have dressed their followers in black or brown shirts — have sought to cut off their members from the full range of social and intellectual contacts that are the reality check of morals and the bulwark of sanity. Here we must stand firmly with Mill in staunch defense of our liberties, first among which is the liberty of self-definition, which all liberties of self-expression and exploration, regardless of their intrinsic value, critically serve. The idea of the nation, even in party ideologies with international ambitions, has stood high among the means of subverting that liberty and manipulating human social identity and attachments. Nationality, indeed, is second only to religious claims in its power and its penchant for subversion of the self.

Far too often in history have the nobler impulses of human beings, the human desire to act and live or die for a higher cause, been exploited by cynical or self-deluding pretenders to the role of champion of the common good. Words like nobility, honor, self-sacrifice, and duty have, as a result, grown tarnished. Their gold braid has been repeatedly exposed as tinsel; the medals on their proud chest assayed as base metal that only briefly and in the brave glint of sunlight and youthful generosity with life itself could pass as rightful emblems of the values for which sacrifices have been preached or demanded: the future, the homeland, the faith, or the nation. It is such imposture above all that gives nationhood a bad name and prompts the idea that nations are ghosts and collectivities, not legitimate realities. The conceptual nub of all such imposture is the claim of the collective to determine for all how each person shall construe his identity and what each individual shall hold sacred.

Elie Kedourie traced the moral claims of nationalism to Fichte's appropriation of the Kantian idea of self-determination.[13] This provenance was meant to expose a logical error. Kedourie bitterly remembered the excesses of nationalism in Iraq and the expulsion of his own family, and of the vibrant Iraqi Jewish community as a whole, in the name of Iraqi nationalism. He saw nationalist ideology as a moral and intellectual outrage: "Of the two great absurdities of our time—" he wrote, "Marxism and nationalism—Marxism is, to be sure, the more attractive absurdity: yet, it *is* an absurdity and a dangerous one at that." Then turning to nationalism, he added, "There is nothing in human history to suggest that because you are a Georgian or an Uzbek, you should risk life and limb, going to the brink of extinction, in order to enjoy living in an independent state."[14] Kedourie's indignation is well placed, and he is right in holding that not every ethnicity needs to constitute itself a nation-state or lose its manhood, its rights, or even its optimal advantage.[15] Yet some groups do seek articulation (and recognition) as nations, and I believe that they can rightly do so. We can find the basis of that right under the rubric of our idea of free association, which is, at bottom, a matter not just of allegiances or affinities but ultimately of the freedom of self-identification. Whether individuals should articulate their social identities in claims to national expression is a matter in the first instance for the judgment of those individuals, and then for the judgment of those whom their choices will affect.

The sense of a need for national recognition by groups that do not presently have it is a topic of legitimate concern to many—not least, the powers in a multinational state or (erstwhile) colonial empire whose actions might inspire the demand. That is exactly what is meant by the pregnant 'when' in "When in the course of human events. . . ." The moral case is not one to be judged exclusively by outsiders, nor by interested parties of one side to the exclusion of all others.

As for the formal dimension of the "absurdity" Kedourie cites, there is a paradox in some collectivity's presenting itself as the true realization of who I am— and of doing so in the name of my right of self-determination. Yet we must state that the idea of national self-determination is no mere equivocation or over-extension of the Kantian idea of personal autonomy. It rests on the (Hegelian) recognition that important components of personal identity are social. Since identities must be self-appropriated, it does not follow from respect for communal identities that a given national identity can be simply assigned and deemed authentic. By the same token, however, neither can such identifications be simply, externally denied.

The heart of Kedourie's objection to the excesses of nationalism exactly parallels Isaiah Berlin's point in *Two Concepts of Liberty*: It is illiberal, smothering, for another (a nationalist ideologue, say) to define for me who I am, who I shall be, who I shall have been. National identity, in this sense, is a "subjective" rather than an "objective" right. But for that very reason it is a claim that can legitimately be made by (or even for) an individual. It is far less easily imposed, although the obligations (as distinguished from the identity) of communal membership, as we saw in chapter 1, can be legitimately enforced and *are* enforced by a variety of formal and informal means.

The difficulty in Kedourie's position is that denial of national identity to those who claim it is the same sort of illiberal or repressive act as is its imposition. It is to avoid the morally problematic posture of enforcing such a denial that democratic states are wise to seek voluntary adherence to the national idea or ideals that animate them. In the same way, such states wisely seek to give reasonable grounds to such adherence — to win the hearts of those without whom a democratic state would be nothing. The wisdom of the American Constitution in seeking to separate faith from the state and the beauty of the Torah's effort to ground the life of the Law in love of the God of justice — rather than the fascist's or fanatic's emptying of self into a corporate non-self — both lie in the recognition that individuality and freedom are the soundest groundworks of civil society and social order and the firmest foundations of communal allegiance.

A participatory democracy has the clearest moral warrant and the most effective political claim upon the allegiance of its citizens. Such claims are most stably secured in an open, pluralistic society, where ideas, rather than ethnicities provide the overarching social bond, and where the paramount idea is that of openness itself rather than some enforced homogeneity of cant or dogma. But the openness we speak of, the openness that fosters tolerance and the harmonious integration of a diversity of cultures and individual outlooks, is not the openness of moral sterility and intellectual vacuity that fosters the confusion of liberalism with license or of creativity with eccentricity. Rather, it is the openness of the open future, a tolerance grounded in respect for the deserts of personhood, and a communally warranted and societally guaranteed trust in the good faith of others who share in the national enterprise.[16]

If nations are not living organisms, still less are they persons. So they hardly can bear the deserts of persons. But far too often in America does the recognition that nations are mere collectivities whose members are persons — the primal and paramount, rightful bearers of desert — swamp and overwhelm in confusion the legitimacy of the nation's claims upon the individual. It is these claims that we need to measure if our liberalism is not to be allowed, under the name of libertarianism, to sag into anarchy. Laski was mistaken to expect the state to become just another social institution, alongside the firm, the union, and the foundation.[17] That way lies the type of anarchy we see now in the former Soviet Union, where every institution follows the bent of its possessors and none must answer to a common law. Libertarians are mistaken, for their part, to model the state on a voluntary association like a gun club or farming cooperative. That way lies another form of anarchy, the madness of survivalist militias, fighting, as if in Afghanistan, to the last tooth and blasting cap.

The state has power because the collectivity has needs: for security and order, health care, research, and education, a level of social integration that today cannot function effectively without coordination and support on a national scale. Even in the days of Plato and Aristotle the notion that a state could act effectively from the base of a small, self-contained city and its immediate environs was a romantic fiction long discredited by history. Today, when we have the means of deliberating democratically (and through accountable representatives) on the scale of the na-tion-state, and when integration of a much higher order and on a much vaster scale than was feasible in antiquity has become a matter of survival, not to mention quality of life, the notion of the state as condominium is a mere wishful and reactive fiction, an apocalyptic legend.

In responding to the myths of ragged individualism, as Sam Beer used to call it in the days before libertarian extremism had reached apocalyptic meltdown and dreamers of Armageddon had begun to carry heavy arms in small towns and rural outposts, we do well to remember that just as individual interests need not conflict but can be complementary, so can the deserts of individuals and those of the collectivities they may constitute or create.

To face what is (at least in liberal societies) perhaps the most vexed case of the possible conflict between individual and group interests, we must consider time and labor, risk and danger, but above all, money. Those who are suspicious of the rights of nations are often curiously unconcerned about the claims a state may make to risk or sacrifice the lives of its own, or those of others, in the nation's cause. Critics are far more prone to complain about the propriety of the state's reaching into their pockets than about its claims upon the lives of their children. The argument has been made, often by politicians and occasionally by philoso-phers, that the purposes for which a state may demand resources of us are morally secondary or even irrelevant; what really matters first or foremost, they say, is whose resources they are.[18]

This position, I think, is unwarranted. One need not regard all property as theft to show the unsoundness of rejecting taxation, or welfare payments, or trans-fers of wealth. One need only recognize the inherence of deserts in beings, and in persons par excellence. For if the state is an agency, it must, like any agent capable of acts with moral consequences, recognize deserts, and not just those of its members, or indeed its more privileged members, or of the artificial entities they may create — corporations, trusts, power groups, churches, lobbies, unions, or foundations — but of all those beings whom its acts, or policies, inactions, or omissions might affect.

Critical among the interests that just regulations must regard are the rights and deserts of human beings (and even corporations) in some way to keep what they have, seek what they need, and use what they have earned. These are rights that only a societal institution can specify in practice and with equity and that only a state can effectively guarantee. I do not argue that the state, by legislating, creates the right to property and therefore has the right to take it away. That nominalist line of argument makes every institution arbitrary and finds no state act or policy more or less justified than any other. States, after all, may regulate all manner of things. One cannot, without permitting tyranny, assume that whatever a state regulates is *eo ipso* its creation, or even that what it creates belongs to it to take away.

Clearly there may be property rights quite apart from any governmental apparatus. How else could states succeed in justly regulating or even respecting the economic interests and relations of anyone? Or are we to say that there is no sense ever in the notion that a state might, under cover of law, steal or take wrongfully or commit any injustice whatever? If justice itself were the mere creation of the state, there would be no normative standard for legislative or other governmental actors to consult in regulating their own official acts and policy decisions, and even consistency with prior actions or existing laws would hold no prescriptive force. For a law cannot reach outside itself to demand adherence to its principle; and a court decision cannot urge, more than it does in its very promulgation, the concurrence of future justices and jurists. *Stare decisis* and legal consistency are warranted by the value of fairness, and that, in turn, by human deserts.

States, I argue, have moral standing because of the good they can do. It is not for what a state has done for me and my individual interests that I may owe it not just taxes but allegiance. Rather, in keeping with our argument in chapter 1, a state's authority stems from (and is limited by) its capability of enhancing the human condition and serving the general good, of which my atomic or narrowly personal interests, or even my familial and communal interests, are just a handful of perspectivally prominent but fractional constituents.

By regulating civil and economic relations, states can enhance the standing and so the deserts of the governed. For it is not just entrepreneurs or laborers who create wealth; inventors, advertisers, and human services workers do so as well. Civil, social, and educational services, public health, and indeed the arts are just as essential to an economy as are capital and labor and just as essential to a society's well-being and quality of life as are the military, the police, and the services of the fire brigade and the ambulance corps. There is an infrastructure that is physical: the sewers, water supply, energy and transportation grids, the system that maintains air quality and facilitates communications. These must be established and maintained, as human relations require, if anyone is to prosper and if society is to develop and enhance our capability of meeting our own and one another's needs. But there is an equally necessary intellectual and spiritual infrastructure — of museums, libraries, schools, colleges and universities, research institutes, public forums, parks and playgrounds, wetlands and wildernesses. There are also public rituals and symbols, holidays and celebrations, in addition to the spaces and occasions in homes and lives that are private but must be publicly protected and respected, the holy days and the times and places of worship and reflection by which the public entity makes room for the emergence and efflorescence of the private. Without the accessibility and vitality of all the elements of cultural infrastructure, a society will soon crumble and its mission be emptied and forgotten.

It is natural and easy to decry the inefficiencies of the state in looking after or providing a physical, civic, or economic infrastructure, or to chafe at the seeming intrusion of state interests into the sacred private space that we may reserve to ourselves as the domain of the spirit (or the body). Some, in this spirit, may express disappointment, irritation, or frustrate territoriality by saying that we would all be better off with less government, and perhaps best off with none. But such discomforts are deceptive, tempting us with the fallacy of taking for granted goods whose source they cut away. Some of those who talk of rugged individualism fail to notice how deeply their sense of self is invested in the stock market and protected by the same network of routine and emergency civil and social services that protects the individuality of everyone else.

The madwoman of Chaillot happily leads all her neighborhood "pimps" down into the bowels of hell. But even as she does so, she presumes that her old sunny neighborhood will remain much as it was, only better. She is, of course, a madwoman and answerable neither to logic nor to morals. But we, who bear both the blessing and the curse of accountability, must be more careful whom we brand a pimp or parasite. The Soviets, lumbered with an ideology that classified marketers as barnacles but made the Party the apotheosis of the Proletariat, watched powerless as their normative distribution system ground to a halt and their Party grew bloated on the excesses of the shadow system whose workings Soviet norms could not authorize or explain, let alone control.

Those who decry government as a mere drag on the economy suffer from a complementary blind spot. For states, contrary to the rhetoric of wishful minimalism, are just as much creators of wealth as are any of those who engage in profit seeking. Regulators, as much as marketers, are productive members of society—as much as miners, farmers, pastoralists, or manufacturers. It would be a worthy resolution for the new century if politicians, venture capitalists, labor leaders, and managers could learn to stop calling one another parasites. There are four myths involved in such name-calling, which in a civil society takes the place of what once was called class warfare. In place of the "haves" and "have nots" we now have the employers, the employed, and the entitled—with government called to the uneasy role of referee, and admonished, in the name of politics, not to dispassion and impartiality but to interest and compassion.

Each group has its myth, and each, it seems, without rising up on its haunches and taking a somewhat higher view of its fellows and its own interests and situation, can see the fallacy only in the myths of the others. The myth of capital is the well-known story of the invisible hand, coupled perhaps with a certain romanticism about risk taking, naively draping the familiar fact that any business enterprise is based on minimizing and diffusing risk. The invisible hand is supposed to level the playing field, as though smoothness were the very meaning of risk taking, and as though play were all that an economy is about. The myth lies in the illusion that all needs, including the direst needs of the disadvantaged, are adequately met simply through the operations of the economy, as the market responds to demand, without any public note of those who may be unable to answer the market's call or any official responsibility for finding the cause and cure of such disadvantage.

The myth of employment is the labor theory of value, predicated on the assumption that the mere making or taking of a thing makes it both mine and valuable — without consideration of the conditions necessary for me to make or take it, let alone make it precious in the eyes of others. In the mythic state of nature, I find myself on a beach or in a garden or on an infinite prairie, where my taking disadvantages no one else. But such surreal landscapes are the stuff of dreams. They tell me nothing about the rights and wrongs of ownership but only celebrate the phenomenology of the first moment of appropriation and prescind from awareness of its costs and consequences, as well as its conditions.

The myth of entitlement is the myth of the ever-normal pot. It rests on the moral demand that needs must be met. But it frames its demand in a strange lack of concern for the means by which they can or shall be met, adequately or inadequately, generously or with hostility. That view is childish. An adult view of politics would look to the economic system by which legitimate needs can be answered and to the social system by which higher deserts can be given articulacy — not only legitimated but concretely and contextually defined and enhanced.

Even the would-be referee has his own myth, the myth of the stone soup. Here government is imagined not to be an economic player, whose actions or inactions, health, sobriety or corruption, have costs and benefits. Rather the state (or public agencies in general) is deemed to make a sufficient contribution to the common stock merely by playing a regulative role, determining what everyone else's contribution must be, within the pretense of the legal fiction that governance (and correspondingly, academic, eleemosynary, and clerical functions) are not sectors of the economy, factors, and interest groups within a society. Government is restrained from breaking even, made a sump of unprofitable and undesired services, and then criticized for inefficiency and waste. State agencies grow and government services proliferate by a law and inertia of their own, without direct accountability to the purposes that would legitimate their activities.

To disentangle these myths, I must argue that it is not because states generate wealth that they have the right to take wealth from individuals. It is because nations have the capability of meeting deserts that states have responsibilities, including responsibilities toward those who can generate or contribute much, or little, or nothing, and including responsibilities toward those who are not party to the state on which the responsibility falls. The striking moral fact — reflected in the exclusion problem — is that the responsibilities called forth by the deserts of beings make their claims where there is agency to execute them, not where there is some prior agreement or commitment to do so. Responsibilities, for that reason, often fall to the state, which acts as the agency of the nation — not merely because the state enjoys a de jure monopoly of ultimate coercive force, and not merely because its forums are the courts of last resort, but because no lesser agency is equal to the need. Indeed, it is the virtuality of its capability that gives being to the state and that causes or encourages it to grow.

There are many tasks that states alone can perform. Only a nation, or some agency constituted by a nation, or a consortium of nations, can place a human being on the moon or regulate nuclear energy and nuclear waste. But these contemporary examples of the economy and power of scale are hardly unique. For only a nation, ultimately, can feed the hungry. As Spinoza wisely wrote, "People are won over by generosity, especially those who do not have means of securing the necessities of life. But to provide aid for everyone in need far exceeds the power and the self-interest of the private individual, for his resources are far from equal to the need, and one person is too limited to join himself in friendship to all others. Therefore the responsibility of caring for the poor falls upon society as a whole and regards, in fact, the common interest."[19] It regards the common interest and not merely the poor because an integrated society can achieve so much more than all its members can achieve in isolation. Hence the pertinence of Spinoza's remark that people are won over by generosity. To minimize alienation, maximize participation, and optimize the sense of a national project and a national system of shared priorities are themselves legitimate and necessary aims of public policy, quite apart from the fact that actions conducive to these ends may also be morally imperative responses to basic human needs.

To argue in this way is not (or should not be) to fall into the myth of the ever-normal pot. The state is not a god or a deus ex machina that can simply rain down wealth to answer human needs. Neither is the nation an unlimited source of wealth. The notion of the impoverished or dispossessed, or of their advocates and tribunes, that others can and must provide for them is as much a source as it is a symptom of alienation and hostility, a cause of social cleavage, not a cement of integration. But here we see clearly both what it is that states must do and why it is that they have the authority to do it: States must not just regulate but must integrate the interests they profess to govern. Concretely: If education to the full extent of individual capacity, or health care to the full extent of the state of the art, or elder care to the extent of human need, is a legitimate desert of the members of a society, then it is equally and by the same token the right and the responsibility of the agencies of that society, and above all of the state as the paramount social agency, to draw upon the resources of that society to meet those needs, *and* to call upon its members to pay their proper share and play their proper roles in meeting these and other social needs, as members of an effectively functioning community.

Private vice is never public virtue, and sheer selfishness conjures up no invisible hand to stir the pot. By the same token, the displaced generosity of vicarious social reformers who rely on the stone soup fallacy — the presumption that everyone else must contribute but that ego need contribute only the idea of pitching in — provides nothing to fill that pot. But an integrated society can answer to the needs of all its members and meet far more than their most basic needs. It is this fact that legitimates the rise of nations. If there are needs, there is work; and if there is work there are wealth and opportunity. It is this, the capabilities of social integration, not just in the pin factory but in the day-care center, the Job Corps, the community college, and the Peace Corps, that affords the wealth of nations.

I say nations, and not merely states, since questions of scale, resource, and the large-scale integration of human energies are crucial here. A state must find not merely goods to allocate but means by which to articulate the interests it governs. Yet, as an institution, it is a mere mode of organization and has no resource of its own. A state, as such, has not the energies and resources adequate to answer the human needs that fall to its care — still less the power to coordinate human efforts on any major scale or to motivate the efforts needed to achieve sustained progress or greatness in science, literature, the arts, technology, philosophy, moral virtuosity, or spiritual prowess. But a nation — through the conjoint efforts that can be spurred by a sense of shared identity and that such an identity can legitimate by reference to the idea of a common (if diverse and localized) national project — can find within itself resource for all these things, and for the generation of leisure, capital, enjoyment, widespread knowledge and understanding, and many other human goods that are valuable intrinsically and worthwhile instrumentally, in promoting still further goods.

If nations are capable of such human goods as these, then plainly the existence of nations is not only legitimate but precious. This is so not because history aligns people in nations, nor even because human beings have a right and affinity to associate with (and identify with) others whom they regard (for whatever reason) as of their own ilk. For such thoughts touch only on the negative dimensions of the moral issue. They tell us only that something is negated or denied when nationhood is withheld. But they do not tell us that nations are, on balance, justified. Nor do we learn that the existence of nations is worthwhile because nations are the only fit way of organizing human activities and enlarging human potentials — they are not — but rather because nations can optimize human potential in a variety of ways that are not readily achieved by other means. So, given the human condition as we know it, it would probably be the case that if nations did not exist it would be a moral obligation to invent them.

If we think of a democracy merely as a group of people who make decisions by vote, perhaps in accordance with Robert's Rules of Order, then the nexus between democracy and nationhood is entirely contingent. But we might take the idea of democracy in a stronger sense: Lincoln's sense of a government of the people, by the people, and for the people. In that case, government would regard as its mission the securing of both positive (or material) and negative (or formal) rights. The state's responsibility, on that account, would be to muster the necessary resources to secure the human right to the development of human potential and understanding, the right to peace and health, and the right to progress, economically, morally, and intellectually. In tackling such a task, I think, only a nation-state or some greater power can be a fully effectual democracy.

But if it is by reference to the human goals they can facilitate that nations are legitimated, why, we must ask, should the optimal level of practical concern for such goods be confined or even preferentially allocated among those who are members of the nation that makes them possible? Why should the goods that nations can promote in behalf of their citizens not be spread to the universe of human beings at large? Can nations legitimately separate themselves from one another or from the broader human condition?

3. Nations and Exclusivity

To the elemental question, how it is that I can be asked to die, or to die by fractions, through the risks expected of me in the common interest, for the common defense, as we like to say, our argument has provided us with an answer: A nation can call on us to offer sacrifices, of our lives as well as our fortunes, not frivolously but in case of need, and not aggressively but in the cause of defense, because (and so only to the extent that) through the sustenance of nationhood, our individual and conjoint aspirations can be fulfilled. It is because nations enable us, acting in concert, to achieve goals that we could never achieve in isolation that nations can ask us to give what is properly our own, can expect it to be given freely, and can place sanctions on the free riders who would stint or withhold what is demanded of them. It is because the life and so the demands of nations are justified in this way, and only in this way, by the goods that nations serve, that nations may *not* call upon us to violate the very principles by which alone their existence is justified.

But what then of our question about exclusivity? No matter how inclusionary any social entity may be, if it functions at all, it functions by differentiating those who are its members from those who are not. If nations exist for the sake of individuals, how can any invidiousness in their actions be fair or right? Or how can nations function without establishing, in practical terms, distinctions between the greater world and their own citizens? For nations are the creatures of self-perceived distinctions of identity, of differences and differentiations between us and them. And national institutions are in large measure the articulation of such perceptions in social and societal practice. The operative social contract is not the mythic one that precedes the constitution of a society, but the effectual one that is the outcome and resultant of that society's dynamic.

Isn't it the very division of the human world into "us" and "them" that transforms the idea of defense, say, from a necessity into a euphemism? Don't the lines and bonds of allegiance that make possible the demand of sacrifice on the part of some create the very boundaries that make such sacrifices necessary? For is it not the case that if there were no "other" there would be no aggression to be feared or defense to be mounted? How then can we justify a loyalty that when generalized seems not only to presuppose but to render inevitable the very sacrifices it calls for?

My answer must be twofold: To begin with, I stand on the ground I laid out at the beginning, when I argued that basic existential deserts rest on need — not membership, agreement, promised requital, purchase, or any other merely formal fact. Thus it is both relevant and necessary to recognize human deserts for which exclusion is entirely inappropriate. When we know that individuals are sick or suffering, enslaved or hungry, it is incumbent on us to act. (Act, again, despite the mythos of the television world, does not mean kill. We may act by way of diplomacy, or by economic, social, ideational, or informational measures long before we may or must come to blows or take up arms.) There may be no bond of kin or contractual agreement between us and those in need. Yet that fact does not mitigate our responsibilities toward our fellow human beings, or, for that matter, toward the claims of the environment.

By that very token, however, to fulfill such obligations, we must have the power to act. And that requirement alone, if nothing else, makes it incumbent upon us to band together in groups far larger than the family, tribe, neighborhood, or clan, and far more formally regulated. Our conjoint actions may be regulated by military articles or by the relations of the marketplace, which are capable in many ways of replacing penury with plenty. Or they may be ordered by the relationships of the penal and civil law, which allow us to organize ourselves into an effectual society. Such a society can sustain action because it sustains the lives and efforts of its members. It trains them, gives them skills and missions, inspires values and a vision that will conduce to the welfare of those fortunate enough to be its citizens—but also to the welfare of the larger world.

Nations, in other words, are justified by the same considerations that justify the existence of individuals. With individuals too there is an inside and an outside, self and other. In both cases, the differentiation is legitimated by (and to the extent of) the worth of a project. We can see now why it is that the demands of justice, like those of charity, which in Hebrew bears the same name as justice, do not stop at the boundaries of the self—or the "we." Moral claims are the claims of beings and can be made only upon beings. This fact places the requisites of action ahead of external needs. Neither principle nor interest stops at the frontier. But to be answerable morally and effective pragmatically—to act at all—a nation, like an individual, must integrate its members and coordinate their energies in ways that it cannot achieve in behalf of others who are not its members. And no living entity can survive or justify itself by seeking to engulf all that there is within its boundaries.

It is because a person is a subject that persons deserve special regard. It is because (and to the extent of) the worthiness of its goals that a nation can claim sustenance from its constituents and legitimacy—indeed, autonomy—in the eyes of the world. It is not the case, I have argued, that nations are justified by the sheer power of the idea of democracy. For even a democracy can be a tyranny, and many a democracy, from Athens to modern times, has committed acts of imperialism. The irreducible preciousness of each person's status as a person does not (as the expression 'self-determination' may suggest) simply translate into a comparable precious power of self-determination on the part of nations. On the contrary, the two kinds of self-determination stand in tension with one another, each demanding qualification in the other, and neither achieving its optimality unless the legitimate demands of the other are met. For no act of a nation can be legitimate that undermines the worth and dignity of the individuals in whose behalf alone the very existence of nations becomes legitimate. But also no act of an individual can be legitimate insofar as it threatens the survival of a nation or undermines the justice that legitimates and sustains that survival.

Just as we must recognize that there is no nation to the exclusion of its members, so must we recognize the Hobbesian truth that the life of individuals would be pretty paltry without the articulation of their separate powers through institutions on a scale that only nations can undertake. Thus, rather than argue that an individual's right to self-determination is fulfilled only through the attainment of nationhood by a people to which that individual belongs and with whose achievements that individual can identify, I argue that democracy is one of the achievements of which nations are capable, and for the sake of which nationhood is worthy of being sought. Indeed, without creating a persuasive or question begging definition, I think that the considerations that justify the existence of nations (as sharply distinguished from those that identify nations de facto) press in the direction of democracy, and liberal democracy at that.

Failure by the high standard of such normative considerations cannot, in view of the hopes and needs vested in the survival of any nation, warrant the purposive destruction or dismantling of a nation. But such failure assuredly can demand adjustment of a nation's ideals, issuing an imperative for a nation to call upon the resources at its command, whether those of its own diverse culture and history or those of the cultures and history of the world around it, to aid it in pursuing a more liberal and more democratic way of life. To fail to do so is to put national survival at risk and to jeopardize even the desert of national survival — since nations are justified only by their capabilities of enhancing the human condition, and they win the allegiance of their members and the credence of others, upon which their survival depends, only by their effectiveness in configuring and effectuating a broad and inclusionary ideal.

We cannot say that nations whose project or idea is inchoate or wrongheaded have no right to exist, for nations are peoples, and minimally their members have a powerful claim on life and liberty, self-expression and human flourishing. But clearly, when a nation's project is at odds with such powerful interests as these (in its own members or among those whom it may exclude), its actions cannot at the same time and in the same respect be sustained or legitimated by those interests. In such a case, there well may be a need for reconfiguration of certain of a nation's institutions, and, in certain extreme cases, of the state that has betrayed the interests it was called into being to serve.

It is true that democracy underwrites nationhood in the sense that a people's democratic right to self-determination can be fulfilled through its attainment of nationhood and may be impeded gravely, perhaps fatally, if that right is thwarted. But it is equally true, and in a way far more important, that democracy is one of the chief achievements of which nations, alone or with distinctive strength, are capable, and for the sake of which nationhood is worthy of being sought. By contrast, the mere subordination of individual aspirations to national projects or programs is, from a democratic and a human, moral standpoint, no achievement at all.

Conventionally it might be argued that nationhood is legitimated by the sovereignty of peoples, and that in turn by the legitimate claims of individuals to autonomy. But I am arguing that the democracy that gives operative meaning to the very idea of human autonomy attains its reality, perhaps optimally, perhaps exclusively, through the vehicle of the nation-state and is not readily sustained without the protection of such a state. I say "perhaps exclusively," since there are many interactions in chemistry that take place on a practical scale and speed only in the presence of some catalyst that has no chemical role in the interaction and yet is necessary if adequate quantities of the reagents in question are to be brought into appropriate relation with one another. The same is true, I suspect, with the economies of scale that national institutions distinctively achieve.

The warrant we have offered for the legitimacy of nations and their actions yields as a corollary the home truth that we cannot justify the violation of human rights on grounds of national autonomy or cultural distinctiveness. Nor can we warrant the frustration of democratic aspirations on the grounds of national sovereignty. For such autonomy and sovereignty themselves are warranted only by the service they can render in establishing democracy and performing other acts that enhance the dignity and well-being of all those affected. Sovereignty, like respect, must be won and earned, again and again. The loyalty and sense of identity that create and sustain a nation reflect the practical effectiveness of its cause and the intellectual and moral penetrance and penetration of its values. The flagging of such loyalties is not a mere mark of wickedness or weakness but the symptom of a shared malaise that needs to be addressed and that bespeaks the failing of an idea, that is, its losing credibility, the loosening of the bonds of identity that may have made it shareable.

All of this has strong implications for the question of exclusivity: The resource and the energies that sustain a nation are themselves sustained by the bonds of reciprocity and integration that unite that nation and that make relations among its citizenry stronger than their relations with strangers. My commitment to drive a car made in America is based in part on my knowing that the rules and standards by which such cars are made, as regards the standard of living and safety of the workers, the respect shown for the environment, and the regard in which the consumer is held—not in advertising copy but in practice—are matters in which I have some indirect say. To the extent that appropriate standards are flouted, my commitment is weakened. But the articulations of my society give me recourse. The same sort of relationship, reciprocal and interlocking, repeated many times over, is the making of a society; and being structured as a society—not a family or even a community, but a community whose relations have a formal structure and an informal web of stiffening to them—is what transforms a people into a nation. A society unravels when its members can no longer believe in one another or trust its institutions. We saw this phenomenon in the devolution of the Soviet system, when demoralized workers were saying, "They pretend to pay us and we pretend to work."

The parallelism here between commerce and other social relations that depend on trust is no accident. Although I owe help and sustenance to everyone, I have a stricter obligation to those who have paid me for my goods and services. The invidiousness of that distinction is overcome only by the fact that commerce is itself of value. For commerce receives a critical impetus from reciprocity and exclusivity. But no small part of the value of commerce arises in the fact that without the resources generated by exchange, my broader obligations would be unfunded. The attorney who works only pro bono will not be available for much pro bono work. The same is true with nations. Nations function through the relations among their citizens, and they function the more effectively insofar as these relations are reciprocal, wide ranging and extensive, materially rewarding, and morally enlarging. An effective and well-integrated nation can greatly uplift the humanity of its members, but only an effective and well-knit nation can hope to do the same for humanity at large.

We have seen clearly why it is that being a court of last resort does not place a nation or its state above the law, or above the demands of justice or morals. For it is only in the interest of those demands that the claims of nations are legiti-mated—or the inconveniences of states tolerated. But one might think that the concomitance of invidious treatment which the existence of nations presupposes and which the formation of states renders canonical urges us to ensure that the nation-state is superseded as rapidly as the inertia of history may allow. This in-ference, I think, is in error, for it is predicated on the assumption that, say, a world state could accomplish all that is now left up to individual nation-states but without the invidious distinctions that now subsist among nations. That assumption may prove false, however, since people seem to need bonds of identification to cement or support the formal ties of reciprocity that unite them in a society and to energize their interactions. It is not easy to assume that such bonds will simply be dissolved or transcended. It is not clear that a transnational identity, if achieved, would kindle the zeal that mere nation-states now articulate effectually enough—and sometimes too effectually. What we do observe, historically, is that efforts to dis-place national bonds of identification have typically involved atrocities and force: warfare against civilian populations, calculated acts of mass starvation, mass trans-fers of population, death camps, and killing fields. It is not clear that a world state will be achieved by less violent measures, if at all. Perhaps the dream of a universal state is no more than a trick of mental extrapolation, flattered into a passion by the hegemonical aspirations that dynasts or dictators of the order of Alexander, Caesar Augustus, Napoleon, or Hitler have used in deceiving themselves and large numbers of followers into killing and dying for what have always proved to be much lesser, and typically ignominious, ends.

The irony has often been remarked that human beings may be more willing to accept a tyranny of "their own" than the benevolent rule of outsiders. Whether such attitudes reflect sheer backwardness and bias, an instinctual aversion for sub-ordination and potential exploitation, or some deeper insight or subtle sensitivity to slights at the hands of the culturally insensitive or chauvinistic, it is very clear that second-guessing the sensibilities behind such concerns (telling people, in ef-fect, with whom they should identify) is the heart of substitution of judgment. Willingness to refrain from thinking such thoughts for another is thus the heart of liberalism. Trying to impose them is the core of paternalism. It may also prove bad policy, if the members of a nation can work more effectively with one another than with the world at large. Education, perhaps, can enlarge our social identities, for clearly our argument has not been that nations are the expressions of static and archetypal ethnicities. But to recognize that nations grow and change with the birth and death and aging of identities and ideas is not the same as to warrant attempts to attenuate those identities by discounting the relevance of our tight commitments, of commerce or charity, of law and politics, or of love or principle, in favor of a universalism that might well prove vapid and vacuous.

We do not know, of course, whether an actual world state would do a better or a worse job of distributing resources and allocating responsibilities than the admittedly patchy system of nation-states has been able to do up to now. Nor can we say with certainty that a world state would be less invidious in practice than nation-states have been. It certainly should be, and that potential would be an essential part of its rationale. But we note that nation-states in practice have hardly lived up to the principles that warrant their existence, and we have not a great deal of reason to believe that a world state would be more faithful to its mandate. We do, of course, long for the day when men will treat one another as brothers, but it is hardly a matter of Machiavellian realpolitik to hope that that day does not come before brothers have learned to treat one another as brothers.

One thing we can say is that a world state would lack the support of the weak but still relevant argument from passive consent that serves as a litmus test of political legitimacy: the argument that if people don't like their government, then in a free society at least they can always leave. The argument is weak, as we noted in chapter 1, because it puts the burden of exile on dissidents and the oppressed. But it has a curious strength that we have noted as well, in pointing to an index of dissatisfaction that is hard to gainsay. It is hard to imagine, short of utopia, a society that shortchanges no one. And the United Nations (if that is meant to be the model or the embryo of the universal state) gives us little reason to expect the emergence of utopia out of its higgledy-piggledy bureaucracy. Even the very best of states need not be best for all. Yet surely human freedom should allow those who are peaceably dissatisfied with a regime to make their exit from its jurisdiction. Even in utopia there might be rival conceptions of how individuals or groups preferred to live their lives. But in a world state the discomfited and the disaccommodated, the dissatisfied, the neglected, abused, or oppressed, would have nowhere else to go.

Notes

Preface

　1. See John Rawls, *Political Liberalism* (New York: Columbia University Press, 1993).

　2. Warren Zev Harvey, review of *On Justice* in *Jewish Political Studies Review* (1993): 144.

　3. Jude Dougherty, "Natural Law and the Torah—Review Essay," in *Crisis* (October 1993): 52–55.

　4. See *God of Abraham*, chap. 1.

1. The Idea of Deserts

　1. From the standpoint of an amoral ego, the strong and bold give up more by entering civil society than do the weak and cautious, for they curtail the sweep of their appetites and limit the free play of the penchant for aggression. The sneaky, would-be free riders, who have no intention of playing by the rules, gain disproportionately, compared with the honest and forthright. *Any* civil society involves some such divergence in the distribution of subjective goods and evils.

　2. *Leviathan*, I, 10. Hobbes has powerful motives to resist equating human worth with whatever prideful prelates or boastful barons may claim. But he goes well beyond the rhetorical satisfaction of deflating such pretensions when he categorically rejects intrinsic worth.

　3. A. E. Taylor, "Some Incoherencies in Spinozism, II," *Mind* 46 (1937), reprinted in S. P. Kashap, ed., *Studies in Spinoza* (Berkeley: University of California Press, 1974), 289–309.

　4. See Spinoza, *TP* II, 12, vol. 3, ed. C. Gebhardt, 280.

　5. Moses Mendelssohn, *Jerusalem*, trans. Alan Arkush, 36–37.

　6. Mendelssohn, *Jerusalem*, 36.

　7. Hobbes, *De Cive* I, 7.

　8. Hobbes, *Elements of Law* I, 14, 10; *De Cive* I, 10; *Leviathan*, I, 14.

　9. Mark Murphy's doctoral dissertation (Notre Dame, 1993) shows Hobbes's continuing debt to Aquinas and other natural law thinkers for such assumptions as the idea that

self-interest is a foundation of human obligation. But when Hobbes translates the scholastic obligation of self-protection into a law of nature, he proves too much, and the fact of suicide becomes an embarrassment to his theory: "I conceive not how any man can bear *animum felleum*, or so much malice towards himself, as to hurt himself voluntarily, much less to kill himself. For naturally and necessarily the intention of every man aimeth at somewhat which is good to himself, and tendeth to his preservation. And therefore, methinks, if he kill himself, it is to be presumed that he is not *compos mentis*, but by some inward torment or apprehension of somewhat worse than death, distracted." *A Dialogue between a Philosopher and a Student of the Common Laws of England*, ed. Joseph Cropsey (Chicago: University of Chicago Press, 1971), 116–17. Hobbes leans on the natural law tradition for the force of his claims that madness, suicide, and treachery are evils. But the view is inconsistent with his more outspoken conventionalism, his claim that there is no wrong or obligation apart from convention.

10. See L. E. Goodman, "Mythic Discourse," esp. p. 60.

11. J. O. Urmson, "A Defense of Intuitionism," The Aristotelian Society, 10 February 1975, *Proceedings*, 116. Urmson here understood intuitionism as commitment to a plurality of principles that may conflict (at least prima facie) and that have no clear (algorithmic) rule for the adjudication of their conflicts.

12. See Garrett Hardin, *Promethean Ethics* (Seattle: University of Washington Press, 1980).

13. See Frank Tannenbaum, *Slave and Citizen: The Negro in the Americas* (New York: 1947); Richard M. Morse, "The Heritage of Latin America," in Louis Hartz, ed., *The Founding of New Societies* (New York: Harcourt Brace, 1964), 123–77.

14. See Goodman and Goodman, " 'Particularly Amongst the Sunburnt Nations' . . ."

15. See the discussion in Moshe Sokol, "Personal Autonomy and Religious Authority," in M. Sokol, ed., *Personal Autonomy and Rabbinic Authority* (Northvale, N.J.: Jason Aronson, 1993), 169–216. For the rabbinic approval of independence of mind, Sokol also cites Deut. 30:12, "It is not in heaven" (*ap.* B. Bava Metzia 59b), and Hannah's feisty if fanciful midrashic dare that if she is not given a child, she will closet herself with a stranger, undergo the ordeal of *sotah*, and expect God to make good on the biblical promise (Num. 5:28) that those found innocent of adultery "shall be cleared and conceive offspring" (B. Berakhot 31b).

16. This is not the place to argue the reality of selves, but selves and freedom are postulates of all normative discourse and deliberation, where indeed selves and freedom are synonymous. Their reality is sufficiently protected against dialectical objection by the need to recognize them both even in stating an objection to them. For the self must be identified indexically even in denials of its freedom (rather than that of something else); and the global denial of human freedom generalizes on the notion that one might lack some particular freedom. It is thus parasitic upon the notions it professes to exclude, those of polyvalent potentiality and an open future. Now this dialectical response of mine does not prove that freedom is real but only that it is possible—that it cannot be excluded a priori. But that precisely is what metaphysical denials of human freedom pretend. For how, if not in a priori terms, can it be shown not merely that one lacks freedom to do this or that but that there is no scope at all for self-directed action. My target here is the common investment of rationalists and empiricists in a certain variety of short selling, writing off actions disclaimed as not authentically our own. The rationalists, amusingly enough, argue empirically that some of our actions are not really ours. The empiricists are correspondingly a priori in urging that none of my actions can be mine. The premise I need is more modest, but it is existential: that there are some actions for which we ourselves bear some responsibility, in view of the impact of our own choices. For further reflections on human

freedom, see Goodman, "Determinism and Freedom in Spinoza, Maimonides, and Aristotle."

17. Cf. Cicero, *De Finibus* III, v–vii.

18. Cf. J.-P. Sartre, *Existentialism and Human Emotions* (New York: Philosophical Library, 1957), 24–28.

19. See Nahmanides, ad Lev. 19:2.

20. A similar argument might be used against our thesis: If a being just is its actions, what remains to cause those actions? But note that our claim is that a being is its program. The plan and capabilities that define a being's actions and render them effectual is its essence both in the Aristotelian sense (as what differentiates this being from all others) and in the Spinozistic sense (as what expresses its nature and identity). The sheer givenness (materiality in Aristotelian philosophy) at the core of every finite existence does not, as such, qualitatively differentiate any being from the rest. But, as each being elaborates its act, proliferates its expression, and exfoliates its capabilities, it gives itself an identity that lends substance to that existential core. We can see here both why matter is necessary to finite beings and why materialism is inadequate as an account of their natures and activities.

21. Operatively, the sniper must be treated as the exigencies of his pragmatic role demand, as long as he represents an imminent danger. Once he is disarmed, his claims as a person return to the fore. He now forfeits many of the civil presumptions that society has accorded him in fleshing out the dignity of personhood, for his actions have defeated many of those presumptions. But he does not lose all of them. And never does he lose the basic existential rights of personhood: He may not be tortured to reveal the whereabouts of his accomplices. Even while armed, his deserts as a person are not nugatory. Thus the moral requirement of phased measures: Deadly force may not be brought against him, even as he fires, if lesser measures would suffice to halt the danger he presents. See page 43.

22. Kantian ethics derives, say, kindness to animals as a humane virtue, not as a corollary to the categorical imperative. One can say that humaneness is part of what we cultivate in treating humanity in ourselves as an end and never merely a means. But that argument is on a par with the celebrated proof that Adam wore a yarmulke, which rests on the verse (Gen. 3:23) announcing that God sent Adam out of the garden: "Do you think he'd send him out bareheaded!" For the nutritional risks of vegetarianism, see *New York Times*, June 20, 1998.

23. Spinoza, *Ethics* 4, prop. 18, Scholium, ed. Gebhardt, vol. 2, 222–24.

24. See Lev. 19:17–19; cf. *God of Abraham*, 160.

25. See Jude Dougherty's review of *On Justice* in *Review of Metaphysics* 46 (1993): 614–15.

26. See G. E. Moore, *Principia Ethica* (Cambridge: Cambridge University Press, 1986; first published 1903), chap. 5.

27. Kenneth Seeskin, "Is Existence a Perfection?—A Case Study in the Philosophy of Leibniz," *Idealistic Studies* 8 (1978): 124–35.

28. Spinoza, *Ethics*, III, prop. 29, schol.; Definitions of the Emotions, 43–44, ed. Gebhardt, vol. 2, 162, 202.

29. See, e.g., Porphyry, *De Abstinentia* III, 20; Ikhwān al-Safā', *The Case of the Animals vs Man*. Cf. the discussion of *zekhut*, p. 40–44.

30. Thus he plays on their views about omnipotence and voluntarism to generate the inference that God created things that would be otiose on their assumptions; see *Guide* III, 17.3, 25.

31. "Time Out," in *The Poetry of Robert Frost*, ed. Edwin Connery Lathem (New York: Holt, Rhinehart and Winston, 1969), 355–56.

32. See Spinoza, *Ethics* IV, props. 35–37; V, prop. 36.

33. See *On Justice*, chap. 1, and *God of Abraham*, chap. 1.

34. See Saadiah on Job 34:17–19, trans. Goodman, 359–61.

35. Hertz explains (ad loc.): "The olives were gently pounded in a mortar, and the first drops of oil obtained were of the purest quality."

36. See Ernest Klein, *A Comprehensive Etymological Dictionary of the Hebrew Language for Readers of English* (New York: Macmillan, 1987), 198.

37. Cf. *God of Abraham*, 215–19.

38. In context the praise in Deuteronomy applies to Gad, but Avot and many subsequent texts apply the words to Moses. Avot goes on to argue that a late repentance does not avail for one who misled the many—traditionally, an allusion to the apostate Elisha ben Abuya. The sins of the penitent misleader "rise in judgment against him," not simply in homiletic imagery, but because they permanently stain his character through their fusion with his persona in his public teaching and example.

39. Cf. Urbach, *The Sages*, 1.496–508; Solomon Schechter, *Aspects of Rabbinic Theology* (New York: Macmillan, 1909; reprint, New York: Schocken, 1961, 1972), 170–98.

40. Jacob Neusner, "Systematic Integration and Theology: The Concept of *Zekhut* in Formative Judaism," in Mark Cohen, Daniel Snell, and David Weisberg, eds., *Near Eastern Studies in Honor of William W. Hallo* (Bethesda: CDL Press, 1993), 170–80.

41. A. Marmorstein, *The Doctrine of Merits in Old Rabbinical Literature* (London: Jews College, 1920).

42. See *Mekhilta de-R. Ishmael*, Va-Yehi; Va-Yissa.

43. See Apollonius Molon *ap.* Josephus, *Contra Apion* 2.14; Origen, *Contra Celsum* 4.31; etc.; Marmorstein, *Doctrine*, p. 27.

44. For the *rodef* see Emanuel Rackman, "Violence and the Value of Life: The Halakhic View," in Baron et al., eds., *Violence and Defense*, 124–25, 129.

45. David Hume, *An Enquiry Concerning the Principles of Morals*, IV, ed. Niddich, 205–6. Human social arrangements foster the illusion that the two-parent family is no longer necessary. But it is only because many more than two persons assist in child rearing that individuals can contemplate the prospect of raising children "on their own." Hillary Clinton has popularized this notion, and neo-conservatives have taken umbrage at the political edge her rhetoric has given the idea. To her slogan "It takes a village" to raise a child, they retort, "It takes a family." But surely what we have here, in bio-social terms, is not an either/or but a both/and.

46. See Gilles Deleuze's extended meditation on this theme in *Expressionism in Philosophy: Spinoza* (New York: Zone Books, 1990).

47. Alasdair MacIntyre argues that natural law may present us with categorical imperatives in the strong, Kantian sense that revolves around the idea of acting on principle; see "How Can We Learn what Veritatis Splendor Has to Teach?" *The Thomist* 58 (1994): 171–95. I too find such imperatives in nature, encoded in the aspiration of all things toward perfection. But, like the love of truth, such imperatives remain to be elicited, interpreted, and appropriated. Their presence does not negate the role of the subject. The book still needs a reader, if it is to be read. Thus even "Choose life" is not a perfect categorical imperative, since its normative force is not without exception, as heroes and martyrs seem to know and to testify by their actions. "Choose life" is a corollary of the love of God and the imperative which that love conveys, of aspiration toward perfection.

48. For the false polarity of deontology and teleology, see *On Justice*, chap. 3.

2. Judaism and Human Rights

1. See Louis Henkin, "Judaism and Human Rights," *Judaism* 25 (1976): 132–33 ff.; contrast L. E. Goodman, "Equality and Human Rights: The Lockean and the Judaic

Views," in the same volume, 357–62. Henkin's article "was updated and appears in the Vatican Jewish–Christian Dialogue 1965–85 Volume (Vatican, 1988) and is the only significant piece cited by Roman Catholic sources"—Richard Freund, *Understanding Jewish Ethics* 2: 177, n. 11. Cf. Stanley Benn, "Rights," *Encyclopedia of Philosophy* (New York: Macmillan, 1967), 7: 195; Daniel Polish, "Judaism and Human Rights," *Journal of Ecumenical Studies* 19 (1982): 40–50; Alasdair MacIntyre, *After Virtue* (Notre Dame: Notre Dame University Press, 1984), 67–69; Eugene Borowitz, "The Torah, Written and Oral, and Human Rights: Foundations and Deficiencies," in Hans Küng and J. Moltmann, *The Ethics of the World Religions and Human Rights* (Philadelphia: Trinity Press, 1990), 25.

2. Francis Galton, the founder of modern, i.e., post-Darwinian eugenics, appealed to clerical celibacy to help explain the relative inefficacy of selection pressures in refining and advancing the human population. See F. Galton, *Hereditary Genius* (1869; 2d ed., London: Macmillan, 1925), 343–45.

3. See, e.g., Francis Oakley, "Legitimation by Consent: The Question of the Medieval Roots," *Viator* 14 (1983): 303–35.

4. Maimonides's Code, the *Mishneh Torah*, is called the *Yad Ḥazakah* or "Strong Hand" as an allusion to its fourteen volumes, since the Hebrew word *yad*, hand, has a numerical value of 14.

5. See H. Malter, *Saadia Gaon: His Life and Works* (New York, 1926; reprint, New York: Hermon Press, 1969), 159–71.

6. The Arabic title was *Kitāb al-Mukhtār fī ʾl-Āmānāt wa-ʾl-Iʿtiqādāt*. As Kafih explains: "In every manuscript of the original version of our teacher, the title is *The Book of Beliefs and Convictions*, and so it was translated [in 1186] by R. Judah Ibn Tibbon [the father of Samuel Ibn Tibbon]. For the text he had before him was that of an early version. But in codex M [Bodleian MS Pococke 148], which is in my view the text of our teacher's final revision, the title is given as I have written it [*K. al-Mukhtār fī ʾl-Āmānāt wa ʾl-ʾIʿtiqādāt*]. And rightly so. For our teacher did not set out simply to gather a compendium of beliefs and convictions, but to demonstrate which beliefs were worthy of choice and which convictions were true in his estimation." J. Kafih, ed., *Sefer ha-Nivḥar ba-Emunot uva-Deʿot*, 1, n. 1; cf. preface, pp. 6–9: "I do not have any doubt that this is the title in his final revision" (9).

7. See Goodman, "Saadiah Gaon's Interpretive Technique. . . ."

8. See Pamela Huby, "Traces of the Theory of Natural Rights in Greek Thought," *Filozovska Istrazivanja* (Zagreb) 37 (1990), 1105–10, in Croatian; English version in *Synthesis Philosophica* 5 (1990): 499–505. In view of the current political situation in the Balkans, these two journals are not easily come by. Even the author does not have a copy. I am grateful to her for a transcript of her English original.

9. Cf. Job 4:2, 7:11 for the moral imperative (and spiritual right) of self-expression—even before God.

10. Susan Ford Wiltshire, *Greece, Rome and the Bill of Rights* (Norman: University of Oklahoma Press, 1992), 112–13.

11. Huby, "Traces," 504.

12. Huby, "Traces," 503.

13. Mogens Hansen, *The Athenian Assembly in the Age of Demosthenes* (Oxford: Blackwell, 1987), 8.

14. Douglas Knight, "Political Rights and Powers in Monarchic Israel," *Semeia* (1994): 93–117.

15. Gerard Watson, "The Natural Law and Stoicism," in A. A. Long, ed., *Problems in Stoicism* (London: Athlone Press, 1971), 216–38; cf. Huby, "Traces," 499.

16. See Moshe Greenberg, "Some Postulates of Biblical Criminal Law," in his *Studies in the Bible and Jewish Thought* (Philadelphia: JPS, 1995), 25–41,

17. See Robert Gordis in M. Konvitz, ed., *Judaism and Human Rights* (New York: Norton, 1972), 190–91; the Rabbis are horrified at Phineas's attack on Cozbi and Zimri (Num. 25); R. Judah ben Pazi envisions Moses and the elders as intending to sanction Phineas for acting without due procedures: They would have placed him under a ban, he urges, but for the intervention of the Holy Spirit. See E. E. Urbach in Baron, Wise, and Goodman, eds., *Violence and Defense in the Jewish Experience*, pp. 104–5.

18. Maimonides codifies the rabbinic law elaborated from these foundations in MT 14, under the rubrics *Sanhedrin* and *Evidence*, trans. A. M. Hershman (New Haven: Yale University Press, 1949), 3–136.

19. Does this seem parochial? It is easy to forget that the Torah was the law of Israel long before it was claimed as the universal heritage of humanity; no later claimant has sought to implement its social legislation systematically. The idea that the "Old Testament" is particularistic and the "New" universal is simply an old polemical charge that plays off the universalism of the Torah against its own more immediate focus.

20. But cf. B. Bava Metzia 115a, Bava Kamma 27b–28a.

21. Cf. Hayim S. Nahmani, *Human Rights in the Old Testament* (Tel Aviv: Joshua Chalchik, 1964); Haim Cohn, *Human Rights in Jewish Law* (New York: Ktav, 1984); Robert M. Cover, "Obligation: A Jewish Jurisprudence of the Social Order," *Journal of Law and Religion* 5 (1987): 65–74; Susan A. Wolfson, "Modern Liberal Rights Theory and Jewish Law," *Journal of Law and Religion* 9 (1992): 399–427. Samuel Stoljar responds to the notion that rights cannot be inferred from claims, commands, or obligations in *An Analysis of Rights* (New York: St Martin's, 1984). See also Milton Konvitz, "Conscience and Civil Disobedience in the Jewish Tradition," in *Judaism and Human Rights*, 161–78; David Daube, *Civil Disobedience in Antiquity* (Edinburgh: Edinburgh University Press, 1972); and Robert Wilson, *Prophecy and Society in Ancient Israel* (Philadelphia: Fortress Press, 1980).

22. See Shmuel Safrai, *The Literature of the Sages*, and *God of Abraham*, esp. chap. 4.

23. Immanuel Kant, *The Metaphysics of Morals*, trans. Mary Gregor (Cambridge: Cambridge University Press, 1991), 169 (363).

24. See A. S. McGrade, "Rights, Natural Rights, and the Philosophy of Law," in Anthony Kenny and Jan Pinborg, eds., *The Cambridge History of Later Medieval Philosophy* (Cambridge: Cambridge University Press, 1982); and McGrade's discussion of the medieval appropriations of Aristotle on this topic in "Aristotle's Place in the History of Natural Rights," *Review of Metaphysics* 49 (1996): 803–29. Cf. Brian Tierney, "Villey, Ockham and the Origin of Individual Rights," in J. Witte and F. S. Alexander, eds., *The Weightier Matters of Law: A Tribute to Harold J. Berman* (Atlanta: Scholars Press 1988), 1–31; cf. Tierney's "Origins of Natural Rights Language: Texts and Contexts, 1150–1250," *History of Political Thought* 10 (1989): 615–46; and his "Aristotle and the American Indians," *Chistianesimo nella storia* 12 (1991): 295–322. Alonso de la Vera Cruz, *Defense of the Indians: Their Rights*, ed. and trans. E. J. Burrus (St. Louis: Jesuit Historical Institute, 1968).

25. I quote the JPS translation of *The Prophets* (Philadelphia, 1978). To do justice, as Genesis 18:25 shows, means, in Hebrew, as in English, to do what is right: uphold the innocent and condemn the guilty—in a practical way, to recognize their deserts. *Shiftu* here connotes recognition of rights, just as the English 'condemn' entails not merely judgment but a finding of guilt.

26. A. S. McGrade, "Righting Some Wrongs about Rights," paper, December 28, 1993, American Philosophical Association, Atlanta. This paper contains a fine review of the con-

troversy over the idea of rights in medieval discourse; cf. McGrade's "Ockham and the Birth of Individual Rights," in Brian Tierney and Peter Linehan, eds., *Authority and Power: Studies on Medieval Law and Government* (Cambridge: Cambridge University Press, 1980), 149–65; Alan Gewirth, "Rights and Virtues," *Review of Metaphysics* 38 (1985): 739–62.

27. Martin Golding, "Justice and Rights: A Study in Relationship," in Earl E. Shelp, ed., *Justice and Health Care* (Boston: Reidel, 1981), 23–35; cited here, p. 30.

28. H. Bracton, *On the Laws and Customs of England*, ed. G. E. Woodbine and S. E. Thorne (Cambridge: Harvard University Press, 1968), 23; cf. Golding, "Justice and Rights," 29.

29. See Golding, "Justice and Rights," 27.

30. For the connection of Bentham's notion that rights are "rhetorical nonsense—nonsense on stilts" (*Anarchical Fallacies*, ed. Bowring, 2: 501, para. 2) with his horror of the fear of ghosts and abhorrence of legal fictions, see C. K. Ogden's introduction to Bentham's *Theory of Fictions*, xv–xvi, citing Bentham's *Constitutional Code*, ed. Bowring, 9: 83–84. See chap. 4 below, note 2.

31. See Golding, "Justice and Rights," 54, 57.

32. McGrade, "Righting Some Wrongs," 10.

33. See Golding, "Justice and Rights," 28.

34. David Novak, "Is There a Concept of Individual Rights in Jewish Law?" *Jewish Law Association Studies* VII (1994) 129–52, cited here, p. 137.

35. Novak, "Is There a Concept," 138–39.

36. See Mishnah Sanhedrin 11.6, Makkot 1.1–6; cf. Bava Kamma 7.3, Bava Batra 3.4.

37. Cf. Novak,"Is There a Concept," 146–47.

38. See *On Justice*, pp. 34–39, 160–62, 185–86.

39. *Mekhilta de R. Shimon ben Yohai*, ed. J. N. Epstein and E. Z. Melamed (Jerusalem: Mekitse Nirdamim, 1955) 211.

40. The point bears on our discussion of pornography in chap. 4; see p. 118 below.

41. Besides the sources already cited, see Abraham Katsch, *The Biblical Heritage of American Democracy* (New York: Ktav, 1977); D. Ritschl, "Der Beitrag des Calvinismus für die Entiwicklung des Menschenrechtsgedankens in Europa und Noramerika," *Evangelische Theologie* 40 (1980): 333–45; and the balanced account in Freund, *Understanding Jewish Ethics*. Cf. *God of Abraham*, esp. chap. 4.

42. Muhtar Holland, *Al-Ghazālī on the Duties of Brotherhood* (London: Latimer, 1975). See Goodman, "Friendship in Aristotle, Miskawayh, and al-Ghazālī."

43. See James Barr, "Ancient Biblical Laws and Modern Human Rights," in D. A. Knight and P. J. Paris, eds., *Justice and the Holy* (Atlanta: Scholars Press, 1989), 25.

44. Cf. Walter Harrelson, *The Ten Commandments and Human Rights* (Philadelphia: Fortress Press, 1980); Freund, 2: 144–45.

45. See *God of Abraham*, chap. 5.

46. See Maimonides, *Guide* III, 27, 33; *MT* I, II.

47. See *ED* IX, 1, Kafih 262–63; Rosenblatt, 324–25. For Rāzī, see Goodman in *EI²*, *Studia Islamica*, etc.

48. See Goodman, "Razī's Myth of the Fall of the Soul."

49. See Saadiah, *The Book of Theodicy*, trans. Goodman, 128–29.

50. See al-Ash'arī, *Kitab al-Luma'*; A. J. Wensinck, *The Muslim Creed: Its Genesis and Development* (London: Cass, 1965; 1932); George F. Hourani, *Islamic Rationalism: The Ethics of 'Abd al-Jabbār* (Oxford: Clarendon Press, 1971).

51. See Eric Ormsby, *Theodicy in Islamic Thought: The Dispute over al-Ghazālī's "Best of all Possible Worlds"* (Princeton: Princeton University Press, 1984).

52. *Book of Theodicy*, 127.

53. *Book of Theodicy*, 358–60. The passage quoted from the Book of Job is here rendered according to Saadiah's Arabic translation.

54. Compare Maimonides's gloss of "Will He who planted the ear not hear . . ." (Ps. 94:9) at *Guide* III, 19, Munk 3: 340 ab.

55. Thus the emphasis on *general* providence in God's speech from the storm wind as Saadiah reads it; see *Book of Theodicy*, 393–94.

56. *Book of Theodicy*, 123–24.

57. *Book of Theodicy*, 128, 141.

58. See Job 21:34; cf. 13:8, 16; *Book of Theodicy*, 128.

59. Saadiah, *ED* VI, 4; IX, 5, 8 = Rosenblatt 246, 338, 349; and ad Job 33:29, *Book of Theodicy*, 354.

60. *ED* IX, 4; Kafih, 269, Rosenblatt, 334.

61. See B. Berakhot 5a, citing Lam. 3:40, Ps. 94:12, and Prov. 3:12.

62. Kant, *Lectures on Ethics*, ad fin.

63. *Book of Theodicy*, ed. Kafih, 14–15; trans. Goodman, pp. 126–27.

64. See *Book of Theodicy*, on Job 39.

65. See Goodman, *Avicenna*, chap. 3; "Ibn Bājjah," in Leaman and Nasr, eds., *History of Islamic Philosophy* (London: Routledge, 1996) 294–312.

66. See *Guide* I, 54, 27, 19; *ED* II, 12; Kafih, 109; Rosenblatt, 130.

67. See William Montgomery Watt, *The Formative Period of Islamic Thought* (Edinburgh: Edinburgh University Press, 1973), esp. chap. 4.

68. A. S. McGrade, "Righting Some Wrongs," 6. Cf. *God of Abraham*, 97–98.

69. Thomas Aquinas, *Summa Theologiae* IIa IIae, q. 104, a. 5; q. 10 a. 8; McGrade, "Righting Some Wrongs," 5.

70. 1 Sam. 8:11–18, JPS translation, in *The Prophets* (Philadelphia, 1978).

71. As Freund notes (*Understanding Jewish Ethics*), Henkin's argument that there was no notion of rights in biblical Judaism makes (selective) use of the prophetic account of the establishment of the Israelite monarchy. Yet Samuel's objections are couched as warnings against encroachments on the people's established rights, and the prophet protests his own consistent respect for those rights. From Samuel's standpoint, monarchy was a melancholy necessity to be acknowledged, not an ideal to be achieved. But the case for a monarchy is made, by way of deference to popular demand, and this capitulation suggests, even by the prophet's acquiescence, both a right of the people to be heard as to their form of government, and a variety of rights and interests which a central government, despite its costs, must be called upon to respect and serve.

72. Freund's theme is the multiplicity of voices and dialectic of outlooks in the canon. He cites 1 Sam. 9 for a monarchical view, opposed to the critical view of 1 Samuel 8. But the two chapters stand side by side, and the tensions between them are not those of logic. As Knight writes ("Political Rights and Powers"), "While the two stories depict diametrically different divine assessments of royalty, there is actually no direct conflict in terms of popular sentiments: if Israel demands a monarchy in one account, they do not resist when God volunteers it in the other narrative." Even this seems a little strong: Samuel (reluctantly, like a man facing retirement) sees the need, as God does; and God knows the potential for abuse at least as well as Samuel does. But recognition that power corrupts does not mean rejection of all institutions, and knowledge that the people's servants may serve goals of their own does not eliminate the people's need for servants. In the eyes of the prophets, the young Saul was rightly chosen, because he was the best man for the task to which he was called. The old Saul, a tragic figure, was no less rightly replaced.

73. Maimonides seems to have been annoyed at having to treat a Muslim potentate for secondary impotence, arising, perhaps, from sexual overindulgence. He characterizes

the Rāzīan complaint against physical sufferings as an unwillingness to accept the fact that not all existence is for one's own sake alone and that nature did not constitute us with an infinite sexual capacity. See *Guide* III, 12, and *The Treatise on Cohabitation* (written for al-Malik al-Mustaffar, the Ayyubid sultan of Hama, in 1190 or 1191), trans. Fred Rosner in *Maimonides: Medical Writings* (Haifa: Maimonides Research Institute, 1984).

74. The Rabbis had much negative experience with the billeting of Roman troops and with Roman demands for taxes in kind, the latter a symptom of the inflation rampant in the Roman Empire of the third century. See ARN 20, B. Sanhedrin 98b, Bava Kamma 113a, Bava Batra 8a, 9a; and the discussion in Safrai, p. 25, citing Tosefta Eruvin 5:22.

75. For the Rambam's response to the ideal of the philosopher king, see A. Melamed, *The Philosopher King in Medieval and Renaissance Philosophical Thought* (Atlanta: Scholars Press, forthcoming).

76. *Guide* I, 46. "The Arabic word *sulṭān*" (cf. the Hebrew *shilton*), as Bernard Lewis explains, "is an abstract noun meaning authority and rule, and was used from ancient times to denote government," *The Legacy of Islam*, ed. J. Schacht and C. E. Bosworth (Oxford: Oxford University Press, 1974), 169.

77. The monarchical role is legitimated by its military function. But Maimonides sees the king as a magistrate too, since kings may serve as *nasi* (Sanhedrin president) and are elected by a prophet or Sanhedrin for their competence and uprightness, which take precedence over the familial claims. See *MT, Hilkhot Melakhim* I, 2, 7, 8, citing Deut. 25:19, 1 Sam. 15:1–3, 2 Sam. 7:16 with Ps. 132:12, 89:31, 33, etc.

78. Accordingly, we should not allow our familiar democratic rhetoric to obscure from us the fact that although a president or a prime minister is an officer of the state and accountable to the people, and is far from being an arbitrary tyrant, he is not, for that reason, any the less an exemplar of the Aristotelian principle that "the rule of one is best."

79. "The Code of Maimonides," *Review of Metaphysics* 3 (1950): 519–22.

80. "Eight Chapters," 5, Gorfinkle 32, trans. 71; cf. *Guide* III, 15; I, 73.10.

81. "Eight Chapters," 4, 24, trans. 62–63; cf. *Guide* I, 58, 59, etc.

82. See, e.g., Nizām al-Mulk, *The Book of Government or Rules for Kings* (written between 1086 and 1091), trans. Hubert Darke (London: Routledge, 1960); al-Ghazālī, *Naṣīḥat al-Mulūk* (written between 1105 and 1110), trans., F. R. C. Bagley as *Ghazālī's Book of Counsel for Kings* (London: Oxford University Press, 1964).

3. *Abortion and the Emergence of Life*

1. Cf. G. R. Dunstan, *The Artifice of Ethics* (London: SCM, 1974), 53.

2. *Guide* I, 72; II, 6–12. See my "Maimonidean Naturalism," in *Neoplatonism and Jewish Thought*.

3. See Ibn Tufayl, *Ḥayy Ibn Yaqzān*.

4. Al-Ghazālī, *Al-Munqidh min al-Dalāl*, ed. F. Jabre (Beirut: Commission Internationale pour la Traduction des Chef-d'oeuvre, 1959), 50–51.

5. See Goodman, "Did Al-Ghazālī Deny Causality?"; cf. "Ghazālī's Argument from Creation."

6. See Goodman, "Ordinary and Extraordinary Language."

7. Such thinking, ascribed to "Moses," is criticized in Galen, *De Usu Partium* XI; cf. R. Walzer, *Galen on Jews and Christians* (London: Oxford University Press, 1949), 11; J. Schacht and M. Meyerhof, "Maimonides against Galen on Philosophy and Cosmogony," *Bulletin of the Faculty of Arts of the University of Cairo* 5 (1939): 82; tr. 70.

8. See Goodman, "The Greek Impact on Arabic Literature."

9. See al-Ashʿarī, *Kitāb al-Lumaʿ*, ed. R. McCarthy, 77–79

10. *TF* 17, ed. Bouyges, 195 = *TT* 17, ed. Bouyges, 517.

11. *TF*, ed. Bouyges, 203–4 = *TT*, ed. Bouyges, 536.

12. *TF* 1, 57–58 = *TT* 1, 37–38; cf. Aristotle *Metaphysics*, Theta 2.

13. *Qurʾān* 36:77–82; and al-Ghazālī's discussion in *Faḍāʾiḥ al-Bāṭiniyya*, ed. A.-R. Badawi (Cairo: National Printing and Publishing House, 1964), 48.

14. *The Book of Theodicy*, trans. Goodman, ad Job 10:10; 231; cf. H. A. Wolfson, *Philo* (Cambridge: Harvard University Press, 1962), 2: 200. I translate the text of Job here as in Saadiah's Arabic version.

15. Al-Ghazālī, *Iḥyāʾ ʿUlūm al-Dīn*, Book 35, pt. 2 (Cairo, 1967–68) 4: 324–25.

16. *Iḥyāʾ*, Book 35, pt. 1. For Maimonides's treatment of natural and volitional causes, see Goodman, "Determinism, Freedom and Responsibility. . . ."

17. *Guide* III, 13, 25, 32; "Eight Chapters," 8. See pp. 69–70 in this book.

18. See David Novak, "Some Aspects of the Doctrine of the Self-Contraction of the Godhead in Kabbalistic Theology," in Goodman, ed., *Neoplatonism and Jewish Thought*; cf. Stephen Benin, *The Footprints of God: Divine Accommodation in Jewish and Christian Thought* (Albany: SUNY Press, 1993).

19. *Guide* III, 22, ed. Munk, 3: 46 ab; cf. Ibn Tufayl, trans. Goodman, 114–27.

20. In his Commentary on Avot (ed. Rabinovitz, 182; trans, David, 100–1) Maimonides treats the ten items as paradigms of the miraculous in nature: The list is not meant to be exhaustive. The general principle is that God does not alter the order of creation: The Sages "did not believe in temporal changes in God's will but held that at the outset, in creating things, He set it in the nature of each thing that all that would be done with it could be done. Whether what would be done was commonplace and thus 'natural' or a novelty reserved for rare occasions and thus a portent, it was all the same." Maimonides is more welcoming than Al-Ghazālī to the polyvalency of human volition, but he departs from Al-Ghazālī here only in restricting to the original creation the imparting of the necessary natures to things. And even that point was anticipated when Al-Ghazālī urged that God's creative action could produce temporal changes from a timeless plan; see *TF*, 50.

21. See *Guide* II, 48, for the fish; I, 67, for the finality of creation.

22. *Guide* II, 36–38; see Goodman, "Matter and Form as Attributes of God."

23. Cf. Mishnah Ketubot 3.2; Deut. 32:31, 1 Sam. 2:25. For the "reckoning," see Maimonides, *MT* XI, iv.

24. See The Laws of Hammurabi, 209–14, in E. R. Driver and John C. Miles, eds., *The Babylonian Laws* (Oxford: The Clarendon Press, 1955), 2: 79.

25. See *God of Abraham*, chap. 3, esp. 101–2.

26. Stephen Ricks, "Abortion in Antiquity," *Anchor Bible Dictionary* (Garden City, NY: Doubleday, 1992). Ricks surveys the Lipitishtar, Sumerian, and Hittite laws.

27. Cf. *God of Abraham*, 19–22, regarding pagan child sacrifice.

28. W. W. Tarn, *Hellenistic Civilisation*, 3rd ed., rev. by the author and G. T. Griffith (London: Edward Arnold, 1952; reprint, 1966), 100–2, where further evidence is presented.

29. Trans. Lancelot C. L. Brenton (London, 1851; reprint, n.d., Zondervan).

30. Abraham Geiger inferred that some ancient Jewish law must have ruled as the *LXX* provides; see *Ha-Mikra ve-Targumav*, 280, 343. But the *LXX* does not need a legal authority if, as the translators believe, it *establishes* one.

31. Cf. the oath of Asaph in the seventh century and that of Amatus in the sixteenth, as expressions of the same abiding Jewish moral sensibility: F. Rosner and S. Muntner, *Annals of Internal Medicine* 63 (1965): 317–20; H. Friedenwald in *The Jews and Medicine* (Baltimore: Johns Hopkins, 1944), 368–70.

32. *De Specialibus Legibus* III, 108–9, trans. after F. H. Colson (London: Heinemann, 1958), 7: 545.

33. Tacitus writes: "Things sacred with us, with them have no sanctity, while they allow what with us is forbidden . . . all their customs, which are perverse and disgusting, owe their strength to their very badness." Tacitus betrays his penchant for disinformation by contradicting his own story about the image of an animal in the Temple of Jerusalem (*History* 5.4, vs. 5.9). He betrays his groundless hatred not only by ascribing the prohibition of infanticide to an unreasonable (in Jews!) desire to reproduce, but also in explaining *shemittah* as an extension of "the charm of indolence" from a weekly to a septennial cycle. The fugitive (5.2) and disfigured (5.3–4) race of Jews, Tacitus writes, hate and are hated by all the gods. Jews attract converts and clients from the outcasts of other nations (5.5). The historian's negativity remains unabated even when he singles out the Jews' kindness and honesty toward one another, their avoidance of relations with foreign women, fearlessness in battle, and rejection of infanticide. See Moses Hadas, trans., *The Complete Works of Tacitus* (New York: Random House, 1942), 657–66.

34. *Spec. Leg.* III, 110–11.

35. *Spec. Leg.* III, 112–19; cf. Josephus, *Antiquities*, 4.278.

36. Maimonides, *MT, Hilkhot Yesodei ha-Torah* 5.5, glossing 2 Sam. 20:4–22 and following Resh Lakish, Y. Terumot 47a.

37. Maimonides, *MT* XI, iv, 8.15, with *Migdal Oz*, ad loc.; cf. David Feldman, *Marital Relations, Birth Control and Abortion in Jewish Law*, 278.

38. Maimonides, *MT, Hilkhot Rotzeah* 1.9.

39. See *Mekhilta* to Exod. 21:12–14; J. David Bleich, "Abortion in Halakhic Literature," in F. Rosner and J. D. Bleich, eds., *Jewish Bioethics* (New York: Sanhedrin, c. 1979.), 155–56.

40. See also Ḥullin 58a, Gittin 23b, Nazir 51a, Bava Kamma 88b, cf. Temurah 31a and the responsa cited by Rosner in "The Jewish Attitude toward Abortion," in M. Kellner, ed., *Contemporary Jewish Ethics* (New York: Sanhedrin, 1978), 267 n. 7.

41. David Novak, *Law and Theology in Judaism* (New York: Ktav, 1974), 118; cf. R. Moses Schick, *Responsa Marharam Schick, Yoreh Deah*, 155; R. David Hoffman, *Responsa Melamed Leho'il, Yoreh Deah*, 69.

42. *Shevet me-Yehudah*, 26 ff; cf. R. Nahum Rabinovitch, *Ha-Darom* 28 (5729), 19 f., cited in Bleich, "Abortion in Halakhic Literature," 148.

43. See Naḥmanides, *Torat ha-Adam*, in *Kitvei Ramban*, ed. Chaim Dov Chavel (Mossad ha-Rav Kook, 1986), 2: 29; and on Tosfot B. Niddah 44a.

44. See R. Ezekiel Landau of Prague (1713–93), *Noda bi-Yehudah* 2 (Vilna, 1904), Ḥoshen Mishpat 59; Yom Tov Lipmann Heller (1579–1654), *Tosfot Yom Tob* to Mishnah Niddah, cited in Novak, *Law and Theology*, 119.

45. *Ḥavvot Yair*, 31; cf. *Zekhuta de-Avraham*, cited in *Ḥemdat Israel*; and *Responsa Ateret Ḥakhamim, Even ha-Ezer*, 1; R. Jacob Emden, *Responsa She'elat Yavetz*, 1, 43.

46. See B. Shabbat 135b, treating Num. 18:16.

47. B. Sanhedrin 57b, glossing Gen. 9:6 Gen. Rabbah 34.14. In B. Berakhot 50a we read: "Even the fetuses in their mothers' wombs uttered their song" at the parting of the Red Sea. The midrashic poetry here treats the fetus as a virtual subject. It too celebrated the redemption, but the word "even" shows that it was not a person when taking part in that event.

48. *Ḥiddushei R. Ḥayyim Levi* (1936) to Maimonides's *MT, Hilkhot Rotzeah* 1.9; Feldman, *Marital Relations*, 279.

49. *Pri ha-Aretz* III (1899), cited in Bleich, "Abortion," 158; Feldman, *Marital Relations*, 286.

50. *Teshuvoth Maharit*, 1, no. 99. As Bleich notes (153), the Maharit regards abortion

as a form of "wounding," therefore justifiable, like surgery, for the sake of maternal health. But fetal interests are still not overridden *ad libitum*.

51. *She'eloth Yavetz* (New York, 1961), no. 43, and Bleich, "Abortion," pp. 152, 159. Rabbi Emden's rulings on these two points are widely disputed by other halakhists. Notably he remarks ad Tosafot Niddah 44b: "Who is it that permits the killing of a fetus without reason?"

52. See *Jewish Monthly* (August-September 1989): 21.

53. *Teshuvoth Beit Yehudah* (Livorno, 1758); Rabbi Z. Uziel, *Responsa Mishpetei Uziel*, pt. 3, 46–47; *Responsa Beit Yehudah, Even ha-Ezer* 13; *She'elot Yitzhak*, 69; *Tzitz Eliezer*, vol. 9, 51:3; Bleich, "Abortion," 139; Rosner, "Jewish Attitude," 265.

54. *Tzitz Eliezer* 9 (1967), 236, 13 no. 102. That the permission involved a prospective Tay-Sachs birth indicates the gravity of the justifying fetal abnormality and the certitude of the prognosis required to move a rabbinic jurist on this point: Tay-Sachs disease can be detected *in utero* and is invariably and agonizingly fatal in infancy. For the problems of mass screening for Tay-Sachs carrier status, see Goodman and Goodman, "The Overselling of Genetic Anxiety"; F. Rosner, in Rosner and Bleich, Jewish Bioethics, 178–90. For R. Plocki's decision, see his *Hemdat Israel* (Pietrokow, 1927).

55. Among the key early Christian texts, *Didache* 2:2 treats the prohibition of abortion as a corollary of "Love thy neighbor as thyself," and 5:2 speaks, in rabbinic style, of abortion as destroying the image of God; cf. *Epistle of Barnabas* 19:5, 20:2; *Apostolic Constitutions* 7.3.2.

56. *Havvot Yair* (Lemberg, 1896), 31.

57. David Novak, *Jewish-Christian Dialogue* (New York: Oxford University Press, 1989), 9–11.

58. " 'Be Fruitful and Multiply': Issues Relating to Birth in Judaism," in Rela M. Geffen, ed., *Celebration and Renewal: Rites of Passage in Judaism* (Philadelphia: JPS, 1993), 12–31; see 16–19.

59. David Feldman in *Jewish Monthly* (August-September 1989): 23.

60. Laura Geller in *Jewish Monthly* (August-September 1989): 25.

61. David Novak, "Be Fruitful . . . ," loc. cit.

62. Responsa *Koah Shor* no. 20; *Hiddushei R. Hayyim Ha-Levi* to Maimonides's Code; Feldman, *Marital Relations*, 277, 279.

63. See Maimonides *MT*, XI, iv, 8.15, and *Migdal Oz* ad loc.; cf. Feldman, *Marital Relations*, 278.

64. Cf. Paul Ramsey, *The Ethics of Fetal Research* (New Haven: Yale University Press, 1975), 28.

65. In J. Noonan, ed., *The Morality of Abortion* (Cambridge: Harvard University Press, 1972), 107.

66. See L. E. Goodman and M. J. Goodman, "Prevention," esp. 31–32.

67. In 1990 the Centers for Disease Control estimated the number of abortions in the United States at 1.4 million. With the aging of the population, the annual number declined to 1.3 million in 1993 and 1.2 million in 1994, a rate for 1994 of 21 abortions per 1,000 women aged 15 to 44, or 321 per 1,000 live births. In 1985 there were some 1.6 million abortions annually. Annually, some 3 percent of the women of reproductive age were obtaining abortions in the early 1980s. In metropolitan areas, where most abortion services are located, there were over 1,500 abortions per 1,000 live births, and the number of abortions had been exceeding that of live births since 1976. Nationwide in the 1980s and 1990s, some 30 percent of the pregnancies that did not end with stillbirths or miscarriages were terminated artificially. See S. K. Henshaw et al., "Abortion Services in the United States,

1984 and 1985," *Family Planning Perspectives* 19 (March-April 1987): 63–70; Associated Press, January 4, 1997.

4. On Liberty Reconsidered

1. Lucian, *The Sale of the Philosophers* (2nd century), trans. by Paul Turner as "Philosophies Going Cheap," in *Lucian: Satirical Sketches* (Baltimore: Penguin, 1968).

2. What Bentham wrote: "reasons for wishing there were such things as rights, are not rights . . . want is not supply—hunger is not bread. That which has no existence cannot be destroyed—that which cannot be destroyed cannot require anything to preserve it from destruction. *Natural rights* is simple nonsense: natural and imprescriptible rights, rhetorical nonsense,—nonsense upon stilts." *Anarchical Fallacies*, originally published in E. Dumont, *Tactique des Assemblées legislatives* (1816) and collected in John Bowring, ed., *The Works of Jeremy Bentham*, 2: 501. Bentham speaks sagely when he goes on to urge us to specificity, not jumbling legislative proposals in "an undistinguishable heap . . . under any such vague general terms as property, liberty, and the like." But the weakness of his approach becomes evident when he argues, in the same paragraph, "as there is no *right* which ought not to be maintained so long as it is upon the whole advantageous to the society that it should be maintained, so there is no right which, when the abolition of it is advantageous to society should not be abolished." Cf. Bowring, 3: 217–19; 8: 242–53, 327–28; and see the texts and discussions in C. K. Ogden, *Bentham's Theory of Fictions* (Paterson, NJ: Littlefield Adams, 1932; reprint, 1959).

3. See R. Sartorius, ed., *Paternalism* (Minneapolis: University of Minnesota Press, 1983).

4. Joel Feinberg, *Harm to Self: The Moral Limits of the Criminal Law* (New York: Oxford University Press, 1986).

5. A paradox naturally emerges here, since some of some social pressures might naturally take the form of expressions of opinion. The tension is not merely theoretical. The dialectic of political correctness is one expression of its power: Some forms of speech and action, deemed, say, progressively heretical, are privileged as such; their criticism is presumed censorious—at least in social contexts governed by fairly homogeneous norms— while other forms of social criticism are suppressed, under rationales drawn from Mill's own arguments. The closest Mill comes to addressing the difficulty is in acknowledging that it "is neither possible nor desirable" to expect no one's feelings toward another to remain uninfluenced by the other's personal deficiencies, say, of taste, good sense, or character. Mill counsels sensibly that we should caution our acquaintances about the estrangement which their foolish attitudes or offensive behavior might engender. This parallels the biblical obligation of reproof (Lev. 19:17). But that mild obligation of fellowship *(re'ut)* does not endorse a right or responsibility of bringing concerted social disapproval to bear; and Mill's counsels, similarly, do not extend to public actions undertaken with a view to altering behaviors that seem, say, self-destructive—or repressive. Mill writes, simply, "What I contend for is, that the inconveniences which are strictly inseparable from the unfavorable judgment of others are the only ones to which a person should ever be subjected for that portion of his conduct and character which concerns his own good, but which does not affect the interest of others in their relations with him" (*On Liberty*, 134–35).

6. See Herbert S. Frankel, "The Concept of Colonization" (Oxford: Oxford University Press, 1949); "The Tyranny of Economic Paternalism in Africa: A Study of Frontier Mentality, 1860–1960," *Optima* supplement (Johannesburg, 1960).

7. For the philosophical import of Mill's 35 years at the East India Company, see Lynn Zastoupil, *John Stuart Mill and India* (Stanford: Stanford University Press, 1994).

8. Gertrude Himmelfarb seems to write apologetically when she stresses that Mill's examples of justified despotism come from the distant past. See *On Liberty and Liberalism*, 21. Mill's strictures against Chinese culture (*On Liberty*, 129–30) and against the French and Spanish peoples of his own day (*Representative Government*, 213) show how contemporary and near to hand were the applications of his view that some peoples and cultures are simply not ready for liberal government. The very arguments in which Mill links liberalism with progress are mired in a chauvinism that broadcasts disapproval toward others— from the ancient civilizations of China and India to the opposite shore of the English Channel. Social criticism is always in order, and traditionalist societies are hardly exempt from it—although the old Tory response to Whiggery stands by: that exploitative capitalism can carry individualism too far when it battles against long established traditions. But beyond the niceties of that debate, the fact remains that colonialist paternalism or neomercantilist benign neglect sits a little too cozily with a willingness to write off the traditionalism or communalism of, say, the entire Third World as Asiatic lethargy or African backwardness, tropical or subtropical torpor—leaving the shrewd dealer from an industrial nation not only with the profits but also with the comfort of moral superiority in the collectively claimed virtues of vigor, individualism, and ambition. Mill does not voice colonial or imperial designs against France or Spain. He turns his argument in the direction of a vague hope that the energy and industry of individuals from these European nations (and trading partners) will, with the aid of institutions like those he commends, lead to the gradual reforms that will make liberal institutions possible, or palatable, in new locales. But aiming to hold up even *these* foreigners as an object lesson and a foil before the jingoism of his audience, he does not shrink from dismissing the French at large as "essentially a southern people" for whom "the double education of despotism and Catholicism has, in spite of their impulsive temperament, made submission and endurance the common character " (213). Nor does he balk at remarking (on the same page) that "the most envious of all mankind are the Orientals." The fascination of the exotic and the practices of opium exportation and full-scale imperialism help to explain how global dismissals of entire cultures can be turned from a hope and expectation of progress in Europe to a weary denial that it will begin any time soon in Asia. But lurking behind civil (or cousin-like) disdain and mercantile or colonial contempt is always the chance of war, in which stereotypes like those that Mill freely indulges become as much a part of the armamentum as guns and armor. For the dialectic of environmental racism and the notion of a "southern" temperament, see Goodman and Goodman, " 'Particularly Amongst the Sunburnt Nations. . . . ' "

9. The warrant for free trade, Mill urges, "rests on grounds different from, though equally solid with, the principle of individual liberty asserted in this Essay." The trouble here is not Mill's argument for the utility of free trade, but the absoluteness of his faith in its efficacy and—as with free speech—his unwillingness to consider values that might count against it. In classic Utilitarian fashion, Mill is more than willing to sacrifice varied interests to what his Benthamite calculus expects to be the general good: "In many cases an individual, in pursuing a legitimate object, necessarily and therefore legitimately causes pain or loss to others, or intercepts a good which they had reasonable hope of obtaining. . . ." The inability of Mill's standards to differentiate those cases of this kind that require regulation or remediation from those that do not—except where "fraud, treachery, and force" may be in play—is one good reason for preferring the Mosaic attempt to integrate law and morals over the secularist assumption that the two should be held apart. Monopoly, nepotism, and usury are just a few examples of unfair practices that do not involve fraud, force, or treachery.

10. Thus, in the Hebrew idiom, one can live as well as die "for the sanctification of God's name"—and the former is by far preferable, where the choice is possible.

11. Philo, *De Abrahamo* xxxvi, 201–4; see *God of Abraham*, 23–24; cf. the treatment of play in Philo, *Questions on Genesis* iv, 188.

12. Philo, *Quod Omnis Probus Liber Sit*, 1, 15, 17; cf. 20.

13. *Quod Omnis Probus Liber Sit*, 141.

14. See *God of Abraham*, pp. 84, 97–98, 123, 140, 182–84.

15. *Jerusalem* (1783), ii, trans. Samuels, 171. In the same last two pages, Mendelssohn writes: "Brothers, if you care for true piety, let us not feign agreement where diversity is evidently the plan and purpose of Providence.... Why should we make ourselves unrecognizable to each other in the most important concerns of our life by masquerading, since God has stamped everyone, not without reason, with his own facial features? . . . Reward and punish no doctrine, tempt and bribe no one to adopt any religious opinion! Let everyone be permitted to speak as he thinks, to invoke God after his own manner, or that of his fathers. . . . Let no one in your states be a searcher of hearts and a judge of thoughts; let no one assume a right that the Omniscient has reserved to himself alone" (trans. Arkush, 138–39).

16. Eugene Garver, *Aristotle's* Rhetoric: An Art of Character (Chicago: University of Chicago Press, 1994), 82–83.

17. Gertrude Himmelfarb, *On Liberty and Liberalism*, 47–48.

18. Mill, *The Earlier Letters*, ed. F. E. Mineka, 1: 153.

19. Mill, *Autobiography*, 116–17; cf. the more open elitism of *The Early Draft*, ed. Stillinger, 139, and the "rejected leaves," 188–89; Himmelfarb, 52–55.

20. Todd Gitlin, *The Murder of Albert Einstein* (New York: Farrar, Strauss and Giroux 1992), 37.

21. Collins and Skover, *The Death of Discourse*, 116

22. Collins and Skover, *Death of Discourse*, 74.

23. I owe this last thought, about associative psychology, to my colleague Elijah Millgram.

24. Locke's naturalism reserved to the individual the freedom to act and choose; Rawls's argument from virtual consent does the same. It was the Hobbesian idea that no rational chooser would give up the right to chose in matters affecting his own life and ultimate welfare that led Locke to the ideas of inalienable rights and limited sovereignty, and Rawls to the notion that no rational subject would surrender the right to choose. But in the present context Rawls's reassurance has only the force of a tautology. Meanwhile, Mill's anxieties about paternalism and his confidence in the Hobbesian rational ego allow his formulations to extend our liberties into a freedom to negate our rights and surrender our reason, undermining not only the rights themselves but their Lockean rationale.

25. Cass Sunstein, *Democracy and the Problem of Free Speech* (New York: Free Press, 1993).

26. *New York Times*, December 22, 1996, section 2, p. 1.

27. *New York Times*, February 21, 1997, p. B-3. For the misrepresentations of fact in *The People vs Larry Flynt*, see Matt Labash, "The Truth vs Larry Flynt," *The Weekly Standard*, February 17, 1997, pp. 19–26.

28. Indeed, the claim is widely made that it is censorship for the state to decline to offer public support for the production and display of pornographic art.

29. Sunstein, *Democracy and the Problem of Free Speech*, 10–11, 18–21, 215

30. Collins and Skover, *Death of Discourse*, 149–50.

31. See Jesse Green, *New York Times Magazine*, September 15, 1996, pp. 38–45, 54–55, 84–85.

32. Mill's essay was intended to be popular and topical, but it was not a mere occasional piece. As Himmelfarb has shown (*On Liberty and Liberalism*, esp. pp. xv–xviii), it

was a carefully crafted and painstakingly revised essay, in the light of which Mill made critical publication decisions affecting the balance of his oeuvre.

33. Willmoore Kendall, "The 'Open Society' and Its Fallacies," *American Political Science Review* 54 (1960): 972–79.

34. For the nexus of the family-planning movement, Zero Population Growth, eugenics, and the contraceptives industry, see Germaine Greer, *Sex and Destiny: The Politics of Human Fertility* (New York: Harper and Row, 1984).

35. Note the disparity here with the public relations posture of public health campaigns. Adolescent sexual activity, drug abuse, unwelcome pregnancies, and other disapproved acts are described as inevitable when access to condoms, needle exchanges, or abortions are in question. Such access, we are assured, is not to be construed as condonement. But the very mention of the hypothesis that spousal murder or abuse may be part of a larger pathology that might or should be socially addressed is branded, from a public relations standpoint, as blaming the victim.

36. *Hustler* used to run a regular cartoon feature, "Chester the Molester," designed to facilitate the judgment that violent and violative behaviors, including some pretty gory fantasies, were not only amusing or funny but also commonplace and in that sense ordinary, normal, and acceptable.

37. Philip Durham explains how Dashiell Hammett set "the violence-is-fun technique" at the core of his fiction: "The Continental Op soon became physically and personally involved in violence, getting smashed up thoroughly in 'One Hour.' It was not long, as in 'Women, Politics, and Murder,' before he thought violence was sheer pleasure, 'I began to throw my right fist into him. I liked that. His belly was flabby, and it got softer every time I hit it. I hit it often.' And the mood continued in 'Dead Yellow Women' where the Op observed Dummy Uhl, who with 'all the middle of him gone—slid down to the floor and made more of a puddle than a pile there.' As the Op continued down a hall, 'cracking everything' that got in his way and being 'cracked' back, he began to enjoy the violence, which was technically accentuated by one-sentence paragraphs. 'When he crouched above me I let him have it. / My bullet cut the gullet out of him. / I patted his face with my gun as he tumbled down past me.' " Philip Durham, "The *Black Mask* School," in David Madden, ed., *Tough Guy Writers of the Thirties* (Carbondale: Southern Illinois University Press, 1968), 51–79. We even see in Hammett's sensate writing the birth of the climactic scene of *Prizzi's Honor*: "Gooseneck fired at Kewpie at the moment she threw a knife at him. Kewpie 'spun back across the room—hammered back by the bullets that tore through her chest. . . . ' Gooseneck was in similar trouble as he stopped shooting and tried to speak, while the haft of the girl's knife protruded from his throat. 'He couldn't get the words past the blade' " (Durham, 62–63). That last irony, about trying to get words past a knife blade, is meant to be funny as well as sensate. It educates a sadistic taste by overlaying laughter onto horror. For the nexus of Hammett's topics and technique to his politics, see Sheldon Grebstein, "The Tough Hemingway and his Hardboiled Children," in Madden, *Tough Guy Writers*, 35.

5. The Rights and Wrongs of Nations

1. For the image, see Jer. 51:33; Dan. 2:35; Hab. 3:12; Amos 1:3; 2 Kings 13:7; Isa. 21:10, 41:15

2. The notion of an ascriptive trait derives from Talcott Parsons's work in *Toward a General Theory of Action* (Cambridge: Harvard University Press, 1959) and "Pattern Variables Revisited," *American Sociological Review* 25 (1960): 467–85. Parsons's intention was

to differentiate characterizations based on achievement from those based on stereotypes or markers beyond an individual's control. But, as Dahbour points out (*Philosophical Perspectives on National Identity*, 7), there is a tendency, in thinking about nationality, to seek "more fundamental" identifiers, "not to be thought of as arbitrary principles of classification . . . e.g., people who speak Tamil or were born in Estonia." Valorization as "fundamental" of such identifiers as "stereotypes, or other distinguishing markers of personhood that set off one set of persons from another," is a way of unraveling the very distinction Parsons set out to draw. Granted that stereotypes play a significant role in marking group identities, both for insiders and for others, the fact remains that ascriptive characteristics alone, because of the externality of their selection and application, cannot ground personal identity and are never adequate descriptors — let alone sufficient criteria — of national identity.

3. Cf. John Dewey, *The Public and Its Problems* (New York: Henry Holt, 1927; reprint, Denver: Alan Swallow, 1954); cf. Dewey's *Liberalism and Social Action* (New York: Putnam, 1935).

4. See p. 44 above.

5. For the arbitrariousness of racial markers, see Goodman and Goodman, " 'Particularly Amongst the Sunburnt Nations.' "

6. Omar Dahbour, "National Identity as a Philosophical Problem," in his *Philosophical Perspectives on National Identity*, 2

7. I resist the idea that nations are cultures or "societal cultures." Judith Lichtenberg ("How Liberal Can Nationalism Be?" in Dahbour, *Philosophical Perspectives*, 54–55) gives qualified endorsement to that view, "shared by Kymlicka, Tamir, Lind, and other participants in the current debate." See Will Kimlicka, *Multicultural Citizenship: A Liberal Theory of Minority Rights* (Oxford: Clarendon Press, 1995); Yael Tamir, *Liberal Nationalism* (Princeton: Princeton University Press, 1993); and Michael Lind, *The Next American Nation: The New Multiculturalism and the Fourth American Revolution* (New York: Free Press, 1995). A lot depends, as Lichtenberg points out, on what is being contrasted with nationalism (or any term). All of the books she cites on this point intend to impart legitimacy to various forms of cultural pluralism, so they tend not to stare hard at the question of what unites a nation. But, to begin with, it seems syntactically awkward to me, courting a category error, to equate nations with cultures: It seems odd to say that nations are cultures if nations are peoples, and peoples *have* cultures. Moreover, there is a smack of stereotyping if nations are described externally as though they were (perforce) homogeneous in culture. And if the satisfying totalization of such characterizations shifts into gear as a prescriptive and internal proposition, it readily becomes downright oppressive. Far better to think of whatever it is that can be shared by the populace of a nation as rather minimal and generic, definable perhaps only on a meta-level, and not necessarily in the language of a catechism or the iconography of some rotogravure book of the quaint costumes and customs of many lands. One outcome of the equation of nations with cultures is the exacerbation of conflicts and confusions over just which groups (if any) are "entitled" to nationhood. Solomonic resolutions are then proposed in terms that range from abolition of the nation-state to the fostering of multicultural festivals and celebrations. Thus an argument that began with a quest for even-handedness in the distribution of a presumptive good (national self-determination) ends up rejecting the notion that there is any such good — or finesses the question in a shower of crepe paper and patronization in the public parks. If we avoid equating nations with cultures, we can, on the other hand, at least conceive of the possibility (or recognize the actuality) of multicultural nations. Such a conception, by itself, does not magically dissolve every frustrate minority's claims to nationhood, let alone offer a touchstone of legitimacy to discriminate among such claims, but at the very least it avoids de-

legitimating (or treating as wholly artificial) every multinational state. If we follow through with the logic of this chapter, which predicates the success of nations on their capacity to hold together and act effectually as nations, then our analysis lays down a challenge to the states that nations create: not by legitimating every national claim insofar as it is a national claim, but by suggesting what sorts of thing the adherents of a national idea or identity (including the national idea or identity of a multicultural nation) need to do to keep that identity alive and functioning.

8. Margaret Gilbert, *On Social Facts* (Princeton: Princeton University Press, 1989), 17–18, 146–236.

9. Cf. the thoughtful reflections of Nicole Fermon, "The Female Fulcrum: Rousseau and the Birth of Nationalism," in Dahbour, *Philosophical Perspectives*, 21–41.

10. See Edward Bristow, *Prostitution and Prejudice: The Jewish Fight against White Slavery, 1870–1939* (New York: Schocken, 1983), 54–88.

11. *New York Times*, June 8, 1997, p. A-10.

12. Cf. the extended argument of David-Hillel Ruben in *The Metaphysics of the Social World* (London: Routledge and Kegan Paul, 1985).

13. Elie Kedourie, *Nationalism* (Oxford: Blackwell, 1993; first published, 1960).

14. Elie Kedourie and George Urban, "What's Wrong with 'Nationalism'? . . ." in Uri Ra'anan et al., eds., *Nation and State in Multi-Ethnic Societies: The Breakup of Multinational States* (Manchester: Manchester University Press, 1991), 224.

15. For the political and moral complexities of claims to national self-determination, see Donald Clark and Robert Williamson, eds., *Self-Determination: International Perspectives* (London: Macmillan, 1997).

16. What is the impact of this reasoning on Zionism — or of Zionism on this reasoning? This question belongs to the Philosophy of Judaism rather than to the broader concerns of Jewish philosophy. Therefore I hesitate to disrupt the flow of the argument by responding in the body of the text. Yet honesty and clarity demand that the question be answered, and not in a way that yields to the fashionable disparagement of Zionism: Israel, that is, the Jewish people, deserve a state and in fact need one as a condition of national survival. Too long did the Jewish people confront the violence of history without a land as refuge, without a tax base, without an army to defend them against nations that made war upon their civil populations. "Never again" is the moral imperative born of that historical experience. Applying our argument to the case at hand, we must say that clearly no society can expect to achieve stability through homogeneity, whether ethnic or ideological. That sort of homogeneity simply does not exist, and the means by which it is sought generate instability, not stability. They negate the intellectual and even the ethnic dynamic that drive the historical process. This does not mean that there is place or no role for a Jewish state. On the contrary, the world needs a Jewish state at least as much as the Jewish people needs one. But the Jewishness of that state is to be understood and defined in practice neither through ethnic nor through ideological uniformity. The attempt to render Judaism (or any religion, be it Christianity, Islam, Buddhism, or Hinduism) the established religion of a state insidiously but swiftly destroys that religion as a religion, even as the same policy undermines the credibility of that state. For a valuable object lesson on this point, with regard to the undermining of Buddhism by its treatment as an established religion in Japan, see Notto R. Thelle, *Buddhism and Christianity in Japan: From Conflict to Dialogue, 1854–1899* (Honolulu: University of Hawaii Press, 1987), 21–25. What Judaism should be, in the State of Israel, is a source of inspiration and of humane values that enlarge and inform the spirit of the laws and that motivate a sense of allegiance that not only articulates the historic aspirations of the Jewish people but also invites the civil allegiance of all those who come under the law's sway.

17. See Harold Laski, *Studies in the Problem of Sovereignty* (New Haven: Yale University Press, 1917; reprint, 1929).

18. Cf. Robert Nozick, *Anarchy, State and Utopia* (New York: Basic Books, 1974).

19. Spinoza, *Ethics* IV, app. cap. 17, Gebhardt, 2: 271, lines 5–13. The passage is muffed in Curley's generally outstanding translation. It has a misprint, "case" for "care," in rendering *cura*, and seems to overlook Spinoza's contrast of private with public interest (*utilitatem*), thus weakening the punch of Spinoza's argument: that there is a public interest in sustaining the poor, since they too should be brought into the social contract, even though the most saintly among us cannot literally be a friend to all.

Bibliography

Al-Ashʿarī, *Kitāb al-Lumaʿ*. In *The Theology of al-Ashʿarī*, edited by R. J. McCarthy. Beirut: Catholic Press, 1953.

Avot. *The Sayings of the Fathers*, edited by J. Hertz (New York: Berman House, 1945).

Avot de-R. Nathan (version B). Translated by Anthony J. Saldarini. Leiden: Brill, 1975.

Baron, S. W., G. Wise, and L. E. Goodman, eds. *Violence and Defense in the Jewish Experience*. Philadelphia: JPS, 1977.

Bentham, Jeremy. *Works*. Edited by John Bowring. London, 1843.

Berlin, Isaiah. "Two Concepts of Liberty." In *Four Essays on Liberty*. Oxford: Oxford University Press, 1969.

Collins, Ronald K. L., and David M. Skover. *The Death of Discourse*. Boulder: Westview Press, 1996).

Dahbour, Omar, ed. *Philosophical Perspectives on National Identity*. Published as a special issue of *Philosophical Forum* 28 (1996–1997).

Feldman, David. *Marital Relations, Birth Control and Abortion in Jewish Law*. New York: Schocken, 1975.

Freund, Richard. *Understanding Jewish Ethics: Major Themes and Thinkers*. 2 vols. San Francisco: Mellen, 1993.

Al-Ghazālī, *Tahāfut al-Falāsifa*. 2d ed. Edited by M. Bouyges. Beirut: Catholic Press, 1962.

Goodman, Lenn E. "The Epicurean Ethic of Muammad Ibn Zakariyāʾ ar-Rāzī." *Studia Islamica* 34 (1971) 5–26.

———. "Rāzī's Psychology." *Philosophical Forum* 4 (1972): 26–48.

———."Rāzī's Myth of the Fall of the Soul: Its Function in His Philosophy." In *Essays on Islamic Philosophy and Science*, edited by George Hourani, 25–40. Albany: SUNY Press, 1975.

———. "Rāzī," *EI²* vol. 7, pp. 474–77.

———. "Ghazālī's Argument from Creation." *International Journal of Middle East Studies* 2 (1971): 67–85, 168–88.

———. "Did Al-Ghazālī Deny Causality?" *Studia Islamica* 47 (1978): 83–120.

———. "Maimonides' Philosophy of Law." *Jewish Law Annual* 1 (1978): 72–107.

———. "The Greek Impact on Arabic Literature." In *The Cambridge History of Arabic*

Literature: Arabic Literature to the End of the Umayyad Period, 460–82. New York: Cambridge University Press, 1984.

———. "Determinism and Freedom in Spinoza, Maimonides, and Aristotle: A Retrospective Study." In *Responsibility, Character and the Emotions: New Essays in Moral Psychology*, edited by Ferdinand Schoeman, 107–64. New York: Cambridge University Press, 1987.

———. "Matter and Form as Attributes of God." In R. J. Long and C. Manekin, *A Straight Path: Essays in Honor of Arthur Hyman*, 86–97. Washington: Catholic University Press, 1987.

———. "Ordinary and Extraordinary Language in Medieval Jewish and Islamic Philosophy." *Manuscrito* 11 (1988): 57–83.

———. "Saadiah Gaon's Interpretive Technique in Translating the Book of Job." In *Translation of Scripture*, edited by D. M. Goldenberg. ed., Philadelphia: Annenberg Research Institute, 1990. *Jewish Quarterly Review* supplement, 47–76.

———. ed. *Neoplatonism and Jewish Thought.* Albany: SUNY Press, 1992.

———. *On Justice: An Essay in Jewish Philosophy.* New Haven: Yale University Press, 1991.

———. "Mythic Discourse.," In *Myths and Fictions*, edited by Shlomo Biderman and Ben-Ami Scharfstein, 51–112. Leiden: Brill, 1993.

———. "Judah Halevi." In *History of Jewish Philosophy*, edited by Daniel Frank and Oliver Leaman. London: Routledge, 1994.

———. *God of Abraham.* New York: Oxford University Press, 1996.

———. "Friendship in Aristotle, Miskawayh, and al-Ghazālī." In *Friendship East and West: Philosophical Perspectives*, edited by O. Leaman, 164–90. London: Curzon, 1996.

Goodman, M. J., and L. E. Goodman. " 'Particularly Amongst the Sunburnt Nations . . . ' —The Persistence of Sexual Stereotypes of Race in Bio-Science." *International Journal of Group Tensions* 19 (1989): 221–43, 365–84.

———. "The Overselling of Genetic Anxiety," *Hastings Center Report* (October 1982): 20–27.

———. "Prevention," *Hastings Center Report* 16 (1986): 26–38.

Hardie, W. F. R. *Aristotle's Ethical Theory.* Oxford: Clarendon Press, 1988.

Harvey, Warren Zev. Review of *On Justice* in *Jewish Political Studies Review* (1993): 144.

Hertz, J. H. *The Pentateuch and Haftorahs: Hebrew Text, English Translation, and Commentary.* London: Soncino, 1937; reprint, 1952.

Himmelfarb, Gertrude. *On Liberty and Liberalism: The Case of John Stuart Mill.* New York: Alfred Knopf, 1974.

Hobbes, Thomas. *A Dialogue between a Philosopher and a Student of the Common Laws of England.* 1681. Edited by J. Cropsey. Chicago: University of Chicago Press, 1971.

Hume, David. *An Enquiry Concerning the Principles of Morals.* 1777. Edited by P. H. Niddich. Oxford: Oxford University Press, 1982.

Ibn Rushd, *Tahāfut al-Tahāfut.* Edited by M. Bouyges. Beirut: Catholic Press, 1930.

Ibn Tufayl, *Hayy Ibn Yaqzān.* Translated with introduction and commentary by L. E. Goodman. New York: Twayne, 1972. Reprint, Los Angeles: Gee Tee Bee, 1990.

Ikhwān al-Ṣafāʾ, *The Case of the Animals vs Man before the King of the Jinn.* [ca. 970] Translated by L. E. Goodman. Boston: Twayne, 1978. Reissued, Los Angeles: Gee Tee Bee, 1987.

Jerusalem Talmud, Shabbat. Translated by Jacob Neusner. Chicago: University of Chicago Press, 1991.

Kant, Immanuel. *Lectures on Ethics.* Presented ca. 1775–1781. Transcribed by T. F. Brauer, Gottlieb Kutzner, and C. Mrongovius. Translated by Louis Infield. New York: Harper and Row, 1963; first published, 1930.

Maimonides. *Dalālatu 'l-Hā'irīn* (*Guide to the Perplexed*), 3 vols. Edited with French translation by S. Munk. Paris, 1856–1866. reprint, Osnabrück, 1964.

————. *Perush le-Masechet Aboth*. Edited by M. D. Rabinovitz, Jerusalem: Kook Foundation, 1962. Translated by Arthur David as *Commentary to Mishnah Aboth*. New York: Bloch, 1968.

Mekhilta de-Rabbi Ishmael, 3 vols. Edited by Jacob Lauterbach, Philadelphia: JPS, 1935.

Mendelssohn, Moses. *Jerusalem*. 1783. Translated by Allan Arkush. Hanover, N.H.: University Press of New England, 1983.

Midrash ha-Gadol. Edited by Mordecai Margulies. Jerusalem: Mossad Ha-Rav Kook, 1947.

Midrash Tanhuma. Edited by S. Buber. Vilna: Romm, 1885.

Mill, John Stuart. "On the Spirit of the Age." 1831. In *Mill: Essays on Politics and Culture*, edited by Gertrude Himmelfarb. New York: Doubleday, 1963.

————. *The Earlier Letters (1812–1848)*. Edited by F. E. Mineka. Toronto, 1963.

————. *Bentham*. 1838. In *John Stuart Mill on Bentham and Coleridge*. New York: Harper and Brothers, 1950. Reprint, 1962.

————. *On Liberty*. 1859. In *J. S. Mill: Utilitarianism, On Liberty and Considerations on Representative Government*, edited by H. B. Acton. London: Dent, 1972.

————. *Utilitarianism*. 1861. In Acton.

————. *Considerations on Representative Government*. 1861. In Acton.

————. *Autobiography*. New York: Columbia University Press, 1924.

————. *The Early Draft of John Stuart Mill's Autobiography*. Edited by Jack Stillinger. Urbana: University of Illinois Press, 1961.

The Mishnah. Trans. Herbert Danby (Oxford: Oxford Universtiy Press, 1933). Includes Mishnah Avot.

Pesikta Rabbati. Edited by M. Friedmann. Tel Aviv: Schocken, 1963. Translated by William G. Braude. New Haven: Yale University Press, 1968.

Porphyry. *De Abstinentia*. [ca. 260], Translated by Thomas Taylor as *On Abstinence from Animal Food*. London: Centaur, 1965.

Saadiah Gaon al-Fayyūmī, *Kitāb al-Mukhtār fī 'l-'Ā'mānāt wa-'l-'I'tiqādāt (Sefer ha-Nivḥar ba-Emunot uva-De'ot)*. Edited with modern Hebrew translation by J. Kafih. Jerusalem: Sura, 1970. Samuel Rosenblatt's translation in *The Book of Beliefs and Opinions* (New Haven: Yale University Press, 1948) is flawed and often unreliable.

————. *The Book of Theodicy: Translation and Commentary on the Book of Job*. ca. 940. Translated by L. E. Goodman. New Haven: Yale University Press, 1988.

Safrai, Shmuel. *The Literature of the Sages*. Assen: Van Gorcum, 1987.

Spinoza, Baruch. *Opera*. Edited by C. Gebhardt. 4 vols. Heidelberg: Winter, 1925.

Urbach, E. E. *The Sages: Their Concepts and Beliefs*, 2 vols. (Jerusalem: Magnes Press, 1975).

Index of Citations

General Index

Abel, 58
Abortion, 32, 79, 87–97
Abraham, 42, 54, 58, 109; his blessing, xiv; confronts God, 39
Accommodation, divine, 36, 85, 109; social, 26, 34
Active Intellect, 54, 71, 85–86
Adam, 37, 83
Adeimantus, 5
Advertising, 113–15
Adultery, 125–26
Afghanistan, 128, 150
Aggadah, 61, 93, 108
Agency, national, 142–46, 150
Ahab, 56
AIDS, 103, 118, 133
Akbar, 101
Akiva, R.: on equality, 58; on God's image, 26
Al-Ash'arī, 63, 82, 170 n. 9
Alexander, 160
Alexander, F. S., 53
Alexandria, 109
Alienation (*see also* Violence), 18, 47–48, 62, 68, 79, 127, 154
Alpert, Richard, 115
Altruism, 132
Amatus, oath of, 171 n. 31
Ambitio, 34
American Civil Liberties Union, 76, 117
Anarchy, 9, 15, 56, 72, 149–50

Animals, 25–26, 29, 31, 53, 63, 69–70, 113
Anthropocentrism, 36, 68
Antinomianism, 17
Apollonius Molon, 165 n. 43
Appropriation, moral, 16, 20, 42, 48, 140
Aquinas, Thomas, on rights, 53–54, 71
Aristotle: on capacity, 82; on civil life, 9, 44, 50–51, 71, 105–6; on ethics, 27, 62; on monarchy, 170 n. 78; on music, 135; on rhetoric, 112
Arts, 21, 35, 135
Asahara, Shoko, 115
Asaph, oath of, 171 n. 31
Asceticism, 63
Ascriptive traits, 139–41
Ash'arites, 69
Ataraxia, 6
Athens, 50–51, 157
Atonement, 41
Augustus Caesar, 160
Aum Shinrikyo, 115
Australia, adoption policy, 145
Authenticity, 16–20, 62, 66–67, 108
Authority (*see* Government)
Autonomy, moral, 10, 15–21, 48; national, 146–48, 157–58
Avicenna, 49, 68
Avtalyon, on *zekhut*, 42
Ayer, A. J., on abortion, 96
Azariah, 86
Azariah, R. Eleazar b., on Ben Zoma, 41